Firing began to come in from the southwest. "Shit, that does it," I thought. "We're completely surrounded."

The firing was becoming more intense by the moment, and we were returning everything we had. It didn't seem to be making any difference. I grabbed my pistol and shoved it into the back of my waistband. I wanted my "insurance" handy when the final moments came, not stuffed in a holster and inaccessible.

The men were really hurting. Danny kept passing out only to rouse himself and try to rejoin the fight. Keith's fire was growing slack also. Mark and Bill were doing okay, but they were immobile. Their groans of pain were about to kill me. With the radio dead, I knew we were on our own, and the prospects of getting out of this alive were very slim. I had to do something. . . .

4/4: A LRP'S NARRATIVE

Gary Douglas Ford

IVY BOOKS • NEW YORK

Ivy Books
Published by Ballantine Books
Copyright © 1993 by Gary Ford

Library of Congress Catalog Card Number: 92-97071

ISBN 0-8041-0913-3

Manufactured in the United States of America

First Edition: March 1993

PREFACE

How does one begin? This book has been on the back burners of my mind since the war ended. The first attempt at recording any of it was in October 1969 when, in a fit, I sat down and wrote out twenty pages describing a particular event, amounting to three paragraphs. In July 1974, I wrote 170 pages on my first tour because I had begun to feel I was forgetting it, and I didn't want to forget anything. That effort resulted in pure vitriol. I've mellowed considerably since then. It turned out I already had lost a lot. Those many months spent with F/51 LRP were too important to me, took up too much of my memories, no matter how vague, to be allowed to die. I knew when I came home that I wanted to tell my own story some day, and I felt the story of the company should be told, but I never felt it would be my place to do so. I was just a kid. That would be a job better left to someone with a better education, I thought. As it turned out, of the approximately 474 men I have identified as having been with the company at one time or another during the seventeen months of its existence, only thirty or so of us were there the entire time. That does allow me a certain perspective. Besides, those in the individual teams on the ground were the ones who really knew what LRPs and Rangers were really all about. The rest would be very dry, I'm certain.

As for my story, I felt too much of it would not be believable. I had forgotten the soldier's saying: "Ya know the difference between a fairy tale and a war story? A fairy tale begins, 'Once upon a time . . .', while a war story begins, 'You won't believe this shit!' " Probably a lot of it won't be believed, but there is a very critical audience out there that I must answer to: the men of Company F, Long Range Patrol, 51st Infantry (Airborne). They will know I speak true.

Most of *this* version was written as a novel three years ago, written in longhand, about 250 pages worth of material in nine days. I was obsessed with it at that time, but it did help me to exorcise some old ghosts. I had been encouraged and assisted by Denna Fleck, then a history instructor at El Reno (Oklahoma) Junior College, but the obsession was my own. With a novel one can get away with certain things that you often can't or don't want to say in a historical piece. But the truth is better and should always be told, no matter what the consequences. However, I still wasn't ready to tell my story. Too much was missing, and I didn't want to tell only part of the story.

Over the last year or so, I have been assisted in many ways by men of the company whom our association has located. Clyde Tanner of Lockport, New York, provided the after-action reports that in many cases helped to jar my memory, or provided dates of events I still remembered. But the records are not accurate, no fault of Clyde's. Someone at the time kept faulty notes. Walt Butts, the company first sergeant at the time, helped with many details, as did everyone else I have talked to, but still the book was going nowhere. I even received encouragement from John Rotundo, one of the coauthors of *Charlie Rangers*, the story of John and his fellow author, Don Ericson's, time with Company C, 75th Infantry (which evolved from Company E, 20th Infantry, LRP, F/51st's sister unit). We'd met at the 75th Ranger Regiment Association Reunion in July 1990.

Bob Gilbert, retired sergeant major (USA) and current president of the 75th Ranger Regiment Association, really got the ball rolling. He put me in touch with Gary Linderer, author of *Eyes of the Eagle*, which chronicles his time with F/58th LRPs. His second book, *Eyes behind the Lines*, is his time with Company L, 75th Rangers, after the changeover. Gary very kindly hooked me up with Owen Lock, his editor at Ballantine Books, who decided I had a story worth telling. Gary has also provided a lot of information and encouragement. As Bob and Gary have both said time and again, LRPs and Rangers had to watch out for each other then, and we still try. (To assist the reader, LRP, in case this is the first such book you have encountered on the subject, is pronounced LURP or LERP and means Long Range Patrol.)

I am further in debt to Marty Young of Page One Books, in El Reno, for her assistance in editing my messy manuscript. Owen Lock put me in touch with Michael Lee Lanning, author of *Inside the LRRPs: Rangers in Vietnam*, and Lee has very kindly assisted with editing, and many other points, also. William "Bill" Michael Walsh, Jr., of Evanston, IL, has been of great help in pinning down details of a period that often escape me, but are extremely important to both of us. Nothing of this book could have come about had I been left to my own devices. The list, great or small, could go on forever, but in most cases I have mentioned, or tried to, those who provided details. I am in their debt and hope this effort will satisfy everyone.

Twenty-three years is a long time. I kept no notes or diary then, so much has had to come from memory despite all the assistance. Letters I wrote to my mother, Vivian Morelock, at the time reveal the fact that I kept a lot of information from her but, even so, was often too graphic in what I did reveal. In many cases, documentation or published works are incorrect; I was there. I know what happened. It is simply my story and observations of the times. I hope only to give credit where it is due, but the final results are to our credit, for all of the men of F/51, but any fault is mine.

I admit that I am not proud of all that I did, but I will also state for the record, one must remember the times and circumstances we lived under. It wasn't all "booze, broads, and drugs" then, certainly no more so than back in the World. At least we were doing a fucking job! Perhaps this work is my way of making amends for some of what I did. I have read numerous accounts of World War II and other wars and was often left with a feeling that the stories had been sanitized, that the brutal truth of war had been allowed to be replaced by the mores of the peaceful times during which those accounts had been written. War is a dirty business, and if you want it clean and decent, read the comic strips. What follows is the truth. The actions taken by me do not reflect the norm for F/51, but there were a few other individualists within the company. Some names have been changed.

There are literally hundreds of stories from F/51 that should be told. I have only touched on a few. Maybe someday more of them will be told. That would be fitting.

All sentences which end with an asterisk (*) are either near or direct quotes from the company yearbook, published by the company, with (captain) Thomas P. Meyer as proof editor, (sergeant) Jerold D. Berrow as editor, (specialist) Mark G. Eastman did the art work, and (specialist) William D. Ellis did the cover and emblems. There is no indication that the yearbook has a copyright, but I'm not about to steal any thunder from the great effort of these four men. I only wish that book could be reproduced for the public to see.

I would also like to thank Jack Glennon of the Vietnam Helicopter Pilots Association (#7 West 7th Street, Suite 1940, Cincinnati, Ohio 45202) for getting me in touch with several members who provided some information I wanted for one particular event. The whole story deserves telling, but most of the participants can no longer be found at this time.

Thanks must be given also to Ms. Fran Randall, my seventh grade English teacher, who encouraged me to write. I hope she understands the effort.

And finally, last, but certainly not least, my sweet Janice who supported me in this effort, even when she didn't understand.

Gary Douglas Ford
El Reno, Oklahoma
May 1991

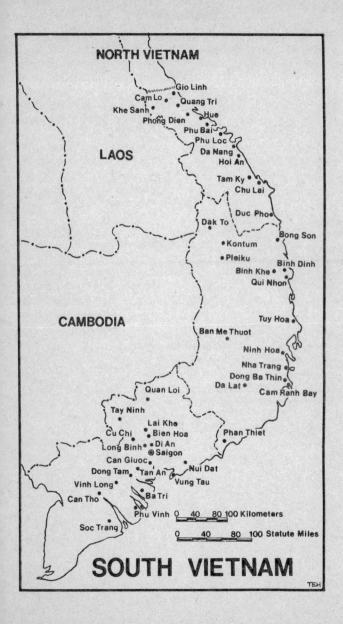

NORTH VIETNAM

LAOS

Gio Linh
Cam Lo • Quang Tri
Khe Sanh • Hue
Phong Dien • Phu Bai
Phu Loc
Da Nang
Hoi An
Tam Ky •
Chu Lai

Duc Pho
Dak To • Bong Son

Kontum •
Pleiku • Binh Dinh
Binh Khe •
Qui Nhon

Tuy Hoa •

CAMBODIA • Ban Me Thuot
Ninh Hoa •
Nha Trang •
Dong Ba Thin •
Quan Loi • Da Lat • Cam Ranh Bay

Tay Ninh •
Lai Khe
Cu Chi • Bien Hoa
Long Binh • Di An Phan Thiet
Saigon
Can Giuoc • Nui Dat
Dong Tam • Tan An
Vinh Long • Vung Tau
Can Tho Ba Tri
Phu Vinh 0   40   80 100 Kilometers

0   40   80 100 Statute Miles

Soc Trang

SOUTH VIETNAM

TEH

PROLOGUE

January 3, 1968. Two UH-1B helicopters flew northeast from Bien Hoa, Republic of South Vietnam, crossing the Dong Nai River, headed deep into War Zone D. The choppers carried two six-man teams under the leadership of platoon sergeant Richard McCoy. Also along in an unofficial capacity was 1st Lt. Albert Snyder, the operations officer with Company F, 51st Infantry, Long Range Patrol.

Our mission was to set up an ambush on a designated trail to deny the enemy the use of this trail as a line of communication and supply. We were also to kill or capture any enemy soldiers who had the misfortune to stumble into our line of fire. I was a member of that patrol.

I was a nineteen-year-old specialist fourth class in the United States Army and had been in country just over five months. I was a volunteer for service in Vietnam and wanted desperately to prove myself in battle. Up until this point, I had seen a little action but nothing significant enough to be worthy of the name. I was beginning to despair of ever getting into battle.

Our target LZ (landing zone) was a big one, large enough to take at least ten slicks (troop-carrying helicopters). That was the good news—if we got into a firefight immediately after insertion, we'd have a better chance of a fighting withdrawal as well as being able to get support from other teams from the company or our reaction force, a platoon from the 199th Light Infantry Brigade. That was the unit we were working for at the time. The bad news was that the LZ was at least a thousand meters from our target trail. That meant an awful long hump through the bush until we got to where we needed to be.

1

The ravages of war were evident from the air. There were many tall tree trunks around the LZ, but bombing and artillery fire had pretty well denuded the vegetation, leaving hardly enough ground cover to conceal a roe deer. The slicks came in, one behind the other, and we unassed in a hurry, sprinting for what tree line there was. Our initial pause was a security check to make certain we hadn't been spotted by Viet Cong (VC) LZ watchers. Those in charge checked their maps and compasses to make certain we were in the right location, and then we loaded up and set out in a westerly direction.

Once we were into the jungle, the scenery changed. Most of the trees were of uniform height, about twenty or so feet high. There was plenty of good overhead cover, enough for Charlie to hide just about anything he had to avoid detection from our overhead flights. The ground vegetation under the leafy roof was another matter. The creepers and wait-a-minute vines formed a vast spider web, impeding our progress considerably, yet not being so thick we couldn't see some distance. No breeze was able to penetrate the thick jungle. A dusty haze just hung in the air and made breathing that much more difficult. A number of large termite mounds lay along our line of march. It was fortunate that experience had taught us not to put a new guy on point; those huge mounds might have easily been mistaken for enemy bunkers by someone less knowledgeable. Our point (point man) knew what he was doing. Looking at the surrounding forest, I was reminded of scenes from J.R.R. Tolkien's *The Fellowship of the Ring*. Except for the fact that the trolls and goblins we would face were likely to be a lot more deadly than the fairytale variety.

The going was rough, and the heat and humidity were overwhelming. A machete might have made our progress easier but the noise—and the obvious path we'd leave—would have been a dead giveaway that we were in the area. My training had taught me that Charlie will usually follow trails or animal paths when he's in his own backyard. By cutting across country, we were less likely to be discovered. We also were less likely to encounter booby traps. That has always been the bane of the "civilized" warrior. Still, it also meant our progress was slow, each vine having to be moved aside or held apart as if we were traversing dozens of barbed-wire fences.

The mission was expected to last five days unless we made

contact. Each man carried approximately eight quarts of water, adding over sixteen pounds of weight to his combat load. The teams carried two M-60 machine guns, with a thousand rounds of ammo each. The gunner and his assistant carried the bulk of the machine-gun ammo, but each team member also carried at least a hundred rounds. Then there were two M-79 grenade launchers with thirty-five rounds of 40mm ammo each, with most of the team members carrying an additional six rounds of 40mm grenades apiece. We had eleven M-16 rifles. The standard load for the M-16s was ten magazines, but most of us carried as many as twenty. This was a combat mission; had it been a reconnaissance patrol, we'd have been much more lightly armed. (Most of the time a light team—six men—went on patrol much more heavily armed than a squad of men in line units, but a heavy team—twelve men—was still more heavily armed, and it was generally felt that the firepower we carried was enough to take on just about anyone.) In addition we carried at least one claymore mine apiece—several of us carrying two—as well as six to twenty hand grenades, trip flares, white phosphorus grenades, aerial flares, etc., etc. I always felt Uncle Sam had given me a lot of good training for my first civilian job when I got out—pack mule.

Water conservation became a serious consideration. What we carried was all there would be. It was the dry season, and there were no water sources along our route of march. Any water found would be suspect. No one was likely to have enough to spare if someone ran out. Listening to the water splashing in our canteens was torture, but you just had to ignore it and drive on.

Breaks were frequent but too short to allow any real chance of recovery before we had to load up and continue. Actually, there was no such thing as unloading your gear; you simply dropped in place and relaxed as best you could. I was just a rifleman, with no status in the chain of command, so I took the opportunity to bitch and mutter under my breath at the seeming insanity of the situation. What was the big rush anyway? It hadn't been made clear to me that we had a time schedule to meet. Patience is not one of my virtues, whatever else they might be.

About midafternoon, we found the ground vegetation becoming increasingly thicker, and we began discovering more footpaths. As far as I remembered from our premission briefing, there were no villages anywhere near us. That could only mean we were getting close to the enemy. This increased my personal concerns. Tired men do not move as cautiously as rested ones, and I was exhausted. Our pace did not let up because of these new discoveries. Getting into a firefight was one thing; being ambushed by someone who'd been listening to our approach for a couple of hours was a totally different matter. We encountered another wall of brush and had to break through it to advance. The man in front of me let a limb go, and it flew back, striking me in the face, sending dirt and debris into my mouth and down my throat. I involuntarily began coughing it up, making more noise than I'd realized. "Ford, keep it down!" Staff Sergeant Lewis, my team leader, hissed at me. What could I say that would make any difference?

A few minutes later, the point came across a definite sign. A fresh pile of human feces had been discovered along our line of march. We stopped to consider this development. I dropped to the ground to get the weight of my rucksack off of my shoulders and to rest for a moment. Despite my exhaustion, I was feeling very tense, as was everyone around me. I was trying to peer deeper into the brush, trying to will the plants to part so I could see what lay beyond.

I was looking to the north when I noticed three men running parallel to our column. One was wearing khaki pants, a white shirt, and a tan bush hat. My first reaction was, Damned civilians are always where they shouldn't be! and just as suddenly realized they had to be Viet Cong! I straightened up to swing my rifle at them, but they had already disappeared from my view, behind a huge termite mound. Bad luck for me, but worse for them. This had brought them directly into the view and line of fire of Tom Santa, one of our machine gunners, who was walking in position right behind me. I looked over to yell at him about the VC, but he'd already seen them. He brought the big gun up and began firing, sweeping right, then left. He didn't have to fire very long. While I couldn't see them fall, it was obvious from Tom's expression the men I'd seen were no longer a part of the war.

We would have checked out the bodies, but there were new developments. The point man had just spotted a large machine gun bunker directly in front of us along our line of march. Fortunately, it wasn't occupied at that moment. It did indicate we were awfully close to the enemy. Charlie didn't build those things out in the jungle just for grins. We also began hearing a lot of voices shouting and yelling in Vietnamese all around us, and the sounds of carbines and rifles being fired filled the jungle. We loaded up again and began moving toward the bunker and then veered left. The shooting was increasing, and I caught glimpses of people moving about in the forest not too far away. Our column moved just a short distance and then stopped in a small clearing with a slight depression in the center. Everyone dropped their rucksacks and formed a circular perimeter, facing out. A couple of the guys were snapping off shots into the jungle. Because they'd actually seen something to shoot at or just as a reaction? I couldn't tell.

Staff Sergeant Jones, the other team leader, set up beside me. We broke out our claymores and covered each other while we set them out. After he'd finished, I began reeling my wire out, doing just as I had done so many nights in the Central Highlands with the 173d Airborne Brigade. I carried the claymore out almost the full one hundred feet of wire and stopped to set it up. The ground was too hard for the folding spike legs, so I propped it up against a large tree, to absorb the backblast, and used part of the wire to tie it in place. When I finished, I stood up and looked back toward our tiny perimeter. I couldn't see any of the team. I had been completely out of sight and without cover during this little detail! Shit! I muttered to myself. If I survive this, betcha I don't do that again! I hustled back to the team, making it without getting shot by Charlie or my own guys. Jones just looked at me as if he'd seen a ghost. All I could do was give him a sick grin.

Things did not look good. The enemy fire was steadily increasing, and despite our not being able to see anyone clearly, it was obvious there were a lot of bad guys all around, and they were not happy to have us there. We had fulfilled part of our mission; we'd found the enemy. As far as I was concerned, it was time to vacate the area and let some of the larger units handle the situation—as our mission dictated and our training required. As if we had any real choice in the matter.

Then the lieutenant decided he wanted a few men to go back along our line of march and check out the bunker we'd passed. Either he'd seen or been told that the enemy was trying to occupy the position. Sgt. Dennis ''Super Sarge'' Lovick,

Tommy Thomas, and I were volunteered. My pucker factor
(wherein one's asshole tightens up so much you couldn't drive
a needle in with a sixteen-pound sledgehammer) increased a
thousandfold as we sortied out from the questionable safety of
the perimeter. Somehow all the shots being thrown at us seemed
well wide of their mark. We got to within a few years of the
bunker and found that it was still empty, but I had the impression
that people were moving toward us. "Fuck this shit!" Lovick
said. "Let's get back." I didn't have to be told twice.

Back in the perimeter, we found that one of the guys had been
slightly wounded by shrapnel. On the other side of the circle, I
saw Ron Kaplan turn to his right, acting for all intents and purposes on instinct. He jumped up and began firing into a brush
wall a short distance away. I couldn't see the enemy soldier who
was shooting at Ron, but I could see his muzzle flash. It was
almost like watching a movie running in slow motion. The enemy soldier's bullets were kicking up dirt as they walked toward
Ron, striking about every foot or so. Knowing he was in a duel
of death, Ron was shooting as quickly as he could. Finally he
seemed to connect; the VC's muzzle blast began to lift as if he'd
been hit, and then his fire stopped. But the last few rounds were
still headed toward Ron. One hit about a foot in front of him,
the next one hit at his feet. The last one struck Ron's right ammo
pouch on his LBE (load-bearing equipment). Sparks and fire
began spewing from the pouch as Ron broke any existing records shedding the gear. He'd been twice lucky. The bullet hadn't
hit him nor had any of his own ammo since his magazines had
been positioned with the rounds facing out. The discarded LBE
lay on the ground, all but forgotten, rounds continuing to pop
off until they were all gone. Fortunately, no one was hit by those
either. At that point, the additional fire didn't seem to matter,
as there were plenty of them flying around us already. The man
next to Ron did get hit by one of the bullets from the enemy
fusillade, through the heel of his boot, but it didn't seem to be
a serious wound.

Then another man was hit by shrapnel. We now had three
wounded.

Sergeant McCoy was talking on the radio, and he raised his
head to tell us the news. "It doesn't look good, people. As far
as we know, the closest LZ that we can get out of is the one we
came in on. C & C [the company commander's command-and-

control helicopter] is on the way, as are the gunships. Slicks aren't far behind, for whatever that's worth. We might have to prepare to E & E.'' Shit, again. Escape and evade. A running firefight when we were as close to the enemy as we were did not seem a proposition with much future. I looked up at what I could see of the sky and guesstimated we had an hour of daylight left, maybe less.

So far I hadn't fired a shot. It wasn't buck fever; I just hadn't seen anyone to shoot at. Besides, something told me that before this thing was over, I might well need what ammo I had very badly. In many ways, in my youth and inexperience, I found it hard to really grasp a lot of the current situation. We were engaged in a very serious battle and might all die, but other than being nervous, I just couldn't accept the fact that I might not see the end of this day.

We continued to maintain our position. Before long we heard the sound of approaching helicopters. Someone popped a smoke grenade to mark our position. The gunships began making their runs, firing up the jungle all around us. McCoy was still on the radio. Then he looked up. ''C & C has spotted a small clearing no more than fifty or so meters away. It's only big enough for one ship to come in at a time, but the pilots are willing to risk it to get us out. When I give the command, we'll blow claymores and begin our withdrawal. The gunships will cover us as best they can.''

Time seemed to hang upon us; then McCoy yelled, ''Blow claymores!'' The twelve or fourteen explosions seemed to come almost as one. I'd instinctively crawled under my rucksack for protection from the backblast, but I was lifted off the ground. It was as if some giant was shaking me. The air was full of dust and smoke. My head was ringing like a hundred church bells were in it. The blast did seem to have the desired effect, though— enemy fire seemed to have subsided somewhat. Or maybe I just couldn't hear it. ''Let's go!'' McCoy shouted.

Extraction would be in reverse order of insertion; my team would be the last one out. We began walking backwards, firing as we withdrew. Now I pulled out all stops and began firing as fast as I could, sweeping left and right, changing magazines as quickly as I could fish another one out of the magazine pouch. I had entered into something like a tunnel; I was totally oblivious to everything and everyone else around me. I wasn't even aware of the chopper coming in to pick up the other team. I pulled out a white phosphorus grenade and then a fifteen-second-delay fuse. It was my intention to arm the grenade and throw it back toward Charlie so that it would explode and start a fire to cover our withdrawal. I unscrewed the blasting cap and tried to insert the delay fuse, only to discover that the threads were stripped on the fuse. I finally gave up and put the original fuse back in, pulled the pin, and tossed the grenade as far back into the woods as I could. Only then did I realize I'd been standing exposed like an idiot, *completely* exposed the whole time I'd been messing with the damned thing. Then, from out of nowhere, a grenade came flying and landed a few feet in front of me. There was no time to react; it exploded, almost knocking me off of my feet. I heard a scream behind me and turned to see Tommy Thomas reeling from shrapnel hits. I had no idea whether I'd been hit or not. I was too engrossed in what was going on to pay attention.

I turned and grabbed Tommy and began running toward the LZ just as the chopper began gently lowering to pick us up. That chopper was awfully exposed, as hovering into an LZ was not one of the Huey's strong points. That pilot had balls! When Tommy and I reached the chopper, as skinny as the belly man was, he pulled us aboard with ease. I landed on the bottom of the ship, my legs lying across the four-by-four used to support the McGuire rig, a device designed for emergency extractions, secured to the floor of the ship. Two more men were pulled aboard, and they landed across my legs. I was pinned and immediately began screaming in pain. I was oblivious to anything else for the rest of the flight back.

We landed back in the company area just minutes before full darkness descended. It had, everyone knew, been a very close call. I was assisted off the chopper, everyone thinking I'd been wounded. Despite the grenade having gone off directly in front of me, I didn't get a scratch. It had hit Tommy, who'd been standing directly behind me, but missed me. Didn't make a bit of sense. It took some minutes before I got any feeling back in my legs and was able to walk. None of our four wounded were hurt badly, so they attended the debriefing before being taken off for treatment.

The information that eventually came down to us was that we'd walked into the base camp of the Phu Loi Regiment, which meant we'd only been outnumbered about fifty to one. This enemy outfit had been able to avoid detection for some time. Now that they'd been located, the 199th and other larger ground units would be sent to engage them. However, once Charlie knew he'd been found, it didn't take him long to disperse. The commanding general of II Field Force, our parent unit, wanted my whole platoon to receive the Bronze Star for Valor for finding that elusive outfit, but all we got out of it were our four Purple Hearts. The man hit in the heel was short (i.e., almost due to rotate out of Vietnam), so they sent him home early. Everyone else soon returned to duty.

While it would have been nice to get a medal, I'd had to admit that my actions hadn't been all that noteworthy. It had simply been a fight for survival, with no heroics on my part. Upon breaking down my gear, I discovered that I had used a lot more ordnance than I realized. It had just been fortunate that I hadn't needed all of the ammo I'd tried to carry out the day before.

I did feel I'd learned a little about myself. A few more combat actions would tell if I really had what it took to be a warrior, but I was not displeased with what I'd learned so far. I did spend some time considering different aspects of the action. I had heard numerous rounds cracking around me but had been too busy during the withdrawal to the chopper to pay any attention. I had felt a great degree of anticipation, but I could not really call it being scared. I wasn't trying to fool anyone, let alone myself. I just desperately wanted to know whether I had conquered my worst fear, that of being thought a coward. Dying did not scare me as much as having that label pinned on me, or having to accept it by my own standards. I had a long way to go before I really knew the answer. I could easily believe there had been several hundred of the enemy around us, but as far as my senses could determine, I had only seen four men. It was almost as if the jungle had been our enemy and we'd been fighting trees wielding AK-47s.

There was one sour note that rubbed most of us the wrong way for a while; one officer was said to have written himself up for a Silver Star for his part in the action. However, the same rumor also had it that the CO, Maj. William C. Maus, kicked it back. Good for him. Guess that's just the way some things are. I wanted recognition in time for things I'd actually done, not for flights of fancy or for talking someone into swearing to a lie. I could not understand how anyone could write himself up for something he did not deserve. I did not understand a thing about medals being worn or awarded for promotion points. Guess I just saw them as a measure of a man. I was too young and naive.

CHAPTER 1

It all depends on one's point of view. For me, arriving in Vietnam was nothing short of a miracle. I had known about the war for years, from movies about the French fall at Dien Bien Phu (*The Quiet American*, which starred World War II hero Audie Murphy) and books such as *The Ugly American*. A popular saying was, "It ain't much, but it's the only war we've got." My father had been in World War II, my grandfather in World War I, and my great-great-grandfather fought for the Confederacy. Going to war seemed as natural a vocation as running the family store. I was so anxious to get into the war, I had dropped out of high school, afraid it would end before I graduated.

But it wasn't as easy as one might think. I'd enlisted for Vietnam, as well as for Airborne training. I had to constantly revolunteer for jump school throughout basic (taken at Fort Polk, Louisiana), and infantry training (Fort Ord, California) until I finally was accepted. The day they handed out orders after we'd graduated from jump school, I waited anxiously, knowing I was on the list. I wasn't. My first duty station was with Company C, 6/9th Infantry, 171st Infantry Brigade, Fort Wainwright, Alaska! What kind of jungle training could I expect up there? As far as I knew, I'd been a pretty good and determined soldier to that point in my training, but after that, my attitude took a nosedive. I felt the army had welshed on our deal, and I was not happy about it.

At the end of my first year in the army, I took a short reenlistment for Vietnam, arriving at Cam Ranh Bay on July 27, 1967. The first impression upon disembarking from the plane was of the overpowering heat and humidity. The sunlight was no big deal. I'd just left Oklahoma, and my last few weeks in Alaska had seen about twenty-two hours of sunlight a day.

Something like 150 of us off-loaded and walked down the stairs to the steaming tarmac to find olive green buses waiting for us. I noted the heavy wire-mesh screens on the windows and figured out all by myself that those were to protect us from hand grenades. We loaded up and headed for the in-processing shed. Besides the heat, one of my first memories was of the smell of diesel-soaked human feces being burned. It seemed to hang everywhere and soon seemed to me to be the most prevalent "fragrance of the Orient."

My group off-loaded and lined up for customs inspection. A couple of air force types advised us of what we could and could not bring into Vietnam. "Firearms, ammunition, explosives, drugs, alcoholic beverages, as well as pornography, are all forbidden for importation into this country." Like we were entering a sterile environment or something!

Next stop, turn in our Stateside fatigues and draw from issue the jungle boots and fatigues that would be our basic wardrobe for the next year. We were then herded into a room, this one more stuffy than the one before, where we received out first in-country briefing. "You are guests in this country and represent the United States of America. Be sure you act accordingly."

"Lifer motherfucker," some kid standing beside me muttered. Obviously a draftee, I thought. I was about as gung ho as the law allowed. "I don' even wanna be here in the first fuckin' place," he continued. Well, to each his own.

I had arrived as "Airborne, unassigned," I had absolutely no idea where I would end up, but having the young paratrooper's arrogance, the last thing I wanted was to end up in a "leg" outfit. Going through jump school had indoctrinated me to a degree; I was proud of my wings, but I didn't buy the old saw that one trooper could whip a dozen legs. Hell, some guys I'd seen couldn't go Airborne because they were too big to get on the plane! Anyway, getting through jump school was the first big accomplishment of my life, like a high-school jock's letter jacket.

We soon arrived at the repo-depo (replacement depot) and

began a never-ending series of roll calls while waiting for orders and assignments. In the meantime, I was trying to absorb the country, to get a feel for what lay ahead. I didn't make any attempts to pal around. I'd read enough about warfare to know, or believe, you don't make friends in a combat zone. Each friend you make, then lose, just devastates you that much more. Color me a loner. Death was just not something I'd had any experience with. None of my family or friends had died while I was growing up, and I wanted to keep that specter as far away as possible. Four guys from my basic training company had been killed in a plane crash on their way home for leave. Two of them, Russell Hudson and Charles Howard, had been in my platoon, and we'd become fairly close friends. That had hurt bad enough. No more.

Finally, I received my orders. I was going to the 173d Airborne Brigade. I was elated! As far as I knew, that was one hardcore, ass-kicking fighting outfit. I was one happy fella when I went to the enlisted club that night for a few beers. It seemed like every other song they played on the jukebox or that the Filipino band sang was, "I wanna go home," and after a while, I was singing along just as loud, and despite the circumstances of my being in Vietnam, meant it.

The next morning, well before the sun came up, all replacements were bused to the airstrip to catch flights to their units. Mine was going to a place called Bien Hoa, just north of Saigon. I ran into one of the guys who'd been on my flight in country, first name Gary also, but I kept forgetting his last name. Despite my reservations, we buddied up, if for no other reason than to share the waiting. Lots of that in this man's army. He was going to the 173d also.

We watched the sun come up over the hills surrounding Cam Ranh Bay, and the day promised to be clear, bright, and beautiful. I had, of course, seen very little of the country so far, but what I had seen looked really nice. I also recognized that I was not there as a tourist. There was a war to be fought, medals and fame to be won, and anything that was not directly involved in that pursuit was beyond my ken. To me, a clear day just meant that our flight would get out on time, and I would be that much closer to my goal.

The flight probably wasn't as long as it seemed; my impatience just made it seem like it took forever. It was also uneventful. As we flew over the thick green jungle, like a deep pile carpet, I wondered how many Viet Cong were at that very moment looking up at us and preparing to shoot us down. I dreaded the thought, only because if I had to die, I wanted it to be in battle, surrounded by the bodies of the enemy, not when I hadn't even seen any action.

Bien Hoa was certainly different than Cam Ranh Bay. Both were hot and humid, but Bien Hoa was also extremely dusty at that time of year. Besides the smell of burning shit, there was also a heavy fog of aviation fuel. Bien Hoa airport was reputed to be the busiest airport in the world. I could believe it.

Once again the milling about and confusion. Someone, obviously with a lot of experience at doing so, got all of the FNGs (fucking new guys) sorted out and loaded onto trucks to take us to our respective outfits. The trucks were deuce-and-a-halfs— two-and-a-half-ton trucks, the defacto taxis for the military services. Ours wound its way through the congested streets along the south side of the main runway and then north on a short loop into the army base. Along the way, we passed a small concrete structure that we were told had been built and manned at a time when the French "owned" Vietnam. Now it was abandoned, of no further use to anyone.

Later, that proved not to be the case. After the first Tet offensive, I heard a story concerning that bunker. One Viet Cong infiltrator had made his way onto the base, secured a machine gun and ammo, and then had captured a hostage. He moved into that same bunker so he would have a commanding view and field of fire over one of the major runways. For some time, he prevented any of our aircraft from taking off or landing, and damaged others. Our forces were restrained from attacking because of the hostage. After the fighting was over and the VC had run out of ammunition, he'd released his hostage and surrendered. I could never learn if the story was true or not, or if so, what happened to the enemy soldier. I have to admit that I liked the story. As the Chinese say, the courage of your enemies does you honor. It was an audacious stunt, and even an enemy who could pull off something like that should be honored.

Bien Hoa Army Base was certainly not Hometown, USA. A civilian should be able to appreciate how neat and orderly most Stateside military bases and installations are; it is not for nothing that soldiers spend so much time on "police call" (picking up trash, cigarette butts, etc.), or other base beautification details.

Bien Hoa didn't quite look like a disaster area, but it wouldn't have taken much to have made it worse. To me, still fresh from Stateside duty, it was unbelievable. It seemed like any type of structure someone wanted to put up for shelter, a barracks, office, you name it, was in evidence. There were tents, pieces of canvas stretched between poles, numerous wood-and-screen edifices for who-knows-what purposes, trailers sprouting dozens of antennae pointing out at a dozen different angles, as well as sandbagged artillery emplacements—sandbags, in fact, surrounding everything. And you know what? I loved it all! This was what I always believed a combat zone should look like, and I really felt at home.

Over the next few days, I would find out what it takes to screw up a good war: REMFs, rear echelon motherfuckers.

Okay, I told myself, we have to have the clerks and supply types, those to bring "us" food, ammo, mail, take care of our pay, tend us when we're sick or wounded. But some of them can be such a pain in the ass! And the officers and NCOs who haven't been in combat are probably the worst.

Before long, we were dumped off at a shack that served as the reception center for the 173d, known far and wide as the "Herd." A big, black sergeant first class (SFC) who greeted us was supposed to be one of the Herd's more colorful characters (no pun intended), but he'd gotten into some kind of trouble and was now stuck with processing FNGs. We also met some of the war heroes who had participated in the 173d's famous "blast," or combat parachute jump on February 22, 1967. They sported the small bronze star on their jump wings to signify that they were different. I'd read something about that in a magazine; seemed to me like most of the photographs were made by cameramen waiting for them on the ground. To hear those guys tell it, Custer's Last Stand and the Battle of the Bulge weren't nuthin' compared to the danger they'd faced. My faith in heroes began taking a nosedive from that moment.

The other Gary was assigned to Company B, 4/503d Infantry; I was going to Company C. We loaded up onto trucks once again for the trip to our company areas. Gary and I shook hands and wished each other luck, probably both doubting that we'd ever meet again.

The trucks had no canvas over the backs, so naturally, the rains began. I had heard about the monsoon, I just hadn't appreciated how quickly it could go from hot and dusty one moment to drenched and muddy the next. I did have enough foresight to know it would get a lot worse before it got better.

As bad as Bien Hoa looked on the outside, I found upon my arrival at the Charlie Company area, situated at the north central part of the army base, it looked a lot worse on the inside. The barracks were the same rough shacks I'd already seen—half of the wall being wood; the upper half was screening, canvas, or cardboard if they ran out of everything else. The interiors had a concrete floor, but the rest of the place was temporary, as if it would all be gone tomorrow. Beside the barracks was a large metal container called a conex, which, we were told, held the personal effects of men killed in battle. I believed it was more likely someone's idea of a way to scare the new arrivals.

The interior of the barracks was a disaster. Apparently the only people in the rear were those going home, recovering from wounds, or awaiting charges for various offenses of military law. Because no one expected them to do anything, and new guys didn't come in that often, nothing was done at all to keep up the place. There was a mixed assortment of wooden and steel cots, with and without mattresses, some with springs, some without, and even a couple of hammocks. Field gear, ammunition, and grenades were everywhere, and the careless way some of the old timers handled grenades really made me nervous. The last thing I wanted to do was to die in a stupid accident before I ever got to the field.

I could shut my eyes and block out the mess I found myself in. I had asked for this, after all. But I couldn't stop breathing. There was an overpowering stench of mold and decay, not unlike what I presumed a tomb would smell like. I almost looked around for dead bodies, but I suspected that was an artificial mess and had nothing to do with the hardships and deprivation of war. It was simply a result of laziness, an all pervasive I-don't-give-a-shit attitude.

But that was not my problem. I was a man with a purpose. I quickly made a nuisance of myself, bugging the so-called veterans about what it was really like in the field. What should I take with me? And on and on. I bugged the supply sergeant about getting issued a .45 pistol, but was advised that *no one* in the 173d carried a pistol. Several someones had had accidents, and they damned sure weren't going to issue one to an FNG!

I put away my gear and tried to find a place to get a drink, but no one wanted a new guy hanging around their club. The food at the mess hall was inedible, so I decided to go to bed early. I got one of the old wooden cots.

It seemed like only a few moments later that I was awakened by a sound probably quite common during the London blitz. The most horrendous explosion I'd ever heard shook me out of my bunk. No one else seemed concerned. What I took for a mortar or rocket attack was, in fact, an artillery battery, directly behind our barracks, firing its nightly H & I (harassment and interdiction) missions at Charlie, the purpose being to disrupt his life and keep him awake. They don't even know where Charlie is, but they're going to harass him. What about the schmucks back here behind the lines? I wondered. The rounds were going directly over my barracks. One short round and good night, Irene! Still, I was surprised how quickly I adapted, sleeping the next few nights under the same conditions with no difficulty at all. It was probably a matter of exhaustion as much as conditioning.

CHAPTER 2

Each new arrival had to go through the 173d's jungle school before being sent to the field. This not only gave you a little more information about what you would face, it also gave you some time to become acclimated. I didn't realize in the beginning just how much of that I would need.

The days before school began were spent getting our field gear, newly issued but hardly new, organized for the most comfortable carry. We were fortunate in having some of those getting ready to go home show us how to rig things. They knew from experience what we'd need and what we wouldn't. Some of our gear seemed to have been created and put into use without anyone's having figured out if it would work for the intended purpose or not. Field adaptations seemed, many times, to work just as well as things designed and produced at a cost of millions of dollars.

The load-bearing equipment (LBE) was first. This was a pistol belt, with suspenders attached to take some of the weight off the waist when all the other items were added. First and up front were two magazine pouches. They'd been designed for the magazines for the M-14 rifle, but four M-16 mags fit quite well. By cutting the trim on the upper lid to the pouch you could lay one more magazine across the top. A nylon strap was folded around one mag so you could pull the strap and get your first magazine out without having to claw for it. A field dressing or other bundle was put into the bottom to raise the magazines up in the pouch—again this was done so you wouldn't have to dig. Two hand grenades could be strapped to the sides of each pouch. Two one-quart canteen pouches were carried at the hip to hold the two canteens, and you wanted to make certain you had at least one canteen cup. An indispensable item in the field, the cup was used for drinking, cooking, bailing water out of foxholes, or urinating in if you couldn't get out of your hole and were too fastidious to piss down your pants leg. At least one first-aid pouch was attached to the suspenders, and from there, you put on whatever else you thought was necessary and whose weight you were prepared to bear. Over time, I discovered that it was a lot easier on my waist to leave the belt unbuckled, taking more of the weight on my shoulders. It didn't help my back or neck a lot, but it cut down on the scarring around my waist.

The rucksack was a fairly small bag, considering how much you actually carried in it, but it had three large outer pockets, and what you couldn't fit into it, you tied to the outside or to the aluminum frame that wrapped around your hips at the bottom. A poncho and poncho liner were the most important items for personal comfort. Shaving gear was mandatory; this was after all an Airborne outfit! Like I needed it. I could easily get by without shaving for a week but was required to go through the motions anyway. Personal items weren't actually frowned upon, but if you got tired of the weight, no one else was going to pack it for you. One item I took along and abandoned on the first night was a mosquito net designed to put over a cot. It was just too much trouble to bother with after your hootch had been strung. (Any edifice that will protect one from the elements is a hootch, not to be mistaken for hooch, bootleg liquor. In our case, a hootch was simply a poncho strung between trees. Many times I'd have given my left nut for the liquid hooch.) Food would be up to you. Eat six meals a day if you pleased, but again, you were humping the load. I was surprised that we were not required to carry an extra pair of boots or fatigues. Other items we would be required to carry would be issued when we got to the field. Right then, it didn't seem all that heavy. An entrenching tool was secured to the outside. There were no bayonets to be issued. For the time being, I would have to make do with a small handmade knife I'd been forced to fork out ten dollars for to another GI who must have seen me coming a mile away. It was a rusty piece of junk, could not cut butter, but it had a good point, so it had some potential as a weapon.

School began the Monday after my arrival. It would seem most of those with permanent assignments in the rear tried to follow a standard Monday-through-Friday, eight-to-five, workday. I had a strong hunch that this luxury would not exist in the field.

For the most part, the classes were quite interesting; they touched on various types of VC booby traps, but we were warned that such dangers could never be learned in toto; Charlie's ingenuity was limited only by his imagination.

There were also classes on U.S., enemy, and foreign weapons, explosives, and other equipment. One day, I was on hand when a big sergeant first class was preparing to fire a LAW rocket (light antitank weapon, a one-shot, disposable bazooka). He was standing on the defensive berm surrounding the base and had squeezed the trigger to fire the weapon when the rocket blew up. As the smoke cleared, I half expected to see a body standing there without a head, but he'd been real lucky. All that had happened was that two small pieces of shrapnel had flown up into his helmet and then glanced off into his scalp. He was treated at the scene by one of the medics and continued with the class. Airborne!

My own traumatic experience for the day involved hand grenades. I'd been scared to death of them since basic training, when I'd allowed the spoon to let up twice, arming and firing the devices. Had they been live grenades, I'd have been killed. So I hadn't even been allowed to throw a real one. I didn't think I'd ever live that down. Now I had to do it for real.

The instructor took two of us up on the berm and handed us a grenade each, saying, "When I give you the word, pull the pins, prepare to throw, and then throw them as far out as you can." I was sweating, bad! I followed his instructions, squeezing the devices as hard as I could. When he called, "Throw!" I had such a death grip, it was hard to let go. I finally released it, but in my nervousness and terror, I merely lobbed it to the outside bottom of the berm. The instructor, ever alert, grabbed both of us, and we went flying back down the slope. That cost me about twenty push-ups.

The last thing on the agenda was an overnight patrol into the so-called demilitarized area surrounding the base. We were cautioned, however, to take the training seriously. Another class, just before ours, had ambushed a three-man VC mortar crew, killing all of them.

I had received my issue of field equipment, and this hike was to be a shakedown so all of us could adjust our gear before we got into the long marches. I'd also been issued my M-16. I'd heard about them and got to see one once in a class in Alaska, but I'd never held, let alone fired, one. I'd gone through all of my training with the M-14 rifle. I was pleasantly surprised at how much lighter the 16 was, but I'd have felt a lot more comfortable if I'd had a chance to test-fire and zero it first. What I was given looked like it had been recovered from a battlefield. I soon discovered it was defective; I couldn't switch it to safe. Some wag made the observation that it really didn't matter since we wouldn't be allowed to carry them with a round in the chamber (loaded), anyway. This was getting better all the time!

Other than walking our butts off, the only thing of note from this little excursion was my first encounter with leeches. A couple of us had been sent back along our original line of march, we were told, to locate a map one of the instructors had lost. While wading through a rain-swollen stream, I must have picked the little bugger up. By the time I caught up with the rest of the company, I could feel the itching and stinging. I pulled up my shirt to find an ugly, black piece of slime stuck to my stomach, swollen as big as my thumb. Of course, he was full of my blood.

I knew what leeches were and that, barring some infection, they weren't generally fatal. But that first one still left me somewhat unnerved.

We moved into a stand of rubber trees to set up our night defensive position, called an RON, for "remain over night," and were directed to dig our fighting positions, foxholes. They were supposed to be large enough for the three men on each position to be able to stand up, have plenty of shoulder room, and be protected to chest level. That is a lot of digging with an entrenching tool. Doing it in the mud after our normal afternoon rainstorm just added to the fun. But this was just one more "skill" that I would need for the coming year. At least that's the way it seemed. I also began wondering what I had gotten myself into.

Sometime well after dark, someone at another position heard movement outside our perimeter. On their own initiative, they had engaged the culprit with a grenade rather than firing their rifle. I had to admit that this made sense. A grenade won't give away your position the way shooting will. I doubt that the instructors would have given any of us credit for having that much sense. Maybe the guy had a previous tour? Net results: no bodies. Must have been an animal.

The return march the next day began leisurely enough, the pace nice, slow, and easy. I had one scare; a man walking a position or so in front of me had a grenade drop from his LBE. He felt it fall, looked down, and thinking quickly, he kicked it away. The damned thing landed right in front of me! Fortunately, it was not armed. The arming device had unscrewed itself, so the body was harmless. Yeah, good move on his part, but it sure scared the shit out of me!

Shortly afterwards, we entered some of the thickest and most tangled woods I had ever seen. The trees were no more than fifteen feet or so high, and I'd swear not one of them had any upper leaves. Most had thorns running up and down their trunks that tore at our uniforms and flesh. Vines and creepers entwined the whole mess. Not a breath of wind could penetrate. Everyone had to pull a short stint on point, chopping through tangle with a machete. It didn't take long to be worn to a nub. Canteens were soon drained as was each man's strength. Once again, I had to wonder what the hell I'd gotten myself into.

The column finally broke out of the mess, and we made a

short march back into the base camp. Classes were over. We'd have about twenty-four hours to rest and adjust our gear, then we'd be off to join our units in the field.

The C-130 cargo plane carrying the new replacements landed at Dak To in the Central Highlands about noon, just after another rainstorm had swept the plateau where the 173d was based. The sun was shining on us, but there were a lot of dark, threatening clouds off to the north, as if the tempest hadn't yet begun.

Tents and sandbagged bunkers were the most obvious structures, as well as the numerous emplacements for heavy mortars and artillery. There were thirty or so men and boys in my group, and we were met by a man who introduced himself as Staff Sergeant Brown. He was pleasant enough, but it was apparent he'd already been through this welcoming a few times. We were split up and shuffled off in the mud to join our individual companies. We were also advised that we would probably have a few days before we went to the field. I made a mental note of its being some time in August, but I could not for the life of me think what the date was.

I'd just met my squad leader, S.Sgt. Ray Jones, a large black man, ugly as homemade sin, even if he did think he was pretty. He was cordial enough, however. Replacements are such a pain in the ass. You wonder if they'll live long enough to learn how to tie their boots, let alone be of any value in battle. One of the very first things he told my group was to be sure and wear our dog tags all the time. He told of an APC (armored personnel carrier) that had been hit by a mortar or rocket recently. All nine men inside had been killed, burned beyond recognition. Many either had not been wearing their dog tags at all, or had been wearing them on nylon cord rather than the issue chains. Most of those men would remain unidentifiable forever. He also told us there would be a lot more information to absorb before we began our next patrol in the mountains.

But that information was not to be imparted, at least not then. Within an hour and a half of my arrival, a runner from the command post brought word to Jones. There hadn't even been time for us to receive an orientation from the company commander or anyone else. Staff Sergeant Jones was directed to get everyone ready; we were going into action. A Special Forces compound at a place called Dak Siang was in imminent danger of being overrun by a large force of Viet Cong, and we were going to support the Green Berets.

Six of us loaded aboard the Huey for the flight out. Though that was my first flight aboard a Huey, the sensation and appreciation were lost in the realization of where it was taking me. After all my planning and scheming, I was going into battle for the first time. And I could not deny that I was scared shitless! I tried to reason with myself that this was just what I'd come to Vietnam for, but I could not shake the feeling of doom.

Dak Siang, like Dak To, sat on a wide plateau with a gently rolling slope on one side, the only side I could see, that terminated at the base of a mountain, which, at first, seemed to reach into the clouds forever. It also looked like it would give a mountain goat a nervous stomach. I couldn't help but wonder why Dak Siang, like Dak To, hadn't been put on the higher mountaintops that surrounded them, but . . . ? Lots of questions would never get answered.

My position was on that slope, looking up at the mountain. We were also told that the Viet Cong were coming from that direction, over the mountain peak and probably straight up again at us. Trying to see the enemy, I looked up into the clouds, but the distance was too great. A 105mm artillery battery that had been brought in with us, slung from the bellies of a couple of big CH-47 Chinook helicopters, was already setting up and had begun firing salvos up into the mountain. We, the grunts, then took the empty crates the artillery rounds had been packed into and filled them with dirt to make our bunkers and fighting positions. No obvious signs of the enemy so far, but I did have a good front-row seat for the fireworks and aerial display. There were numerous sorties by helicopter gunships, as well as AE-1 prop-driven fighter planes, as they strafed and bombed the top of the mountain. I was also witness to a very impressive display of their use of napalm. I could not imagine anyone's being able to survive such a beating. But there was no doubt the enemy was up there; one of the attacking gunships was hit and crash-landed about a hundred yards down the slope in front of my position. A jeep raced down from the compound to pick up the crew. Some were brought back on stretchers, so it was apparent they had been wounded, but I wasn't told how badly.

Later that afternoon another Chinook landed near us, and wrapped in ponchos and slung from poles like someone's trophy tiger taken on a hunt, two bodies were carried off. Staff Sergeant Jones inquired and was told that those guys were two of the Special Forces advisors who had been with the ARVN Rangers fighting the VC up on the mountain. They had been killed in battle.

These were not only the first dead Americans I had ever seen, they were the first dead people, period. I could not see their faces or features. I paused from my digging while they were being carried into the compound and watched, examining my own feelings. There weren't any. I hadn't known them. I felt no sorrow, no anger, nothing. I had already instinctively buried some feelings very deeply so I would not have to face them. Later I would wonder if feelings of any kind would ever resurface.

By dusk, it was determined that the situation on the mountain was well enough in hand that it was unlikely we would receive an attack that day. We rigged up for guard duty and prepared to receive the night.

That first night, I broke the first rule of combat; I went to sleep on guard duty. Staff Sergeant Jones woke me up, none too gently I might add, but his threats of court-martial and firing squads meant little compared to my own mortification. I had let my buddies down. I felt so badly, I could have shot myself. I was left to ponder my fate the rest of the night, sleepless, even when it was my turn to sleep, more afraid of what fate would bring in the morning than of any rifle-wielding enemy. Come daylight, he let me off the hook, simply warning that this damned well better not happen again. You bet your ass, Sarge!

That day was spent in continued improvement of our positions. There were more fighter planes and gunships over the mountain, but it seemed obvious the VC had been driven back over the crest because the strikes were now on the other side. The tableau was over. Just before dark, I was selected to go out on a listening post as part of a detail under Sergeant Jim McElwee. I wasn't very impressed with him at first; he looked younger than me, smaller too—skinny, with red hair and freckles. His toothy grin reminded me of a death mask or Howdy Doody. But I soon learned that he was a damned good soldier.

Six of us were going out. We spent the night sleeping on the bare ground in the tall elephant grass (because it grew high enough to hide an elephant, some type of savanna, I was told).

The only thing about the night worthy of note was that several hours after dark, we heard something big moving through the brush toward us. We listened hard and soon heard a distinct cough. "Tiger," was all Jim said. He radioed back to the garrison that he was going to engage it with grenades so they wouldn't get jumpy when they heard the explosions. Conservation is a wonderful thing, but being stalked for a midnight snack is serious business. Jim tossed out two grenades in rapid succession, and after the blast, we heard a very attention-getting roar. I'd have much preferred hearing that from the safety of a zoo, with good strong bars between myself and the owner. We found a blood trail the next day but no cat. I was relieved for his sake as well as ours.

The battle was reported over and won the next day, so our element was told to get ready to move out. We soon loaded aboard the choppers again to begin our next assignment, a search operation in the mountains near a place called Dak Pek. It was time to get on with the primary goal of winning the war.

CHAPTER 3

It seemed like a very long flight to Dak Pek but only because the Chinook we flew in just wasn't as fast as other aircraft. I watched through the chopper's porthole and tried to learn more about the terrain. It seemed to be all up, mountains everywhere, then the deep clefts of valleys covered by the ever-present forest.

The day was dreary, ground fog hanging in patches and veils in the valleys and along the slopes. The mountaintops were lost in the clouds. I reasoned that there might be hundreds of VC below us, but there was no real indication of their presence.

It was raining when we arrived at a hillside LZ. I could just make out the fringes of what I presumed was the village of Dak Pek, or maybe that was the name of the district, mountain, or whatever. There was a very wide river between them and us. I was told that we were less than twenty miles from the Laotian border, a hiding place for the enemy.

The first order of business, after off-loading all of the equipment, was to dig in for the night. I was issued my quota of ten, dark green, nylon sandbags. These made it easier to construct the bunkers we'd turn our foxholes into. There was also chow to be handed out and packed up, mostly C rations, but they did give us a few LURP rations. The Cs were canned and heavier than the LURPs and had to be heated up with what they called "heat tabs," trioxane tablets. Just touch a match to it, and it puts out a very hot, blue flame. I thought that these were a marvelous invention. They'd have come in handy in Alaska, whenever we stopped for a short break, to allow us to warm up a little. They did produce a gas when burning that could be fatal if breathed in any quantity. The LURPs were freeze-dried and packed in airtight wrappers, much lighter than Cs, but they required half a canteen cup of water to reconstitute. Water, I thought, would not be a problem, since it rained all of the time.

I'd been introduced to the other members of my squad as well as the first sergeant, platoon sergeant, etc., but having a pretty poor memory for names, I missed them the first go-around and figured I'd just get to know them in time. The CO was a Captain Connolly, but my dealings with him would be few. I was too much in a "gosh!" frame of mind, amazed by the sights around me and of being where I was in the first place. My senses were trying to absorb so much at once that I was overwhelmed.

I was also overwhelmed by the weight of the gear I was going to have to carry. Each man was supposed to carry a three-day supply of food, at least ten twenty-round magazines for the rifle (only load eighteen rounds, I was told by those who knew. I never saw a thirty-round magazine that go-around), two hand grenades (I carried four, to try to overcome my fear just by the contact), a couple of smoke grenades, two canteens, a claymore mine, one hundred rounds of machine-gun ammo, a couple of 60mm mortar rounds, and for me, a D-handle shovel. It certainly made digging the foxholes easier, but it just added to the burden.

My personal gear amounted to a toothbrush, shaving gear,

poncho liner, poncho, and letter-writing material. I hefted my load and groaned at the weight and only hoped we wouldn't be walking too far at any one stretch.

After packing up, we were allowed to go down to the river to take a bath. The water was only knee-deep, but the current was about as swift as the law will allow. To make matters worse, the bottom felt like a lava bed. And cold! I'd have sworn that water had come directly from a glacier. After entering the water, I was quickly swept off my feet and wondered if the skin would ever grow back on my butt.

After writing a couple of letters home to family and friends, I settled in to relax before dark. We'd all be on stand to—everyone up, armed, and alert—as dusk and dawn were the traditional times that one's enemy will attack. In the meantime, the three men on each position had to take turns pulling guard duty through the night. I had a feeling sleep was going to become a real luxury.

The night was long, sleep hardly realized, when too quickly the dawn came, and we were loading up to begin the march. We crossed the river and found that the current seemed to have subsided a little, or maybe with the load I was carrying, I just wasn't as buoyant. I'd heard that modern technology had gone a long way to reducing the weight of individual items of equipment that a soldier had to carry. I was also firmly convinced this just meant we'd be given more equipment to carry.

My boots got a good soaking during the crossing and began rubbing me raw immediately. When do we get a break? I wondered. We'd only just begun, and already I was exhausted.

I noted the grass-and-straw huts as we entered the village, and the people outside watching us as we passed through. They weren't staring at us with anger or suspicion, or any other discernible emotion. Perhaps they'd just seen soldiers passing through too many times before.

The road we marched on seemed to lead right to the base of another huge mountain. I wondered how we were going to get through it. Then I got my answer; one by one, the soldiers melded with the mountain. It seemed to go up at a steady forty-five degrees, and then they began to climb. Another skill for the outside; I was being trained as a mountain goat. For the next six weeks or so, I often wondered if mountains had any side but up. And when you came down in the rain and mud, most of the descent was done sliding down on your butt.

My mind refused to accept or consider that this was what I was going to endure for the next year. Lift your foot, grab for the next tree or rock, vine, anything, to help pull yourself up, while at the same time, juggling your rifle and that damned D-handle shovel. We got a break every hour, and if not, maybe the next hour.

The rain never stopped, and the mud permeated everything. I wore it, ate it, brushed my teeth with it, and slept in it. I shit mud. C rations didn't have enough substance to them to allow normal bowel functions, not when your system burned off everything so quickly just to keep you going. Leeches appeared again, then the mosquitos. I assumed they would disappear at higher elevations. Not so, they just wore oxygen masks. During brief breaks, I swatted mosquitos and picked off leeches. Insect repellent was great for both. Tiny little leeches can get into the damnedest places you'd ever imagine—and some parts of one's anatomy are too sensitive for cigarettes and insect repellent.

Another, lesser, enemy were the wait-a-minute vines. Just vines and creepers dangling from trees and attached to the ground. One tripped over them or was garrotted by them. They defied being cut. The muzzle piece for the 16 at that time was a three-pronged affair, open at the end. Great for snapping the wire on C-ration cases. On the few occasions I was able to walk with my rifle pointed out in front of me—as it should have been in a combat situation—I always ended up with a wait-a-minute vine caught between the prongs. This required that I back up, disengage, and try it again. Two steps forward, four back. I never could get too far at any one stretch.

That first night in the mountains, I found out what the real luxuries were: extra boot laces to tie up my poncho to make my hootch, an air mattress that didn't leak, enough insect repellent to battle the flying and crawling enemy, an extra C-ration meal, and *sleep*. We were told the last was in shortest supply and had been back ordered for some time. Other things, such as steak and baked potatoes, strawberry pie, a warm bed, dry clothes, a cold beer, and a hot woman (not necessarily in that order), were not luxuries. They simply existed in legend. I could not imagine there being any end to this.

Despite all the rain that fell, our canteens were still empty most of the time. Everything was tried. We would hold up the column at every little stream or rivulet to fill up, but someone was always yelling at us to hurry up as we were holding up the column. Where we were in such a big hurry to get to, I never did find out. We tried catching rainwater directly in our mouths or by holding canteens to trickles running down trees or brush. At night we'd suspend ponchos between trees to catch the dripping water. It worked well as long as you didn't mind drinking through gritted teeth to filter out leaves, dirt, and bugs.

When we got resupplied, about every three days, it was almost like Christmas. Someone would usually want the chow that others didn't care for such as ham and lima beans, known fondly as "ham and motherfuckers," or "ham and claymores." There were also big cardboard boxes, supplement packages, full of candy, gum, toilet articles, cigarettes, writing paper, and so on. Things a good PX would stock that just weren't available to us in the field. I took up smoking to relieve the monotony and smoked Kents because not as many others wanted them.

One variety of candy that no one else seemed to care for was the Hershey's Tropical Chocolate bar. About six or eight ounces of hard, pale stuff that didn't seem affected by the heat, or digestion. We called them guerrilla bars (maybe it was "gorilla"; they did look something like flattened monkey turds). But since there were always plenty of them left after each resupply, I'd stock up and have plenty to eat through the day. That was also convenient because we never stopped for lunch breaks. I never learned why. I quickly developed a system of knowing just how many I could eat each day and hopefully not run out before the next resupply.

The inconveniences seemed to keep piling up. As I said, each man carried ten sandbags to build bunkers each night. They were certainly much lighter and more durable than the old canvas variety. We'd fill them up, chop down a few trees, and build what seemed like fairly substantial bunkers. I never had to find out. Then each morning when we'd load up for the next march, we'd empty the sandbags, fill in the holes, so Charlie couldn't use them if we had to come back and fight in that area. Then we'd roll the bags up to tie to our rucksacks. A sandbag might hold thirty pounds of dirt or fifty pounds of mud. With the mud in particular, you never got them completely empty. With the sixty or seventy pounds of equipment we already carried, add to that another twenty or thirty pounds of Vietnam.

I believed, and was convinced later, that fighting isn't really all that hard. You do what you had been trained to do or learned on your own, trusting to luck or whatever gods there might be. You simply did what you had to do to survive. One attitude was, if you were lucky, you would be wounded and could get out of the field for a while. If real lucky, a wound that would get you shipped home, preferably not in a body bag, and hopefully, with all parts still present and accounted for. If somewhat less than lucky, you got killed. At least then you'd get a good night's sleep. (I had nightmares about dying and going to hell and having to pull guard duty every night through eternity.) Each day you were healthy was just another day you were committed to the mission, whatever the hell that was.

I know I was too harsh about the status quo. The 173d was a good outfit, tested and bloodied in battle many times before and later. The old hands had been there, seen friends and buddies die. They didn't need to prove themselves to anyone. It was just my misfortune to be with them between battles. I was too impatient with everything and everyone and made a lot of people around me angry on a regular basis. They, in turn, looked at me and generally treated me like the green-assed rookie that I was. Just a wee bit of a malcontent. I felt I was different, though I wasn't trying to avoid combat. I was looking too hard for it and got it all of the time from my superiors.

The dawning of every new day brought little variation other than the scenery. The events of each day were a replay of the day before. Up before dawn and on alert until first light, we'd eat a quick meal, pack up, and march until late in the afternoon. It always seemed like the rain was the heaviest when we were on the trail.

There were people around me, my peers and superiors, and I talked to them, but for the main, I was just numb all of the time. While marching, the conversations were just curses of rage, despair, or frustration. Orders were given, people responded. During the brief interval from the time we stopped in the evenings until guard duty began, we prepared our hootches and ate. The conversations might become a little more lively as each man told of the world he'd left, his plans for the future, and the women he'd had, real or imagined. Some of those guys were awful liars.

After dark, sleep arrived easily. And then would come your turn on guard. The darkness would wrap itself around you, and you really were alone. I always felt alone in the beginning, and the fact that my attitude had brought this about never dawned on me. I saw and heard a lot of things that made no sense. Malaria was a big thing. If you got it, you were seen as having abused government property (your GI body) and had taken another man out of the field. Each soldier was required to take one big "horse pill" every week to ward off one kind of malaria and a smaller pill, "birth control," to ward off another. At night the first sergeant would walk about yelling, "Malaria control time. Roll your sleeves down." "Article Fifteen time. Roll your sleeves down." Rolling your sleeves down was considered the best way to avoid being attacked by swarms of mosquitos.

No unit was able to move through the mountains quietly. Orders were shouted from one end of the column to the other. Stragglers were always being yelled at. Some company commanders had "squawk boxes," loudspeakers attached to their radios (an extra load for the RTP [radio telephone operator] to carry, of course, not the CO) so they could hear their radios if they walked away for a moment to converse with other officers, or to take a dump. (Same thing.)

Every evening there was the general cacophony of a military unit setting up camp, trees being felled, and bunkers being built, etc.

Again, every three days helicopters would come out for resupply, and sometimes we'd get a hot meal. This was quite a break from the do-it-yourself variety. (It only seemed like every other meal they brought was liver and spinach.) And mail, *the* biggest booster of morale as long as it was all good news. Every now and then, some REMF general or colonel had to come out and inspect the troops ("Spruce up that uniform, soldier. Button that shirt. Why are your boots so dirty?") Helicopters could not land in triple-canopy jungle so occasionally a chain saw would be lowered to facilitate clearing a LZ. Seldom would a chopper shut down while on the ground; the visiting dignitary might need to get back to the rear for supper with someone important.

Then, after all of that noise, someone would slip furtively about the perimeter at dusk and whisper to all the children,

"Shush, we don't want Charlie to know we're here." Hell, my mother probably knew where I was.

Yes, I was a malcontent and always on someone's shit list. And to make matters worse, I had an uncanny knack, as someone observed, of "tripping over my dick." One of my first nights in the mountains, I was assisting in putting out trip flares as an early-warning device against infiltrators. As I tried to make my way back into the perimeter in the rain, mud, and gloom, I slipped and hit the trip wire, setting off the flare, illuminating myself and everything and everyone around me with about a million candlepower of light. (Well, it was bright.) No one forgot that little accident any time soon.

A few days later, I was climbing from rock to rock, making my way up another mountain. I took one step too great, and my pants ripped at the crotch. Actually, it was as if the material from just below my waist to my knees had been vaporized. Since no one wore underwear in the field, I had no secrets for the next week of that patrol. (Wonder how that would have set with a female integrated army?) In a way, it made some things easier. No messing with buttons when nature called. Just turn and point. That's when I found out the hard way about where leeches can get. Cigarettes or insect repellent are the best ways to get rid of them, but some places are too sensitive. Such a dilemma.

My boots did not fit properly. They were constantly wet and had stretched—with all the "contour walking"—from a size 8R to a 10EEE, or something along that order. I was in constant agony. Leeches found their way in easily enough, anyway. I finally had to cut a hole in the back of one boot to ease pressure on one particularly bad blister, figuring this was simply opening the door for the little buggers. Not so. They attacked the other foot instead. Guess they were like men chasing women; if it's too easy, it's no fun.

The first ten days in the mountains ended without a single sighting of the Viet Cong. Understandably, that did not bother the veterans. I was pissed. Returning to base camp at Dak To was almost like being in another world. At least for that moment, it was sunny and comparatively dry.

Shortly after our return, a formation was held to present awards, medals, and commendations to individuals from some action at an earlier time. I wasn't all that cynical. I envied those men. Because of the wind, I couldn't hear the words being spoken as the citations were read, but it was a magical moment, nonetheless. Flags fluttered in the wind, the men were drawn up in neat and orderly lines. The sun sparkled on the Silver Stars, Bronze Stars, ArComs (Army Commendation Medals), and Purple Hearts. It impressed the hell out of me. Others received their Combat Infantry Badges. This is what it's all about, I thought. I wasn't concerned about saving the Vietnamese people from communism or with making the world safe for democracy. Not even preventing the Reds from marching down Main Street, USA. That was too abstract a concept at that time and place. What I yearned for was the respect and recognition of my superiors and peers and of my countrymen. I wanted to be a hero.

Rest and refitting lasted about three days. The comforts were little different from the field. There were showers, but the water was still cold. I still slept on my air mattress, under my poncho hootch, under the stars. There were three meals a day, hot chow, if you didn't mind walking about half a mile or so to the mess tent. Walking was still torture, so for the most part, I ate my field rations in the open air as before.

The night before we were to go back out, several of us met some guys from the 173d LRP unit (Long Range Patrol). Each of them seemed to have his own knife, everything from daggers to bowies, or some kind of semiauto pistol or revolver. They were wearing semiofficially authorized, Vietnamese-made, "tiger stripe" camouflage fatigues. I also noticed another difference in their uniforms; they did not wear the hated steel pots. I asked one of them about this, whether they had just shed them while in garrison or what. No, I was told, they wore whatever they pleased in the field—berets, bush hats, scarves tied around their heads, or they went bareheaded. That really didn't strike me as practical, but getting away from the helmet seemed like a great idea. It might well protect one from bullets or shrapnel, but I would have been quite willing to take my chances. Besides, I had an extremely hard head.

The LRPs told stories of five- or six-man patrols ambushing a few VC and finding out too late they'd hit the point element to a battalion (about five hundred men). Sometimes their bodies were recovered afterwards, sometimes not. The action was always close, personal, short and sharp, win or lose. They were just about as enthusiastic as the law will allow.

Not for the first nor last time in my life, I was so excited, I could have actually shit. Of course no one with an ounce of sense would volunteer for such an outfit, right? But I'd broken the soldier's rule of never volunteering too many times already. I had no idea how to get into such an outfit or what the requirements were but I had to find out more about this LRP thing.

As I grew up, my heroes were men like Robert Rogers and his Rangers during the French and Indian War, even if he had sided with the English during the American Revolution; Francis Marion, the Swamp Fox of the American Revolution, and John Mosby who, during the Civil War, all but ruled a large area of the Shenandoah Valley in Virginia that became known as "Mosby's Confederacy." With a small band of men, he had controlled an area so large that it had taken an army to try to rout him out, but never with any real success. I'd also read extensively about Darby's Rangers of World War II.

These were my heros. Men who served, generally with honor, always with audacity, and usually against superior odds. They had style, panache. They were part of a brotherhood I desperately wanted to be a part of. The LRPs sounded like just my ticket. If only my luck would change.

CHAPTER 4

Attired in my brand-new jungle fatigues I loaded up my gear for the next mission. (Now I knew why no one bothered to sew their patches on them. After wearing the same clothes for ten days straight, twenty-four hours a day, they were beyond further use. You just got new ones.) The rain had subsided somewhat, and thanks to the miracle of youth, my feet weren't quite as sore. Maybe this mission would be less mundane and I'd see some action.

I'd caught up on my letter writing while at Dak To and had put in plenty of requests for socks, food, and candy, and a new watch. While busting through a solid wall of brush, I'd emerged only to find my old watch had been ripped from my wrist. Not that time really mattered. I'd also spilled my guts in my letter damning the war and everyone running it. I was too disgusted and discouraged to care any more. This fluctuation of attitude would carry me for the rest of my tour.

The next mission was somewhat different. The mountains weren't quite as high or steep, and the rain did let up some. The area wasn't any more fun than the last one, though. There was still the mud to contend with. Sliding down a mountain was the only way I ever seemed to descend. I reached a point where I'd just throw the shovel and my rifle down, slide down to retrieve them, and do it again. Didn't really seem to matter. I'd been issued a new 16, but it didn't look much better than the last one, and I hadn't had an opportunity to test-fire this one either. Going out and not knowing if your weapon will function or not is no great encouragement.

It bothered me a lot, climbing so many mountains. Being at the very bottom of the pecking order, I had no idea what our mission was. My reasoning was that Charlie was not likely to occupy too many high mountaintops, and if he did, so what? Let him keep 'em. On more than one occasion, I saw men dropping from total exhaustion or from the heat. And it wasn't just the cherries (another name for new guys). The veterans were better conditioned in many ways, but many of them were also worn down from doing the same thing for so many months. I was beginning to build up, or so I thought, but it was still a bitch just keeping one foot moving in front, or above, the other.

It was still August, but we had been advised we'd probably still be working this area come Christmas. That certainly affected morale. What was there, then, to look forward to?

In this new AO (area of operations, also your personal space. If someone got up in your face the response would generally be, "get the fuck out of my AO."), I learned the real problems with elephant grass—the ribbonlike leaves would slice you like a razor if they came in contact with your skin. My face, arms, and hands looked like I'd been in a knife fight. Being wet all of the time from rain or sweat, the wounds never seemed to heal, and I knew I was scarred for life. I had my mother send leather dress gloves from my Alaska tour, and they arrived none too soon. After wearing them for a while, they become so impregnated with dirt, mud, and sweat, as well as blood and insect repellent, etc., they seemed to develop their own characteristics. The smell was certainly something to remember.

If not for our clothes and equipment, we might have been mistaken for a band of Neanderthals searching for our next meal. Often I expected to see dinosaurs grazing in the valleys. Everything seemed so primitive—no, primeval, before the dawn of time. Under other circumstances, a lot of the country we passed through would have been considered beautiful, but that was lost on me. One day we were marching through a forest of some really grand trees that towered high above our heads. I looked up and noticed what I took to be an orangutan following our path through the trees. (I know there are no orangutans in Vietnam, but that's what it looked like.) It wasn't uncommon to hear the roar of large cats at night nor to find their tracks during the day. Someone killed a snake one day. It looked like it was made of green silk. I was told it was a bamboo viper, reported to be quite deadly. I wondered when I would find such a snake the hard way.

The enemy, the Viet Cong kind, still remained elusive. While tromping through the rain one day, the column halted. No big deal. It was just a chance for another break. Word came back from man to man, "Everyone move to the side of the trail and take cover. Point has spotted a couple of VC coming down the trail." At last! We were going to see some action! I waited and waited. I was tense, my hands squeezing my rifle for all I was worth, wondering how I would react when the shooting started. On a more practical point, it would also be an opportunity to lighten my load. I intended to throw all of my grenades and fire a lot of ammo.

After what seemed like hours, word was again passed down the column, "Okay, move out quietly. If we're lucky we can get out of here without Charlie knowing we're here." It seemed like we were actually running away from two enemy soldiers. Like I said, I did not have the ear of the powers that be about what their purpose or mission was or anything else, but at that moment I was more disgusted than at any other time in my life. For a moment, I seriously considered firing off a few rounds into the brush and swearing I'd seen someone, or of tossing out a couple of grenades. But without a body or two to show, I also knew no one would believe me. At the least the act would have been looked upon as nothing unusual for a green rookie; at the worst I might be accused of wasting government property, impeding the war effort (whatever that was), or intentionally warning the enemy. I'd be court-martialed. All I could do was to swallow my anger as I watched the others slink off into the rain and fog, or so it seemed at the moment.

In a very short time, it became so normal for me to be carrying a rifle all of the time, as well as all of the other accouterments of war, that I no longer noticed the incongruity of the situation. Firing my weapon would certainly have been a novelty. You never went anywhere without your weapon and ammo, but I'd almost reached the point where I no longer expected to use them.

Each night we'd rig for guard duty. Claymores would be carried out deep into the jungle, away from the perimeter, and trip flares rigged to trees and bushes in front of the mines. I wondered about putting the mines so far out but was told that the backblast was as deadly as the forward blast. If anyone or anything hit the trip wire to the flares, it would light up the world. I already knew how bright they were. Then you would just blast whatever was out there. I never fired a claymore during that time. I usually expected to go out to retrieve mine each morning, only to find it had been stolen by the enemy, or worse, that some night a flare would go off, and I'd squeeze the clacker, only to catch the blast in my face after Charlie had moved it up the hill and turned it around on us. I had early on made a mental note that if I had to blast one off, it would be from the bottom of my foxhole.

One day I was selected to join the point element for our company. I was going along with people I barely knew by sight, let alone anything about. It wasn't exactly a choice assignment. I still had to carry all of my gear, and we had to start out earlier than the rest of the company. The only advantage I could see to it was that, had I been in charge, I'd have set an easier pace. Not having that option, I didn't know what to expect. There was also the factor that with only six of us out front, we might easily be ambushed by the enemy with little likelihood of support from the rest of the company. That prospect didn't bother me too much. I knew I was invincible.

It wasn't very long before I began to appreciate one advantage of this small group. We moved quietly, hardly making a stir in the tranquility of the surrounding jungle. If Charlie found us, it would be by accident and not because we'd announced our presence with all of the noise usually made by the company.

We wandered about for several hours at a very leisurely pace, since our small group did not have to contend with the general accordion effect always experienced by larger units on the move. The sergeant in charge looked like he was younger than I was, but he'd been there longer. For the most part I just kept my mouth shut and observed. Was this what it would be like in the LRPs?

We passed through a small Montagnard village before noon, the people following us with their eyes. While the looks they gave us weren't openly hostile, I felt no comfort there. It was only my imagination that there was a rifle trained at us from every thatch hut. I'd read in Robin Moore's book, *The Green Berets*, that the Montagnards were generally friendly to Americans, though there was no love lost between them and the South Vietnamese. Whatever the situation was, maybe this particular village hadn't gotten the word. I was glad to shake the dust of that place from my feet.

Before long, we came to a wide plateau our sergeant thought we needed to cross rather than circle. It was about half as long as a football field and maybe twice that wide. The trees surrounding it, and the area in general, reminded me a lot of the countryside around Fort Ord.

Hey-diddle-diddle, we went straight up the middle. I was walking in the middle of the detail. Our pace was fairly relaxed and easy. I noted that the guys in front of me were stepping over what appeared to be a log. As I approached the log, I noticed that it was moving. I'm no herpetologist, but I was reasonably certain that I was looking at the granddaddy of all pythons, at least part of it. What I could see, possibly the midsection, was eight to ten inches in diameter. I could not see either end. I wasn't really too concerned. Despite years of watching Jungle Jim fighting big snakes, I just did not believe one would attack something it couldn't swallow unless it felt threatened. Small children or pigs, maybe. I had every intention of giving it a wide berth.

Just for conversation's sake I pointed the snake out to the sergeant. It really didn't seem like a big deal to me other than another observation of nature. But for some reason ol' sarge decided that snake was a threat to the welfare of his mission. I watched as he raised his rifle, switched to full automatic, and fired a couple of short bursts into the snake's body, first three rounds, then another five or six.

That fucking snake went wild! I saw the grass going down around us like it had been cut with a scythe. I ran like a thief. I had no doubt the snake was mortally wounded, but it wasn't dead yet, and it was certainly one pissed-off reptile. I might well have set a new record for the hundred-yard dash as I raced for the trees, leaving the rest of the team well behind me. They weren't too long in coming, though, including the ever-bright Mr. Sergeant-in-Charge.

"What the fuck did you do that for?" I almost screamed. It was no time for diplomacy, and I was pissed.

"Who the hell do you think you are to question me?" he demanded. It was fairly obvious I was going to be on someone else's shit list again, not a new experience. But I felt right was on my side this time. "They," the powers that be, would understand this outburst of insubordination. A few more words were exchanged, the gist of it being, from my point of view, that the snake hadn't been as great a threat as the sound of the rifle being fired, letting everyone know we were in the neighborhood.

Sarge reminded me quite heatedly that I was still a newbie, a fucking new guy, the inexperienced kid who should have more respect for his superiors. That is also what the platoon leader told me when we rejoined the company later that afternoon. All I could do was to choke my anger down again, wishing I was somewhere else. In fact, I had been guilty of insubordination, but—my reputation being what it was—if I had really been wrong, I believe they would have taken some kind of action against me under the Uniform Code of Military Justice (the UCMJ, as it was generally referred to, the military code of criminal law). Nothing was done, nor was it ever mentioned again. I believed that vindicated me, in a left-hand manner.

* * *

We had another young lieutenant join our platoon shortly after that incident. He was new in country and probably being broken in to take over his own platoon. He was friendly enough and very enthusiastic. I had no idea where he'd gone to school to get his bars, but he was also a Ranger School graduate. He was also an infantry soldier's worst nightmare—a second lieutenant with a map.

When he joined us, he discovered that our platoon was usually the drag platoon when on the march, bringing up the rear. He didn't think that was fair, and it wasn't. It meant we were always having to rush to keep up because the column would spread out. Somehow he managed to get us moved up to the position as point platoon, leading the company while on march. Trouble is, while we no longer spent as much time running to catch up, no one else did either. We didn't move nearly as fast nor as far because we were stopped constantly while the lieutenant tried to figure out just where we were; he'd gotten us lost time and time again. The next day, we were the drag platoon again. No one was hurt, but we sure took a lot of ribbing for the lieutenant's mistakes.

A few days later, the lieutenant tried to redeem himself. The rains had come again, and a river in our path was running too high and fast for us to cross safely.

The lieutenant directed the rigging of a two-rope bridge, one he'd obviously learned about in one of his schools. We would be able to cross on that and stay dry in the process. As bad as I am about volunteering at the drop of a hat, I wanted no part of this. No matter; I was volunteered. That's what comes from being known as the kid with the big mouth. Guess they figured I was expendable. As it turned out and none to my surprise, the lieutenant wasn't any better at building bridges than he was at reading maps.

I climbed onto the shaky affair, loaded with all of my equipment. As I scooted out, I knew something was wrong. The rope wasn't taut enough, and about halfway across, I went asshole over teakettle, ending up hanging upside down. I gave up trying to right myself after a few tries and dropped into the water, using the rope to pull myself to the other side. I wasn't about to go back and try it again. A few more guys had to try the bridge, also; my example obviously not being enough to convince them that this was not a good idea.

After everyone finally got across, one way or another, we set up our night position on the opposite bank. Those of us who had gotten more of a dunking than others had some vicarious revenge later. Word was passed around, and then confirmed by our platoon leader, that during the crossing, the would-be bridge builder had lost his map. That was not a loss from our point of view. The trouble was (and to add further insult to injury), the lieutenant had, against some very specific orders, noted all of the battalion's radio frequencies and coded call signs on the map's plastic covering. The brass had him out late that night, trying to find it. No doubt there was also a lot of scrambling back at headquarters to change codes and frequencies since, found or not, the old ones had to be considered compromised.

The last episode for the great architect/pathfinder, for the time being, was shortly afterwards on another night position. He had a very unsettling habit of checking on "his boys" after dark, with a flashlight. I will give him the benefit of the doubt; maybe he just had extremely bad night vision. Otherwise, one must assume he was just plain stupid. Since it was easy enough to see him coming while making his rounds, everyone on each position either crawled into his bunker or got as close to mother earth as possible in case some VC lurking with a rifle, was waiting to pick someone off. At such times, one will pop the buttons off of one's shirt to get a little closer to the ground. Some people have luck in other ways—the lieutenant was never hit. But I do believe that guys like him don't get killed; they are probably responsible for as many deaths of their own men as is the enemy.

A few days later in another, drier part of the AO, I lost my first in-country buddy. It was not atypical of deaths or injuries in that war. We were walking up a gently terraced hill, much easier on the legs than what we were used to. There was an explosion up ahead. The column halted, and medics ran forward. I heard calls repeated over one of the squawk boxes for a Medevac chopper; someone had been wounded.

Before long, a litter was being carried down the hill. As the carriers passed, I glanced down and saw that the guy on it was the other Gary that I'd arrived in country with. "Well, Gary, what happened?" I asked stupidly. His face was pale, and his eyes told of his pain. His right foot was bandaged, but the shape wasn't right; it wasn't all there. "Hi, Gary. Looks like I'm going home," he replied. He was right, and he knew it. A chill ran through my body. It was the first incident that made me really feel something personal about the war. Gary was just a kid, but now his whole life was going to be changed forever. I did not really feel comforted by the fact that at least he was alive.

Our platoon leader told us later what had happened. It had been a booby trap, nothing particularly elaborate, just a long piece of bamboo split down the middle and held apart by a small stick. Metal connectors were attached to both sides of the slit. Wires then were attached to the metal strips and the whole thing rigged to a battery and hand grenade, using an electronic detonator. Something as small as a squirrel running across the bamboo could have set it off. It was designed to maim, not kill, taking off a foot, a hand, or your nuts. Gary's luck had run out. Four other guys were wounded in similar fashion that same day. We never saw a single VC, and the ones responsible had probably been miles away when our men had hit the booby traps.

Fortunately, again depending on one's point of view, our days in the Central Highlands were about to come to an end. All battalions and companies were ordered back to Dak To to prepare for some big "secret" mission.

CHAPTER 5

Upon our arrival at Dak To, we were advised that the entire brigade was being moved to a place on the coast called Tuy Hoa. There was quite a bit of activity going on, other companies coming in from the field, the earlier arrivals and the

garrison personnel having already begun the dismantling and
packing up of gear.

By this time I'd buddied up with a guy named Parker, a light-
skinned black guy about my age from Detroit. We really had
nothing in common except our shared misery. He was also another malcontent, but we got along pretty well anyway, at least
in the beginning. Over the preceding weeks, we'd spent a lot of
time talking, discussing whatever struck our fancy, lying about
the girls we'd had, and so forth. We even seemed to share a
common interest in books. We'd found an old copy of *Beau
Geste*, well worn and falling apart. As hard as it was for me to
do, as I'd finish each chapter, I'd tear out that section and give
it to Parker, since I read faster than he did. I hated to damage a
good book. We also got into the habit of doubling up together
under a common hootch at night.

Parker and I put our heads together one day and came up with
half a thought. With all of the bedlam going on around us, we
decided it would be a cinch to raid one of the ration dumps and
steal a couple of cases of C rations. The most scrumptious meal
I could imagine at that time included a couple of cans of "Beef,
with Spiced Sauce," one or two cans of "Ham and Eggs,
Chopped," topped off by a can or two each of pecan nut rolls
and pound cake. A bottle of Tabasco sauce would have been
nice but was not available. Parker's imagination was no better
than mine.

We finally found an unguarded dump and easily made off with
a couple of cases each. It was with an awful lot of pleasure that
we could now throw away cans of slop we'd never cared for, as
well as others that were not on the top of our "favorites" list.
We stuffed ourselves all night long. This was as close to heaven
as we could imagine it. A few bottles of ice-cold beer would
have been Nirvana, had such a thing really existed.

It was by then early to mid-September. Most of the days were
so much alike, it wasn't worth keeping track of the date. Few
of my letters home, in fact, were dated. I wasn't anywhere close
to being short (time to go home, or more commonly, DEROS,
date estimated to return from overseas). Unit by unit, everyone
loaded aboard the big C-130 aircraft for the flight to the coast.
Those who'd had the locals sew their brigade patches or jump
wings on their uniforms were ordered to remove them so no one

would know what unit we were with when we arrived. This was supposed to be a secret move for a big offensive. Bullshit!

Our plane landed at the Tuy Hoa air base, another world entirely from the one we'd just left behind. The runway was a grid of PSP, "pierced steel planking," laid out over a yellowish orange sand. And there was no mud to be seen anywhere! It was a beautiful day with a few high, scattered clouds. Everything was nice and dry in the sun. It was also warm, almost roasting. We could smell the salt in the air from the ocean not far away, and the breeze was so fresh and clean that it was almost orgasmic.

After loading all of our gear aboard waiting trucks, several guys noted a few air force types standing around. One of them asked, "Who are you guys?" "None of your business," we replied, as per orders. The air heads started laughing, and one of them held up a sign that proclaimed, "Welcome to the 173d ABN BDE (SEP)." Some secret move! We soon found out that the mamma-sans in the vill were even busy making copies of the brigade patches and other regalia to sell to us.

Company C set up tents and hootches in a bivouac area not far from the beach in a grove of honest-to-God palm trees. The hootches were strung a little higher than normal so we could take advantage of the sea breeze. Few of us gave much thought to mosquitos at that point. This was almost like being on a fucking vacation.

Parker and I made a quick trip to a large PX trailer that had been brought down and parked close to our company area. We had about ten dollars between us for our shopping trip. What did we want? We were like kids in a candy store, the variety of goods was just so overwhelming. We finally decided to buy a half case of canned apricots. After returning to our hootch, we proceeded to open can after can and stuff ourselves as if we'd never have a chance like this again. I quickly became so sick to death of apricots, I didn't think I'd ever be able to look another one in the face again.

Other than that faux pas, I was beginning to feel like I'd just been released from prison. It was so warm and dry at Tuy Hoa, and the sand felt so good between my toes. The wind tried to rustle through the stubble on my head, and the sun felt like a kiss.

Company by company, we were allowed to go to the beach

for a swim in a small man-made lagoon. The water was a beautiful blue, very nice, cool, and refreshing. We were advised, however, not to venture beyond the lagoon. Point one, the riptide was extremely fast, and second, there were sharks out there. I wasn't sure if I actually saw any fins cutting the surface of the water, but didn't feel I had to be warned twice.

Having never been any great shakes as a swimmer, I soon tired of that and instead decided to just lie out on the beach and soak up the unaccustomed sunlight. For one thing, I felt more clean than at any time over the last four or five weeks. My stomach was full, the weather was gorgeous. Maybe things really were beginning to improve. Silly boy!

What we could see of the area so far looked really nice, but behind every silver lining there looms a dark cloud. We knew we had not been brought there, at great trouble and expense, for a vacation. The rumor mill had it that we were going to embark on the greatest offensive since Normandy.

There were a number of briefings about the local Viet Cong, how aggressive and motivated they were supposed to be. If they mentioned the NVA (North Vietnamese Army, well trained regulars), I didn't pay any attention, not realizing there was a great deal of difference between the two forces at that time. Had there been time, I don't doubt that we'd have been run through physical training and dress rehearsals for the coming offensive. We were toughened in many ways from our sojourn in the mountains, but I would not go so far as to say we were uniformly in good condition. Our bodies would require a lot more time than we had to recover from what we'd been through. There was a little time before we jumped off, so most of us took full advantage of it to rest and catch up on sleep.

The coastal area stretched for miles in every direction. The mountains we were going into could be seen, all but encircling the plain, some distance away. Still, compared to what we'd just left, they looked hardly more formidable than a gentle rise in the ground. Someone pointed out a large white object, several miles away to the southwest, that was plainly visible on one of the higher hills. "That's a big natural rock formation they call the Buddha. Looks like a big monkey to me. Ya gotta use your imagination," one of the local soldiers told us. "ARVNs take spies and traitors up over it in choppers and push them out. It makes the rest of them talk better." I could not say the idea really offended me, but neither was I convinced the speaker knew what the hell he was talking about. I was not so naive that I didn't believe such things could, would, or did happen. By all accounts, we were fighting a particularly brutal enemy. Our South Vietnamese allies were, of course, not inclined to be exactly gentlemanly either. It tends to rub off on you after a while. A lot of our people might not participate in anything like that, but many of them would not try to prevent it either. Guerrilla warfare is not for the faint of heart.

After a few more days of rest, we began drawing our gear for the planned assault. My squad received a .50 caliber machine gun. At about ninety-seven pounds for the weapon alone, it's not exactly an assault weapon. Two men had to carry the .50, and others would carry the tripod and ammo. I was informed that it would be my duty to take over for anyone who was hit and carry whatever they had been assigned. For a short time, I thought I was going to slip away from that D-handle shovel, but they caught me at the last moment. "Here, Ford. Ya forgot this," Staff Sergeant Jones told me as he stood there with a big shit-eating grin. He knew I hadn't forgotten any such thing.

H hour, the time for the attack came, and we boarded the choppers. A combat assault, huh? Whether by landing craft from the sea or parachutes or helicopters, is there any easy or safe way to go calling on the enemy? I was getting more and more nervous by the second. Once again, I refused to accept the possibility that I might get hit, but as with every parachute jump I'd made, I couldn't ignore the likelihood of injury.

The moment for the assault arrived, and we were off and running. We flew straight from our former bivouac area on a direct course for the mountains surrounding the plains of Tuy Hoa.

Going into what could easily be a hot LZ is spooky, but landing and finding that the enemy has either fled or was never in the immediate area in the first place leaves you with a strange sense of relief and awe. We off-loaded, and at the last moment, I was directed to assist with the .50, as one of the men carrying it was needed somewhere else. Damn, but that thing was heavy! Fortunately we didn't have to carry it far, but we also would not have the opportunity to man it, either. That would be left to others who had more experience. I felt like the valet who had to carry the bride over the threshold so someone else could enjoy himself on the honeymoon.

This was not to be a flat-land operation, but at least this time my company had a different assignment. We would man the base camp while other companies went out on search operations for the enemy. Someone must have screwed up, but I wasn't going to bring it to their attention. We'd get at least three days of sitting about and would only have to dig one foxhole. What a deal!

My squad's position was on a sloping finger of the crest we were to occupy. Once the orders were given, we began digging in. Now I knew why we'd been given pickaxes; I would have sworn that mountain was made of solid marble. It took us a whole day to dig a position about half the size of our normal hole, only to have the lieutenant come around to inspect and tell us, "It's too far back. Move down the slope about ten feet." You do not move a fucking hole, of course, so we spent a second day digging a new one. And we had to fill the other one in! So much for having thought we'd lucked out.

I really couldn't complain, though. The digging was no fun, but at least we didn't have to hump for those few days. Things could have been much worse.

We had a good breeze blowing across the hill, and for the first time in what seemed like ages, mosquitos were not a problem. Every once and a while, we could hear shooting or explosions in the distance. No one bothered to tell us if the other companies were actually engaging the enemy or if there were just a lot of nervous trigger fingers. We received some incoming fire several times after dark, but no one was hit. This was my first time under fire, so to speak, but none of it came close enough to make me feel the sensation. We were even allowed to return fire down the slope. Now I found out about the flaw of this particular 16; when on full automatic, it jammed after every third round. Great! If I'd had any training with the weapon, it might not have been such a big deal. All that I knew was that I had a rifle with full-automatic capabilities, and I saw no reason to fire in any other mode.

On one of those nights, Jones was wandering about and had directed me to check the wire of my claymore. I moved forward to do so, picking it up and tugging on it gently. Something tugged back. I tried it again, thinking, hoping it had been my imagination. Again there was an answering tug. I hesitated a moment or so, more afraid to fire my weapon and have someone think my imagination had gotten the best of me than of being shot by whoever or whatever was down the hill. Finally, I blasted off a few shots and rolled back into the foxhole. Nothing else happened. When I checked the mine the next day, everything was copacetic. The claymore didn't seem to have been disturbed, and there were no blood trails. Was it my imagination?

On the third night on that hill, my squad was ordered to prepare for a patrol after dark. Jones would be leading it. I was still amazed at how much the area reminded me of Fort Ord. The trees were in small stands, scattered across the terrain, and most of them looked like they were blackjacks. So much for my ability to identify vegetation. The area we would patrol was gently rolling hillside, great for a nice easy hump. I felt strange going out like this, nothing but combat gear and my rifle, no rucksack or shovel to carry. I felt absolutely awkward not having that weight on my back and felt like I was going to fall on my face.

After leaving the perimeter, we stumbled about for a while and then set up an ambush position. We waited and waited. No one came to call, so after a few hours, we loaded up and started back in. Once we began reentering the perimeter, Jones began counting noses; we were one man short. I looked back into the gloom and saw two men coming. That was one too many. Everyone dropped to the ground to confront this new threat. At the last moment, the two figures turned and ran away. They must have been VC, but to have taken them under fire without warning could have been bad news. There was always the slight chance one of them was our lost man and that he'd secured a prisoner. What made me nervous was that I'd been the last man in the patrol; they'd been walking just a short distance behind me, and I hadn't even seen them.

A few minutes later, Pierce, our little-boy-lost, showed up. "I got separated from you guys and couldn't find my way back. Then I seen these guys. I follered 'em. I knew Ford was in front of me, so I hollered, 'Hey, Ford, wait for me,' and they took off. I couldn't keep up with 'em. Then I seen ya'll; so I guess they must'a been VC, huh?'' Good guess.

Some months later Staff Sergeant Jones showed me an article in *Stars and Stripes*. A reporter had interviewed Pierce about his "harrowing" experience. He was quoted almost word for word, except for the fact that he didn't tell them who he'd yelled at. I could have been famous!

A day or so later, the other companies walked into base camp. I fully expected to be told to load up for our turn on patrol, but at the last minute, the orders were changed. Apparently there had been so little contact that the AO just didn't warrant further action. We loaded up for another assault, back down the mountains into the plains and rice paddies.

Someone decided to give us a break. Men had been complaining about the heavy loads they were carrying, so we were directed to package up our personal belongings into our ponchos and they would be brought down to us that evening. I gave up maybe two pounds of personal gear, and was given, instead, two 81mm mortar rounds and another one hundred rounds of machine-gun ammo. The mortar rounds alone must have weighed about ten pounds apiece. I certainly hoped they didn't do us any more favors.

The flight down the hill didn't take long, and we were unceremoniously dumped into an area of large, dry rice paddies to await further orders.

There was a large hill behind us, a village of stone or concrete huts to our front, and another vill of grass or straw huts a few hundred yards to our left. We had been set up in a blocking position. Throughout the day, we watched jet aircraft bomb and strafe the first vill while another unit made a ground assault on the other one. I heard more shooting that day than any day previously but was still unaware of anything coming my way.

Our front-row seat was a good one while the sun was still low in the sky. As the day progressed, it became less so. The sun beat down upon my helmet without mercy until I felt like my head was in an oven. My uniform was soaked with sweat, and I began to itch as if I had diaper rash. It wasn't long before I'd drained both of my canteens, and there seemed no more water to be had. Finally—and against orders—I crawled over to a paddy that did have water in it. I'd been told that the South Vietnamese did not use human waste for fertilizer, but something turdlike floated on the surface. I wasn't certain how effective my dirty handkerchief was as a filter. I kept brushing cigar-shaped objects away from the mouth of my canteen, but I no longer cared.

Parker was also beginning to get on my nerves. He'd developed a real attitude problem (as if I should talk). Perhaps I was adjusting to things a little better while he remained a confirmed malcontent. If anyone said anything to him, he'd reply, "White-assed motherfucker" unless it was Jones or someone else who was black, in which case they were, "Fuckin' Oreos." I was really beginning to lose patience.

Later in the afternoon, we moved out. Our line of march took us through the bombed-out vill. As we were passing one of the smoldering huts, some guy with cameras strung around his neck was snapping his shutter at us. "Hey, soldier," he yelled at me, "Look this way and smile." I was tired, hot, and not in a good mood. "Fuck you," I muttered. He got absolutely huffy. Guess I'd missed another chance to be in the history books.

We wandered about for several more hours until we came to a cone-shaped hill covered by a dense thicket of what looked like briar. Thorns tore at me as I made my way to the top to unload my extra ammo, only to be told that they weren't sure if they'd be able to get our personal gear to us that night. Choppers were coming and going continuously, but I guess they were too busy for that kind of mission. Then I was told my position for the night was back down at the bottom of the hill.

Parker and I were joined by a guy by the name of Tom Santa. I'd seen him around but hadn't really gotten to know him. He'd been in country for a while and had seen some action. Blond and a little heavyset (what seemed heavyset to us at that time would be considered anorexic anywhere else), he was quiet, and while not unfriendly, neither was he outgoing.

We selected a spot near the base of the briar patch. As we began digging in, we took our time so the work wouldn't be done until after dark. That was easy enough since the dirt was full of baseball-size rocks. We had conspired together. All of the lifers would be up on the hill. With all of those thorns be-tween them and us, we strongly suspected they would not be coming around to check on us after dark. I had no desire to dig another hole if I could help it. We didn't; we simply scooped out a small fighting shelf, a sunken platform about six inches deep, six feet long and perhaps eight feet across. If we got hit, we'd be in a world of hurt, but after so many nights of digging in and nothing happening, we were willing to take a chance.

A heavy fog came in after dark. It seemed to glow and pulse as it surrounded us. I could have sworn I saw figures moving through it. VC, ghosts? From my experiences so far, one was as likely as the other. Someone on top of the hill fired a few aerial flares, which lent a greenish glow to the fog, but we still couldn't see anything. "Fuck it," Tom said, "let's get some sleep. We can die rested just as easily as we can die tired. Our biggest enemy tonight is the lifers." Since he had more time in country and experience, as well as the fact that I liked what he was saying, I chose to listen to his advice. Sometimes taking orders isn't so hard.

CHAPTER 6

The night passed without any unpleasantries from the bad guys. There is an old Arab proverb, "Fortune is infatuated with the efficient." Perhaps it also made allowances for the exhausted. Sometimes we just reached a point where we no longer cared.

That day, we began a new phase of the operation, searching out an enemy that had apparently gone to ground. At least the ground was fairly flat. But we now began plodding through the rice paddies. My feet had become accustomed to being wet all the time, but before long, the rest of me had been soaked also. At least this place was warm.

As we trudged along through the paddies, it was almost as if someone had devised a new means of fucking with us. Lieutenant Thompson, our XO, had come out to join us for a day or so. He was not well known to me, being an administrative type who remained in the rear most of the time. From my limited experience, he wasn't a bad guy. He did seem to be one of those people who seem to never get dirty. His uniform was always neatly pressed, his boots spit shined in the Airborne fashion. I was often surprised this wasn't required of us also.

Thompson was what we called a profiler. Despite brigade policy, he wore a .45 pistol on his hip, slung low and tied down. He also affected a green silk cravat tied around his neck. Actually, I hated his guts. As we slogged through the paddies, Thompson and his RTO (radio telephone operator) would pace us along the dikes. "I hope the son of a bitch steps on a fuckin' land mine," someone near me muttered. I almost cracked up. It wasn't that he really wished the lieutenant any harm, but misery does love company, and we were about as miserable as you can get. Since dikes meander about, and we walked in a straight line, we didn't travel nearly as far as he did, but when we got to the next village, he would arrive fresh, cool, and clean. He looked like Hollywood's idea of a soldier; we looked and smelled like the real thing.

We entered a small farmstead and began searching for signs of enemy personnel or arms caches but found nothing, zilch, nada. We continued on to the next site. The rest of the day saw little variation.

Upon arrival at that night's RON, I once again found it necessary to try to reason with the powers that be. The spot designated for Parker, Santa, and me was flush against a solid wall of bamboo several yards thick and twenty or so feet high. "But, Sarge," I tried to explain to Jones, "there's no way anyone can get through that stuff, and I'd bet no bullets can penetrate it, either."

"That is where you are assigned, Ford. The captain wants the distance between positions on the perimeter uniform. This is your spot, so dig in."

I stood my guard that night facing into that solid wall, feeling like a child stuck in a corner for a misdeed. I felt like a damned fool. Orderly perimeter, my ass!

One thing definitely was different about Tuy Hoa. We were beginning to get used to the sounds of shots being fired around us. Or I should say, I was. A lot of the others had heard it all too often in the past. Someone brought to my attention one day a distinct sound of the shooting, a *crack-pop*. "That's an AK-47. Ya can't miss it." He was right. Before long, by sound alone, I, too, could give a pretty good account of the weapons being fired.

On the following day, we continued our search. Our point

had located a large two-story building, possibly someone's country home. We found a few bloody bandages in the attic but no VC, no bodies, and no equipment.

We continued our advance. The paddies in that area were terraced, with one being slightly lower than the one before as the elevation decreased toward a canal. Some were flooded, while others were not. We began receiving small-arms fire from a line of trees that ran parallel to the canal. My platoon spread out and advanced at a run. Quite a few smoke grenades had been tossed out to mask our approach, and the air was full of green, purple, yellow, and red smoke. It seemed unreal. A few rounds passed in my direction, but nothing seemed to come too close. It didn't dawn on me that there might be a couple of bullets flying that were addressed, "To whom it may concern." My attitude seemed to have been that if I didn't actually see someone shooting at me, I wasn't in any danger.

Shortly after we reached the canal, we heard several explosions on the other side. We learned before long that one of the guys from our company, Sgt. Don Fant, had been with a recon element when they had been fired on by a couple of VC in a tunnel. The recon people had gotten the unsociable VC. I'd seen Fant around a few times. A tall, blond, good-looking guy with an easy walk. He was also trained as a Pathfinder. Seemed like a nice enough guy during the few moments we'd spoken before.

A couple of tunnels were found on our side of the canal. Tear gas was thrown in to flush out anyone who might still be inside. A volunteer was needed to go down and check them out for weapons or other equipment. I was always dumb enough to try anything once. It was just fortunate for me that I didn't know half as much then as I learned later. Tunnel rats had to be some of the bravest and craziest soldiers in the whole world, with balls the size of watermelons, and made of cast iron. Yes, I volunteered.

I was given a .45 auto and a flashlight for the excursion. I stripped to the waist and put on my gas mask. Whoever had found the tunnel had already cleared away the concealing vegetation. Now it looked like little more than a large rabbit hole. Let's go, Alice.

Flashlight in one hand, pistol in the other, I dropped down inside and found the first room no more than about eight or ten feet below the surface. What I could see of the tunnel through the smoke didn't seem to go back much more than twenty feet or so away from the canal. I found a pile of equipment, including a nylon poncho and a rolled-up hammock that looked like it was made from parachute material, including static line for the supporting ropes. There was nothing else of any significance. No hidden trapdoors were immediately evident.

As I turned to make my way back out, I struck the side of my gas mask on a supporting pole for the tunnel, breaking the seal of the mask. Gas quickly swept into my mask, and I nearly panicked. I couldn't see or breathe. Somehow, I was able to see just enough light to find my way back to the entrance. I popped out of the hole without assistance and ripped the mask from my face. I ran into the wind and then stood, retching for several minutes, until my breath returned.

While I was recovering, someone had taken the .45 from me. I watched as Lieutenant Thompson approached the Vietnamese officer it belonged to. Several of the Viets had accompanied us that day, but I had had no contact with them until this captain had offered me the pistol. Thompson made it known he wanted to test-fire the pistol. He took it and stepped out a short distance away from our group. He then took up a good one-handed firing position. I watched him as he stood there for several moments, seeming to pull the trigger, but nothing happened. He looked at the pistol, then tried again. Still nothing.

Curious, I walked over to see what the problem was. Thompson was just standing there, holding the pistol in the palms of both hands. As I approached, he looked up at me, and his face seemed to go a little white. "Rusted solid," he said. "This thing wouldn't fire if you gave it a week's notice." Now I really was sick. I was also wondering if it would have been a breach of diplomacy for me to have beaten the snot out of that "allied" officer. Goofy son of a bitch, not taking better care of his weapon! He could have gotten me killed! And I felt just as goofy for not having checked it first. A pistol that won't shoot is no better than a fucking rock.

After a while, we crossed the canal to have a look at the two dead VC. It was quite a sight. One still looked human from the waist down, but above that there was nothing distinguishable as human. It just looked like so much ground-up meat. The other one's chest was pretty swollen, despite numerous puncture wounds. The top of this man's head was missing, as if it had been sliced away on a line running over his eyes and back behind his ears to the base of his skull. Pieces of his skull and brains were hanging in the tree above the tunnel they'd come out of.

Sergeant Fant was there to explain what had happened. "One of our guys spotted them after they fired at us. He went to the entrance to try to talk them out. Instead of answering, they threw a grenade at him. It didn't make it out. When it blew up, it got 'em both and collapsed the tunnel. We dug 'em out."

"I thought you'd killed them," I said.

"Not these two," was all he said.

I had never seen a corpse in this condition before. It just didn't seem to bother me. I looked at them for a few moments and went over and sat down on a log. I decided to have lunch, a can of fruit cocktail.

Some of our men were ordered to bury the dead VC. I just watched, chewing away on the canned fruit. A few moments later, Lieutenant "Let's-build-a-bridge" came over. He wanted to see the bodies also. He stood over the bodies for several minutes, and it looked like he was getting a little green around the gills. He tried to cover it up; "Hey, that looks neat, doesn't it?" He kept on in that vein for a little bit, not sounding terribly convincing. Then he turned around and saw me eating. That was too much! He gagged and ran off into the bushes, and I could hear him retching up his toenails. I continued eating, trying to stifle my laughter.

As we packed up to move out, I noticed the fresh graves. The bodies were covered up, but the hands and feet were sticking out, and at some really odd angles. The grave diggers had also taken some brigade patches and cloth jump wings and had placed them between the fingers and toes of the corpses. This would let any of their friends who came to recover them know who had done the deed. It was sick, but we hoped it would be effective.

Our search continued along the canal. Several more tunnels were found by one of our squads on the other bank, and grenades were thrown in, but apparently no one was home. The rest of the day was a complete bore.

CHAPTER 7

The afternoon after the tunnel-rat action, the company moved to a small spot of high ground in an area surrounded by rice paddies. The island was about twenty-five yards wide and fifty yards long. At one time it had apparently been someone's home because there was the shell of a mud hut in the center, the roof and one wall long gone. The whole place was quite overgrown with weeds and other growth. There were a number of tall trees, and despite the tangle, it was rather peaceful. Staff Sergeant Jones returned from another briefing and advised us we would probably be staying for a few days.

He took my little group to a spot on the south side of the oasis and told us to dig in. We looked around, and Santa spotted a small pit, possibly an old garbage dump. "Sarge, the ground around here is soaked. We'll just dig into water if we have to dig our normal holes. Can we just scoop that out a little?" he asked, indicating the dip.

Jones considered for a moment, then told us to go ahead. "Just don't think you're gonna have it this easy all the time, ya know," he said, just to let us know he was still in charge. It took us about fifteen minutes to complete the job, and then we set about rigging our hootches. Now we could sit back and relax for a while.

As dusk settled in, we went on stand to. Everything seemed very peaceful and quiet. Jones came by to check on us and then sat down for a short visit. It really was nice; the stars were bright, the air was cool, the red tracers were singing through the air.

Red Tracers! It took a moment to sink in. We'd all been sitting at the edge of our fighting position when I noticed one red tracer pass to my left, and within a split second, another passed to my right. I wasn't unduly alarmed until I remembered; there were four regular rounds that couldn't be seen between those glowing bullets. I instantly rolled backwards into the hole and found that the others had already jumped in. That hole probably wasn't much larger than an old-fashioned washtub, but it's amazing what the human body can do when there is just cause. We all fit in quite easily, if a little crowded.

Jones screamed, "Grab your gear!" and we turned toward our hootches to comply. Then we had to pause; there was a steady stream of tracers passing between our hole and our hootches. Without further thought, I jumped up and ran, skipping over the tracers like I was dodging mud puddles. I made it to my hootch, grabbed my gear, and then rushed back to the hole, skipping over or through the tracers again. Somehow I made it without getting a scratch. That wasn't the brightest stunt I had ever pulled, but God smiles kindly on fools.

Once back on the position, we watched the fireworks. There seemed no obvious signs of an attack. Someone with a machine gun, immediately to our left, must have thought we were under an air attack; they were firing up into the air at just about a forty-five degree angle. Most of the shooting seemed to be coming from an oasis about a hundred yards across the paddy from us. I hadn't fired a shot yet; so far there hadn't been anything to shoot at.

To find out what had happened, Jones left our position after the firing began to decrease. He did advise us of one factor; "Charlie uses green tracers unless he's using some of our captured equipment. Maybe so, but there wasn't anything but red. Somethin' ain't right."

Before long he was back with the news. "Seems a couple or three VC were crawling around in the paddy. Maybe they thought it would be a good joke to get us shooting at each other. That's B Company over there"—he indicated the other oasis—"They were the ones shooting our way. Anyway, when the shooting started, Charlie crawled off to the side to watch the show. Don't know how, but Foster [one of our medics, known for carrying more firepower than a lot of the riflemen] found 'em and blew 'em away with his shotgun. Guess the laugh is on them." Rumor had it that Foster had more confirmed kills than most of the rest of the company combined.

The firing finally died down as people began to realize they'd been duped. Everyone settled down for guard duty. I took the first shift. While sitting and staring into the night, I reflected on the day's events. I'd seen my first dead VC, and I'd been shot at. I didn't feel any different. I guess I had been mentally preparing myself for this for too long to be too awed. I couldn't tell if I'd really been scared or not. I only wished I'd been able to do some shooting that counted.

After my turn on guard, I went down to the hootches to awaken Parker for his shift. I gave him my watch, he sat up and told me he was awake, and I went to bed. It didn't take long to fall asleep.

It seemed like only minutes had passed when I felt myself being shaken, none too gently. "Get up, you sons a bitches! Get your asses up on the position. I'll have all of your funky asses court-martialed. Sleep on duty on me, will ya!" It was Jones, and he was not happy. I was kind of foggy, but it didn't make sense. Fuck off from time to time, yes, I was guilty of that. But I hadn't gone to sleep on guard since that first night. I'd learned my lesson then. Besides, I was sure I'd finished my shift. Had Parker or Santa gone to sleep?

Then Parker started in on Jones. "Motherfuckin' Oreo! Don't you put your hands on me!"

Jones was cool. I'd have punched the bastard out, or thought I would. Jones grabbed Parker by the arm and neck and began dragging him away. "I've had just about enough of your shit, boy. You and me is gonna' see what the lieutenant has to say about this." Parker didn't stand a chance of battling with Jones. He was one tough mutha.

Santa and I watched them go. "I hope they shoot the little shit," Tom said. I agreed fully, but that did not let us off the hook. We tried to figure out what had happened.

"Wait here. I'll be right back," I said. I went down to the hootches and checked Parker's. I found my watch lying on his air mattress. I went back and showed it to Tom.

"I ain't taking no fucking court-martial for that asshole," he said.

After a bit, Jones returned, much more calm than he'd left. I'd rather hoped he'd cut Parker's throat or something. "Private

Parker has been placed under arrest for gross insubordination. The captain's RTO is guarding him," he told us.

"Sarge," I began, "maybe I can't prove it, but me and Santa didn't do anything wrong. We were using my watch for guard duty. After you left, I went back and found it lying on Parker's mattress. I pulled first shift; I woke him up and gave him the watch. He said he had it, meaning he was awake. What was I supposed to do, carry him to the hole?"

Jones looked at the watch in my hands for a few minutes. I was starting to really sweat. "I believe you," he finally said. "I figured it would be something like that. That nigger is worthless. You two are off the hook, but you'll have to man the position with just the two of you. I can't get anybody else tonight. I'll see you in the morning."

I was quite relieved and also mildly shocked. I was not accustomed to hearing one black calling another one a nigger, but I wasn't going to argue with him over it. I knew I was quite capable of getting into all the trouble I could handle without the likes of Parker making things more difficult.

The night passed without any further problems. Tom and I were only a little more tired than normal come daylight. As far as I was able to learn, Parker only got an Article 15, company punishment, with a fine. He'd already been busted about as low as he could go. A few weeks later, I was told that he got a little "soldier's punishment." He'd gone off on another tirade, screaming and berating a kid named Gomez about some silly nonsense. Gomez just stood up and knocked Parker out with one punch, sending him flying into a flooded rice paddie. No one saw a thing.

Our patrol that day, October 1, 1967, was a little easier; the ground was somewhat drier, and we moved at what, to us, was a fairly leisurely pace. We heard some shooting up ahead, but nothing seemed to come in our direction. Around 1000 hours, we came to an old schoolhouse. Our point had been fired on by someone inside. They had the building circled now, and another squad had done some fire and maneuver and had taken the building. I noticed that the walls were pocked with bullet holes, old ones as well as new. There was a large stone slab imbedded in the wall above the lintel with the numerals 1954, probably the year the school had been built.

I went inside with the others, more out of curiosity than because I had any real business in there. The place was full of debris, and I noticed empty shell casings that certainly weren't from any M-16. The squad that had taken the building discovered a concrete slab, hiding what they believe was the sniper's spider hole. Our platoon sergeant wanted someone to clear the hole and make certain there wasn't anyone still inside. He looked around at everyone, and then he looked at me. "You want to do this, Ford?" he asked.

"You bet, Sarge!" I answered without a moment's hesitation.

Everyone else cleared the building. I made certain I was alone and then addressed myself to the hole, or where it was supposed to be. "Just you and me now, turkey," I said to the poor, unsuspecting VC I hoped was still there. I pulled the pin from one of the grenades I'd been carrying all of those weeks. I was no longer afraid of them, though I had not yet thrown one. Now was the time.

I tossed the grenade on top of the slab and watched it just long enough to be certain it wouldn't roll off. Then I ran across the room, hit the window ledge with my left hand, and vaulted through the window with my rifle in the other hand. The grenade went off just as I hit the ground. I ran back to the front of the building, up the stairs, and into the main room, firing into the now exposed hole. Of course, I was firing full auto, with my rifle jamming every third round, but I did not let this little problem slow me down. Then I tossed another grenade into the hole and repeated my run; across the room, hit the window ledge, and out, again hitting the ground just as the world was rocked by the explosion. As I recovered and ran for the steps again, I heard some of our guys, covering me from the tree line, yelling at me, "Yeah, Ford! Go get 'em," or, "Give 'em hell, Ford!" They were clapping and laughing and cheering me on. I felt a thrill run through my body and almost stopped for a bow. I felt like the guy who'd just scored the winning touchdown in a football game. As fleeting as it might have been, for a moment I had the undivided attention of my peers. It felt good.

I ran back into the building and emptied another magazine into the hole, again somewhat laboriously, from a position around the corner from where the hole was. I reloaded and walked over to the hole and looked inside. Nothing! I could see a large crack in the foundation of the building, where the VC had obviously gotten away, probably long before I'd even begun my John Wayne impression. Hell, he might have been hiding out there in the weeds cheering me on, also.

Still, it was fun. Several of the guys came up, clapping me on the back and telling me what a good job I'd done. That made it worth the effort. Besides, it wasn't like I was going to have to pay for the ammo and grenades I had, in retrospect, wasted. At that moment, a dead VC would have just been icing on the cake, but it wasn't really necessary.

We continued with our patrol but didn't find any other VC. There were a lot of signs that they had been in the area, but they'd all scattered. Someone rounded up on an old woman who must have been about 150 years old. Despite my earlier acclaim, I was given the job of escorting her the click or so back to our base camp. At least they didn't have anyone else accompany me. I'm certain they felt I could handle "granny" by myself. When I tried to take her arm, she jerked away, possibly thinking I was going to rape her. "Lady," I said, "I might be horny, but I ain't desperate." As if she understood every word that I said. Later, she was flown out for interrogation or relocation. I'd just felt a little silly, walking along and holding her arm, like she was my favorite aunt and I was taking her for a stroll. Still, guess it doesn't hurt a soldier's image to be seen as something more than an animal. Good public relations.

The day's patrolling finally ended, and we returned to base. I wondered just how much longer we were going to stay there until we had to load up and move off somewhere else. Patrolling without my rucksack made me feel positively awkward, and I almost missed it.

Hot chow had been brought out for us that night by the time we returned. I dumped my gear, other than my rifle and ammo, of course, at my hootch and made directly for the chow line. We took up our normal five-meter, so-a-grenade-won't-get-ya-all interval. I could understand that, but having to stand at parade rest seemed a little silly.

While I was waiting my turn to be served, Captain Connolly walked up to the platoon sergeant. "Sergeant," he began, "we just got a radio message. High command, General Westmoreland specifically, has ordered each company to send ten men back to Bien Hoa to be part of a new Long Range Patrol company that is being formed. I want you to ask for a couple of

volunteers from your platoon. They want only the best.'' I knew
what that meant; no company commander in his right mind was
going to cut his own throat and send away those men he considered his best. Usually they send the fuck-ups. What they didn't
always seem to realize, though, was that someone who might
be considered a fuck-up in one unit will often excel in another.

In an instant, I remembered everything I had heard about
''LRPs''—small groups operating far from friendlies. Usually
outnumbered, sometimes wiped out when they'd bitten off more
than they could chew. Only an idiot would volunteer for such an
outfit.

''Sir, begging the Captain's pardon. Specialist Fourth Class
Ford would like to volunteer for this new company,'' I said.
There was no doubt in my nonmilitary mind that this was exactly
what I had been looking for.

The captain and platoon sergeant both stood there looking at
me for a moment. I knew what sarge was thinking: This kid is
still a fucking cherry. Hasn't seen any action to speak of or
proved himself to me yet. But then, for that very reason, he's no
real loss to us either. The captain turned to him, ''That okay
with you, Sergeant?''

The sergeant looked at me for a few moments longer, then
said, ''Pack up your shit, Ford. You won't need to wait for chow.
Give your grenades, extra ammo, and other gear to someone
else. You'll be going back to base tonight.'' I was already flying,
as happy as a pig in mud.

It didn't take me long to divest myself of all my gear, including my precious letter-writing material, to those who were staying behind. I joined the group of other volunteers who were also
going. Some I didn't know, but others were more or less familiar; there was Warren Lahara, an ''old man'' of about twenty-
seven or so. Short and stocky, coal black hair, a natural bullshit
artist. He was a draftee, but he'd volunteered for Airborne training, so he was okay; Sgt. Jim McElwee, the little red-haired
guy who loved a good battle; Sgt. Don Fant, one of the best
natured men in the company and a Pathfinder, part of the Airborne elite; Sp4. Tom Santa, my ''roommate'' for the last few
days, probably one of the quietest guys I knew; Staff Sergeant
Jones, my squad leader since I'd arrived. (I liked him, even if
he did ride my ass from time to time—as if I'd ever done anything wrong! Probably thought I was a perennial fuck-up.) And

a guy I didn't know very well, Roger Roberts from Tulsa. Also going along was S.Sgt. Ronald Brown, the man who had first welcomed my group to the herd back at Dak To. All I knew about these men was pretty good; it seemed they were being allowed to go because they had done a good job and deserved the chance to go on to better things.

I'd been the first to volunteer, but I was still almost bumped. There were eleven of us lined up to go. They could not get away with only sending nine, but they damned sure weren't going to send more than they had to. The captain and first sergeant counted noses again, and then my platoon sergeant said, ''Ford, you stay.''

I almost cried, I was so upset. ''But, Sarge, I was the first one to volunteer!'' as if my plea would have made one bit of difference.

The sergeant was just about to put me in my place when Captain Connolly interrupted. ''Just a minute, Sergeant. Let him go.'' Then he turned to his RTO, another of the Pathfinders, like Fant. ''I'm sorry, son, but I'm going to have to keep you. I need your skills with that radio too badly.'' That was it. I was going. Of course, unspoken by the captain was, And besides, I'm well rid of Ford. It didn't matter. I could have kissed the man. I was so happy I could have flown back without the chopper.

A big Chinook soon arrived, and we loaded aboard. There was a lot of discussion about what we were getting into, but most of the guys were just as happy about the new twist of fate as I was. I didn't know many of the men from the other companies; most I would see on a daily basis, but only a few would I really get to know. We really only had one thing in common— we were damned glad to be getting out of the field for a while, no matter what lay ahead. Our grunt days were over.

CHAPTER 8

Once we arrived at the army compound at Tuy Hoa, we turned in our field equipment and rifles, these belonging to the 173d. I was not upset to give that junk back. Then a short physical to make sure we were in a sound enough condition to be of service to this new outfit. After that, praise be, we were told we would have free time until we left for Bien Hoa. Ghost time! (Any time spent goofing off was ghosting; a person so engaged is a ghost.) Once again, luxuries can be a relative thing. Our sleeping accommodations were large wall tents, our beds, folding canvas cots. This was as close to being inside a building as I had experienced over the last seven or eight weeks. There were also showers, but still no hot water.

I didn't have much money on me (the ever-popular military payment certificates, MPC, or Monopoly money), but I wasn't going to let that stand in my way. I hitched a ride to the air force base to enjoy real civilization. Ya have to give it to those air heads; they knew how to live. I went to a movie, *Dad, Poor Dad. Mama Hung You In The Closet and I'm Feeling So Sad*, possibly the worst movie I had ever seen. I had a couple of hamburgers and hot dogs that tasted more like sawdust than meat and then just wandered about alone. I had a ball. I'd have killed for a beer or two but couldn't afford it after that little splurge.

Hitchhiking back to the army compound that night, I was picked up by two guys in a jeep. Along the way we picked up another GI. They dropped him off first. As he was dismounting, he held out a pack of cigarettes and offered one to each of us. I took one and dropped it into my pack, since I already had one lit, thinking he was just being friendly. I did think it odd that the other two declined. I had seen both of them smoking earlier.

After returning home, I entered a tent to see what movie was playing; don't remember now, but it wasn't much better than the one I'd just subjected myself to. I reached for my pack and shook out the next cigarette. Lighting it, I took a deep drag, and almost gagged! "What the hell is this," I wondered, "Must be a Raleigh or an L&M." I took another drag, thinking I'd give it another chance before throwing it away. Second one wasn't so bad, so I continued.

In a few minutes, Lahara came running up to me. "Ford, you fucking idiot! You want to go to jail?"

"What do you mean?" I asked.

"You know what you got there?"

"Sure. It's the worst cigarette I ever had." Why was I suddenly having trouble following this conversation?

"That's pot. Grass. Marijuana. Don't you know nuthin'? Where did you get that shit anyway?" he asked.

I looked down at the butt. "No shit!" I exclaimed.

I'd never smoked marijuana before, couldn't say I even knew anyone who had. And I'd never had any intention of trying it, either. I walked out of the tent, and Lahara followed me. "Besides, if you're gonna smoke it, do it right. Drag it deep into your lungs and hold it." Nothing like a crash course in sin. He was very helpful. I just looked at what was left. It didn't look any different than any other filter cigarette. I dropped the butt to the ground. I felt fine; it was just a coincidence that I went to bed early that night.

We remained in Tuy Hoa for another couple of days and then were flown back to Bien Hoa. The 173d had vacated the base, moving north to Pleiku. We were transported to our new company area, which had previously been the Herd's 2d Battalion, 503d Infantry, area, on the east side of Bien Hoa Army Base. This was great! Wooden barracks, iron cots with mattresses, hot showers, and toilets that flushed. Granted, it wasn't the Waldorf Astoria, but things were certainly looking up.

I don't know which is more confusing, an outfit just forming or one that is disbanding. During the days, the powers that be kept us busy beautifying the new company area, but the nights were pretty much our own. A lot of guys went downtown to party and to get laid. I'd run out of money, and pay day was too far away, so I'd have to wait.

I did begin to run into a few old buddies. Chris Flory stopped by one day. He was from Houston, Texas, and we'd gone through basic training together. Our visit was short but pleasant. I never saw him again. I also never figured out how he found me.

The next day, I ran into several other guys I'd been stationed in Alaska with. Mike Frazier from California, a product of the easy life-style of his native state. We got along well, and both had a desire to test ourselves in the crucible of battle. Bruce Avant from Kentucky, a quiet guy, tall and thin, who surprised me by volunteering for Vietnam. It didn't seem to fit him. Anthony Cicerano, a tall, good-looking guy from New York, one of my cubicle mates from the same squad. (Tony was a lot bigger than I was, but we spent a lot of time wrestling. I didn't exactly win, but I was small enough that he'd always had trouble pinning me down. Used to piss him off.) And Bass. We never did get along. He'd challenged my authority one day when I'd been in charge of a work detail. We'd decided to go to the barracks basement and settle the matter. He won. It could have been worse, I imagine. Perhaps it changed his opinion of me a little that I was willing to try, but it still did not endear us to each other. For the remainder of our time together, we hardly spoke two words to each other. Suited me just fine.

Having people around that I had known before was nice, but it also meant that I might have to face watching people I had become familiar with die some day. I didn't want to deal with that. However, Frazier, Cicerano, and Avant went to 2d Platoon, Bass to 1st Platoon, and I was assigned to 4th Platoon. We soon came to learn we would not be working together at all.

The following day, we met our new company commander, Maj. William C. Maus. He informed us right off the bat, "That's Maus, M-A-U-S, not M-O-U-S-E." And of course, soldiers being the deviants that they are, he was soon being called Major Mouse, but not for very long. Almost as a whole, the company soon came to have a lot of respect for the man. The major, soon to be promoted to lieutenant colonel, was a tall, lanky Texan and a West Point graduate. I liked him.

Having a major for a company commander was also something of a clue that the outfit was going to be different. Almost always, the CO of a company is a captain. We would also have four line platoons instead of the normal three, plus headquarters, communications, and a motor pool. This new company was designated Company F, Long Range Patrol, 51st Infantry, and the best part, we would also all be Airborne. At first, due to some glitch in the issuance of orders, we thought our company designation was Company F. 54th Infantry. We had gone about stamping and stenciling everything to that effect until the correct orders with the right designation reached us. Some silly-assed clerical error, I guess.

Officially, we came into existence on 25 September 1967. There was another separate LRP company formed at the same time. Company E, LRP, 20th Infantry, which would work for I Field Force. In the beginning, our authorized strength was 198 officers and men. The actual assigned strength would fluctuate greatly over the coming months, from as low as 187 to a high of 235. It still seemed like we were shorthanded most of the time. Company E would have a similar strength, also bound to fluctuate at times, but this still made our companies much larger than most of the other LRP companies, some of which were no bigger than a reinforced platoon.

Our authorized shoulder patch would be that of II Field Force, a shield, with a white crusader sword in the center, on a field of blue, surrounded by pieces fitted to form a spearhead, red at the top and yellow below. The only thing that would differentiate us from a host of jerks, clerks, and combat typists also assigned to II Field Force was the allowance of a blue and white Airborne tab. Once again the powers that be had selected something without regard to the wishes of the users. What we preferred, and what in fact remained *our* unit patch was one variant of the patch worn by the Ranger battalions of World War II, designed in 1942 by a Sgt. Anthony Flint, ours being designed by Major Maus. This was a scroll with swallow tails at each end, designating F CO at one end, 51ST INF at the other, and AIRBORNE above LONG RANGE PATROL in the center. This patch had red trim, white letters and numerals, on a black background. It was similar to the patch worn unofficially by the Ranger companies of the Korean War and similar to the pattern used by many other LRP companies.

A brief history of the 51st Infantry was given; it was originally formed in 1917 and assigned for duty with the 6th Infantry Division, with which it remained until 1943 when it was converted and redesignated as Troop C, 10th Constabulary Squadron, part of the 14th Constabulary Regiment. There were numerous other redesignations, inactivations, and reactivations until 1967. Campaigns in previous wars included the Meuse–Argonne and Alsace in 1918, then Normandy, Northern France, the Rhineland, Ardennes–Alsace, and Central Europe during World War II. Unit decorations included the Presidential Unit Citation (Army) for the Ardennes in World War II, while a part of the 4th Armored Division; the French Croix de Guerre with Palm for Normandy, as part of the 10th Armored Infantry; the French Croix de Guerre with Palm for battles along the Moselle River; and the French Croix de Guerre with Fourragere, these last two being also with the 10th Armored Infantry. There would be no tanks to support us in Vietnam, but that was fine with me; when it came time to shit and git, I didn't want no damned tank hindering my withdrawal. Now it was time for us to add to the 51st's history.

We were also told of Long Range Patrol having been created in the fifties and that this type of unit had been chosen over the Rangers. While many units had formed Long Range Reconnaissance Patrol companies or teams, many of these guys were having to perform double duty (hump the bush as a line doggie one day, be pulled back to run a special mission, and then go back to the line the next day with little or no recognition for the services they provided), none of this was done "officially," that wonderful military phrase that takes precedence over logic. We would be the first Ranger-type unit authorized since the Korean War. Heady stuff, that. There would be much to learn.

"Each platoon will have additional training at the Special Forces MAC/V Recondo School at Nha Trang. Upon completion of that training, you will begin actual field operations," Major Maus advised us. "The backbone to this company will be the six-man team for reconnaissance, the light teams. Heavy teams will consist of twelve men for ambush patrols. In the meantime, we will begin training on our own, including physical training, road marches, and runs. Weapon craft will be enhanced, and you'll be taught the use of different radios, codes, and so on. Training, in fact, will never end." God! I hated training. No matter how necessary it might be, I always felt like it was more like playing. I just could not take it seriously.

True to his word, the next day we were up by oh-dark-thirty, well before daylight, to begin our first run. And not at all surprising to me, it was an absolute bitch! I'd gotten tougher in the 173d, but certain muscles had all but atrophied. I was sore for days. What really amazed me, though, were the smaller guys who managed to keep up. At five feet eight inches and perhaps 130 pounds, I thought of myself as small. We had several guys under five feet five inches who just would not quit. I admired their stamina, their *guts*!

The physical training was part of a weeding-out process. Since the major was no dummy, he knew that he'd been sent more than a few yardbirds and eight balls, people he could not afford to keep around if there was to be any real success of making the company a working proposition. There were several interviews, many questions asked, and the right answer had to be given. We began to notice that a few men we had seen around the area were no longer with us. Recognizing my own shortcomings in military protocol, and what had been referred to often as my attitude problem, I began wondering how much longer I would be there. I dreaded the idea of failure and of being sent back to the Herd. However my answers had been judged, the weeding out soon stopped. I had made it. Maybe they just decided to give me one more chance.

Equipment soon began to arrive and was promptly issued. The first and most impressive items were our M-16 rifles, still in their cardboard shipping boxes, apparently fresh from the factory. No more battlefield junk. They still had the cardboard tube in the barrels, to absorb moisture I guess, and the bright red muzzle covers to keep out dust. Most of us would wrap green tape around the red surface, since it would help to keep out dirt and debris, but, of course, the first time you fired the weapon in battle, there went the muzzle piece, shot away and peeled like a banana. At that time, most ground infantry units were still using the M-14, the "elephant gun," much heavier if one is going to be carrying it constantly, but airborne units were armed almost completely with the "Matty Mattel Special," as we called the 16.

The rest of our equipment was brand-new also, from rucksacks to pistol belts. Someone, somewhere had some stroke. We would also be wearing the tree-pattern camouflage fatigues, for field use only, but that still made us one of the first units after Special Forces who got to wear these very practical uniforms in the field, rather than the standard-issue olive green jungle fatigues that everyone else wore, from line troops to cooks. I was feeling better about the outfit all the time. Charlie soon began calling us "the men in the tree fatigues." (In time Charlie would have another name for us: he called us *Bien Kich Du*, which, very roughly translated means spy.* We also had the distinction of having a price established on our heads by the Viet Cong. [At one time this price was monetary, later (sic) a decoration was added for a captured LRP, with a high priority rating.*])

And last, but certainly not least, we would no longer have to wear those damned steel pots. What I'd been told those weeks before by the brigade LRPs had been true. Each man was issued a new bush hat, and most of us wore them proudly and gladly. There are always the individuals who must be different. Berets were not uncommon in F of the 51st, but it would not have surprised me to see a Stetson or sombrero, or even a Nazi coal-scuttle helmet. Some of those guys had a strange sense of humor.

Our field rations would be the LURPs exclusively. In the beginning that seemed like a great deal—they were much lighter than C rations, but you did need water to prepare them. There were eight varieties of the meals: chicken and rice, chicken stew, beef and rice, beef stew, beef hash, spaghetti with meat sauce, chile con carne, and last, and certainly least, pork with escalloped potatoes. The first six were my standard fare. The chili with beans, less so. Took too damned long for the beans to soak up the water. The last, no way!

The packages came with the same variety of extra items as C rations—powdered coffee, powdered cream, sugar, sometimes a packet of powdered cocoa, some type of dessert bar, a spoon and toilet paper. The one item missing was cigarettes, the little four-pack of tobacco products packaged during the Spanish-American War. These had always seemed so dry. The reasoning seemed to be that LRPs shouldn't smoke in the field; it'll give away their position. Some did subscribe to this practice; others didn't. A bottle of hot sauce added a great deal of flavor to the LURPs. As good as they were, having, in fact, only six meals to choose from, I began yearning for C rations after a while. However, food was not as great an issue with the LRPs as it had been before. We ate well in garrison, and with most patrols lasting no more than five days, usually, many of us got into the habit of carrying only one meal per day. We were also instructed that it was best to prepare the meal before we went out so the smell of burning heat tabs, or the noise made by opening the packages, wouldn't alert any passing VC. Once again, it was a great theory; I just didn't care to eat something that had been sitting in my rucksack in the sun since I'd prepared it three or four days before.

The two-and-a-half-ton trucks and jeeps we were issued seemed to be brand-new also and would have suited our needs just fine. However, in the true military fashion, some of our people decided we also needed a few three-quarter-ton trucks. They were a bit more handy than the big trucks, and most of the jeeps were usually tied up transporting officers or senior NCOs, or would be out on radio-relay sites. We couldn't get them issued to us. We had all of the vehicles we would need, *they* said. So like many other things needed, we simply stole them from other units.

The company area was beginning to really shape up when, in true army logic, someone decided to move us to another area. We loaded up and moved off to the northwest area of the base.

Our new home had previously been occupied by Company E, or E Troop, 7/9th Infantry, a recon unit with the 173d. As we passed into the company area for the first time, I looked up and noticed the arch above the gate, with their unit designation in high relief. "All we have to do is break the bottom off of the *E*, and we can call this F Troop," I said, alluding to the television series. It was a term often used, but did not exactly gain complete acceptance. There were some similarities, except for one striking difference—no Indians.

As Jerold Berrow, one of the editors of the company year book, would state, "We soon came to appreciate the isolated area and the privacy it afforded."* Perhaps, Jerry, but it would not have hurt my feelings to have kept the hot showers and modern toilets.

The barracks, two rows of eight each, were much roomier than what we'd left behind, and they had concrete floors. There was a large mess hall, several training buildings, the headquarters building, supply, etc. Officers would live in the BOQ (bachelor officers quarters), a separate building at the southeast corner of our compound. A few senior enlisted men and the first sergeant had separate shacks for their use. There was also a large, sandbagged bunker that would serve as our tactical operations center (TOC)—this was another difference between our unit and other companies. Most companies did not have their own TOC. For a while, we had another unique feature to the TOC—our own aerial balloon, raised on a steel cable after dark with wires running its length to increase the range of our radios. However, the balloon broke loose one day and began to drift away. The air force was contacted, and they sent up a fighter to shoot the thing down. After that, we had to start sending men from the commo platoon out to isolated sites for relay purposes. Quite often they would, themselves, be under attack by mortars or small-arms fire and would still have to relay information for teams that were in contact.

The company had an artillery liaison officer attached to us full-time. His job was to control all artillery missions laid on by the company, to plot and fire all targets, to program H & I in our AOs, and to always accompany the C & C ship whenever it was airborne.* The arty officer went by the call sign Shocker and that name stayed, even after the first one moved on and another took his place, and then another one after that. These men worked for 7/9th Artillery at Bearcat, II Field Force V Artillery, 2/40th Artillery of the 199th, as well as the 101st Airborne Division Artillery and others.*

And in time, we would have our own outdoor movie theater. However, the johns were simply elaborate outhouses (six-holers), and showers would be of the cold-water variety—simple stalls with spigots like most showers, but the water came from steel shipping containers for bombs mounted on a platform behind the shower room. Water had to be trucked in every couple of days. But it beat what I'd known over the previous months. The buildings were all painted a pasty green that I never really got used to.

We had something else that became, for a short time, quite a morale booster—our own museum. In it were displayed interesting items we captured while on patrol or otherwise located in the field. One of the first weapons captured by one of our teams was a U.S. M-1 Garand rifle, probably captured from Americans or Viet personnel at an earlier date. And later, we even captured an M-16 that looked newer than the ones we carried. It was just nice to wander around and get a feel for what we had accomplished. Then some chickenshit at II Field Force decided a unit such as ours wasn't "authorized" its own museum so we had to shut it down. We often did wonder sometimes just whose side they were on.

As we began setting up living facilities in the new area, we learned more about our mission and other useful information. We would not be a part of a larger unit such as a battalion or a brigade; we would work directly under II Field Force. They would farm us out to units that did not have their own LRRP (Long Range Reconnaissance Patrol as opposed to simply Long Range Patrol, a difference the exact mission of which is open to discussion) or LRP capabilities. The 199th Light Infantry Brigade would receive the first benefits of our intelligence gathering, since they were one of the larger units in the Bien Hoa–Long Binh area. They would also provide our ready-reaction force in case we got into serious trouble.

In the 173d, our shelters had been poncho hootches; our beds, air mattresses. Now, when in the field, we would sleep under the stars on bare ground, usually with nothing more than half a poncho or a poncho liner covering our bodies. There were no medics assigned to the company, so a lot of our training included extensive first-aid classes. There was even instruction in performing a slight operation for someone choking, called a cricothyroidotomy.* This involved cutting a small hole in the trachea to allow an injured man to breath if his mouth or face had been hit in such a way that he couldn't draw air. The operation is similar to a tracheotomy but less traumatic for both the victim and the one giving the aid. In anticipation of receiving some supersecret radios that, fortunately, never arrived, they even tried teaching us Morse code. I never did have any success learning the dit-dahs.

Since our field living conditions were going to be even more primitive than the other line units, a great effort was made to make life in the rear more pleasant. The food was pretty good, and there was no shortage of it. Beds were fairly comfortable, and mail was about as regular as anyone could expect, being ready almost daily. I was beginning to feel differently about a lot of things, except perhaps for the constant harassment by the lifers (anyone with intentions of remaining in the service for twenty years). While we were in the rear, police calls were held every day, there were morning formations every day, seven days a week, and our living areas had to be ready at all time for inspection. Beat the hell out of living constantly in the bush, but only to a degree.

And then there was the chance to get to town on the occasions when I had a little money left over after payday. I was young and horny and bothered not at all by morality. Prostitutes, the only Vietnamese I had any real contact with, other than bartenders or laundresses, were usually no more than five or six dollars for a quickie, so I tried to avail myself of their services as often as I could get away with it. It was not what one would call romance, however. Doing one's business on an army cot with nothing separating me from the next "couple" but an army blanket strung on a line, while the two girls carried on a steady conversation . . . Well, it could be downright distracting. One guy swore his whore read a newspaper the whole time. But it beat the alternatives, I think.

However, there was one exception. I'd heard about Miss Mi. To put it delicately, she was reputed to be the best in the business. I was determined to meet her. She resided in the East Hotel, which happened to be in the off-limits section of Bien Hoa. One fine day, between paydays, I made my way to that hotel for a visit, traveling alone as usual, and unarmed, since I wasn't given any option. (GIs were not allowed to go armed when they went into town other than on official business. We might hurt someone or offend the natives, I guess.) A house girl escorted me to Miss Mi's room. It must have been her living quarters because it was too ornate, had entirely too much furniture to be simply a crib. There was a canopied four-poster with a mattress thick enough to suit anyone's taste, a closet full of dresses and shoes, a toilet, and what I knew was a bidet. I also knew what they were used for.

Miss Mi was probably less than five feet tall, long black hair, and much more well endowed than most Oriental females I had met so far. I estimated that she was in her middle to late thirties, old enough to have begun servicing the French before they left Vietnam. Which is probably where she learned most of her tricks.

As I entered the room, she came to me and treated me as if I were a suitor, chattering away in a high, singsong voice like the staccato of a machine gun, as if I could understand every word she said. She put on a record and led me through a few steps of a dance. Then she began to undress. I watched, all eyes.

Her figure was gorgeous, her breasts full, her nipples long and thick. I noticed that she had a lot more pubic hair than the other Orientals I had met, including a mass under her arms. Under the circumstances, I did not find this unattractive. I had read enough to know that this is a cultural thing and considered quite erotic in some parts of the world. She did smell nice.

It was a thoroughly wonderful visit. Her whole attitude was completely relaxed and friendly. She treated me quite pleasantly, before, during, and after. She was in fact a lady during the whole visit. The term whore just did not seem to fit her. A consummate actress, yes. And all of this for eleven dollars. Best deal I'd ever had. I vowed to return.

CHAPTER 9

Platoon sergeant Walter P. Butts was to be our, dare I say it, platoon sergeant. One of the toughest, gruffest bastards ever to leap from an airplane. The man seemed to know every general and colonel of any consequence in the army, and had trained most of them when they were "snot-nosed, shavetail lieutenants." One of the original members of Special Forces, he was sometimes a hard act to swallow, but I wish I'd had a tape recorder to catch all of the stories he told. I think he'd seen his first action with Andy Jackson at the Battle of New Orleans. Well, he seemed old to me. And he did love his "kids." I'd seen him a couple of times in the 173d, screaming as we busted our asses in the bush, "Good training! Good training!" I used to wonder when the real stuff would begin. I always thought he was crazy; come to find out, I was absolutely right.

Our platoon leader was 1st Lt. Albert Snyder. Bespectacled, blond hair, what there was of it, cut in a flat top. We all kept our "bug traps" cut short. I would not have much contact with him in the beginning.

S.Sgt. Ray Jones (would I never get away from that man?) would be my squad leader for all intents and purposes. Jones, Butts, and Snyder were not always the ones we'd answer to, since more often than not, we were under the control of our team leaders. Jones and I would continue to get along as well as we had in the 173d: he was always on my ass about some infraction of military rules or regulations. The man never seemed to sleep.

But the *team*, once again, was the backbone of the company. Initially I felt like I had it dicked. S.Sgt. Ronald C. Lewis was to be my team leader. A tall, skinny black guy, he had about seven years in the army, most of it in Germany. He was a master of the manual of arms and the parade ground. That man could march, and he loved to strut his stuff. The assistant team leader was Sgt. Dennis Lovick, a small guy from Chicago, who we soon began calling Super Sarge. I never got around to asking why. Glasses and hair shorter than the law required. When he cracked up at a joke, often one of his own, the whole company knew it from his high, hyena laugh. Tom Santa also joined us, just as quietly as ever. Tommy Thomas would be with us, too. Very slim, also blond, he was from the south. And last and least, Benjamin Maxwell, a very dark Negro. He was quiet to the point of bringing on paranoia. He never did seem to try to fit in with the rest of the crowd. We were designated Team 4/6, the sixth team of 4th Platoon.

I learned, not long after our arrival, that I was supposed to be working in the military operational specialty (MOS) of 05B2P, a radio operator. I had no more training in this MOS than any other grunt. Guess that's how they shipped me down from the Herd in the place of Captain Connolly's radio operator. I was strictly 11B2P, this being "Light Weapons, Infantry, Airborne." Soon I would gain the MOS of 11F2P; "Infantry Operations and Intelligence Specialist, Airborne," enlisted grade, E-4. No wonder Uncle Sam uses convoluted letters and numbers!

In the beginning, we spent a lot of time working to develop a team spirit. Most of our off-duty time was spent discussing families, our plans for after the war, and so on. Staff Sergeant Lewis did not, of course, deign to associate with us except when he had to. He was, after all, a career soldier. We were told that while he would lead us, he preferred to associate with his own kind. And the horse you rode in on, too!

We even adopted a team mascot. It was an ostrithon. This was a very rare hybrid animal, a cross between an ostrich and a python. It did have the bad habit of attacking our guests, but it was polite. While it would squeeze them to death, it would fan them with its wings to keep them from becoming overheated. I think Lovick came up with it. Very unusual animal.

Still, and for the most part, we worked well together and got along. We were pretty well agreed that when we hit the field, Charlie had better watch out. Oh, the arrogance of youth and inexperience. We also held each other's heads on more than one occasion after a night of celebrating our upcoming victories.

The company area was fairly spacious, and we came to know it well after many accumulated hours of police call, as well as during our constant training. A destroyed helicopter, missing its tail and rotors, was rigged up on huge sawhorses, north of 2d Platoon barracks, for us to practice quick insertions once we began operations.

We also spent a lot of time practicing rappelling from helicopters in case there were no LZs large enough for the chopper to land. Rappelling is nothing more than a controlled descent down a rope by means of a Swiss seat, a rope cut to the proper length being wrapped around your body to form a seat and having a snap link or carabiner hooked into the front of the seat and then attached to the main rope that you will be descending.

A lot of the rappelling exercises were also done from a thirty-four-foot tower built by or for the 173d, just like the ones used at Fort Benning at jump school. These would allow a man to practice his door-exiting procedures when he got ready to make an actual parachute jump. You'd be strapped into a harness, and the harness was attached to a steel cable. Each man would take a position in the doorway and, on command, would leap out and go into the correct body position. Your drop might have been about fifteen or twenty feet, or so it seemed, and then you'd slide down the cable to arrester cables at the end, recover, and continue on with training, unless you did it wrong. Most Airborne candidates go out of the tower four or five times. I did it over forty. I had a theory that, in every class, one man is selected as the goat. That man can do nothing right, no matter how hard he tries. In tower week I just happened to be the goat. The first and third weeks, I had no problems at all. Well, no more trouble than total physical and psychological exhaustion.

I had no idea if the tower had been built specifically for the "blast"—the combat jump—the past February or if the Herd had just tried to keep themselves prepared in case some other jump mission arose. The company had the engineers add two-by-six boards across one side of the tower support poles so we could swing out the door and descend. It was a lot of fun, after you learned to accept and trust in the fact that the rope would hold you.

Most of our rappelling, other than that done from the thirty-four-foot tower, was done from a height of just one hundred feet. Great fun, unless you did a fatal hookup. I was witness to such a demonstration one day.

One of the cooks, Franky Skipper, had decided he wanted out of the mess hall so he could become a combat soldier. I was given the task of breaking him in. While he outranked me, I was the man with more experience. At least I had more than he did. It was great having Franky with us when we pulled berm guard; he was so afraid that he never went to sleep, staring into the darkness for hours.

One particular day, we were having another round of rappelling training from a helicopter. I have always been afraid of heights, but I always tried to do that which scared me the most. I had already been up a couple of times and was in line waiting to go again. I noticed that Franky kept shuffling back, letting others go ahead of him. I finally persuaded him to step up to the front. We watched as another chopper ascended. A man stepped out on the skids, prepared to drop. Which he did. He was no more than ten or fifteen feet from the chopper when he separated from the rope—a fatal hookup. He'd wrapped his line backwards into the snap link. Everyone present watched him fall. There was nothing we could do for him. Before he hit the ground, Franky was back in the mess hall, never to leave again. Often, over the coming months, when Franky would have one too many, he'd lament about his lot in life. "I tried to join you guys in the field, but they needed me in the mess hall." Sure, Franky. You tried. It just was not what he'd been trained for.

The man who fell landed on his face. He lived, but he never came back to us.

The McGuire rig was another matter altogether. This was a system where a couple of four-by-fours were strapped to the floor of the cargo compartment of the helicopter. Ropes were attached to three sets of nylon-web harnesses, attached at the ends. If a team was in trouble and needed to get out, and the choppers couldn't land to pick them up, the rope and harnesses would be lowered. Three men would fit the harnesses around their bodies so they could be lifted out. The men left on the ground then found their firepower cut in half if they were under attack at the time. No one wanted to be the first to test this device in combat.

Practicing with these contraptions was both thrilling and terrifying. We would hook up and be lifted into the air, dangling below the choppers like easy targets. Despite the thousands of pounds of weight those nylon ropes were supposed to be able to hold, I always felt like I was doomed. Traveling at thirty to forty miles an hour, suspended by a mere thread, made jumping out of an airplane with a parachute seem almost tame.

However, patrolling was to be our primary specialty, so that's what we spent most of our time practicing. Each team would spend hours lined up in team formation, moving slowly and quietly around the company area, every other man watching intently in one direction while the man in front and behind watched the other way. We also got a lot of practice in a small patch of woods and tangle just to the south of the company area. Each team would consist of, front to rear: the point man; the compass man, keeping the team headed in the right direction; the team leader in the third position for control purposes and keeping an eye on the terrain and his map; the RTO walking as number four, carrying an AN/PRC 25 radio† constantly in touch with either base camp, or as was more often the case, one of the radio-relay sites manned by other men from the company (because quite often we were too far out to have direct contact with the company). Number five was the pace man, keeping track of

†The batteries for the radios only had enough life to last about twenty-four hours so each man had to carry an extra one, another couple of pounds to add to our load.

just how far we'd traveled by stepping off and counting each pace in meters and then tying a knot in a line for every hundred meters. Of course we practiced this in the open; it's a lot harder keeping an accurate count when moving through the brush. You seldom took a full one meter step. The last man would be rear security, usually the assistant team leader.

We would almost always travel cross-country to avoid detection. To travel on trails invited ambush and having the tables turned on us or—the greater likelihood—an encounter with booby traps. But in case we did run into the enemy, we spent a lot of time practicing immediate-action drills. We practiced constantly so we would be prepared to deliver maximum firepower in any direction, and then the plan was to break contact and fall back. To wit, if the contact was to the front, point would spray the target with a full magazine; the team would already have dispersed to the sides, depending on each man's area of responsibility. Point would fall back through the center of the team, and then each man, in turn, would deliver another magazine toward the threat and fall back, the last man delivering a white phosphorus grenade to Charlie. We also called it "fluid suppression," and *didi mau*.* The team would then fall back to a predesignated rendezvous point to regroup and count noses. This was the time to make contact with the rear and request immediate extraction. A six-man team, even as heavily armed as we were, could not sustain contact for very long against usually superior numbers. Our job was to find the enemy, and then we were to be pulled out. To do otherwise was insane. "Do unto Charlie, and split," was the more simple way of putting it.

We had gotten the word in early November of two Americans having been captured by the VC. Charlie was reported to have immediately shot one and strangled the other one. Many of the men made their individual arrangements and plans for the what-if-I'm-captured? I began trying to secure a pistol, not with any idea of it serving me in battle, but I could fire off a last few shots at the enemy as he closed in, in case I was wounded and could not get away. I planned to save the last bullet for myself. For a while, I had a grenade taped to the suspenders of my LBE, with the spoon facing out. Just pull the pin and instant checkout. I had no intentions of being taken prisoner. An attitude like that, taken so soon and so seriously, can warp your perspective for a long time to come.

In late November, we heard about the 173d being engaged in a big battle at a place called Hill 875. While the 2d Battalion, 503d, had taken the brunt of the casualties, 4th Battalion had been hit hard also. Rumor had it, and it was almost impossible to get the facts, that many of our buddies had bought the farm. One hundred and fifty-eight had been killed, another 402 were wounded. Enemy casualties were supposed to be about sixteen hundred. I had missed out on my big battle after all, but there was just enough information coming back that I didn't feel like I would have been better off than where I was. Besides, it was commonly believed when we had left to join the LRPs, it was we who were going into the most dangerous paths, not the guys who'd stayed back with the Herd.

The company had yet to field a team, when we came damned close to being disbanded. There had been several IG (inspector general) inspections, and we kept flunking them. What the hell did we care about inspections? We were combat soldiers, in name if not in fact. The major had to do some serious shuffling and talking to get the point across; we either played by the army's rules, or it was back to the line. I couldn't have been the only thick head in the company. We finally passed the awesome inspection after six failures. But we'd made it.

The initial groups to attend Recondo School finally returned, and the first teams from the company went out on 22 November 1967. I was chomping at the bit as usual, wanting desperately to go out also. The 4th Platoon was scheduled to be the last platoon to go to the training. Then to make matters worse, someone decided that 4th Platoon would go in two groups instead of one. I was in the last group, and no amount of pleading or begging would get anything changed.

In mid-November several of us were selected to go before a board of review for promotion to sergeant, E-5. I was one of those "lucky" men. I did not delude myself that they had finally recognized my true leadership abilities. Perhaps someone with a warped sense of humor had decided. "Hey, Ford is always bucking authority. Let's make him a sergeant and let him see what it feels like to be in charge." All that it really boiled down to was, considering my time spent in Alaska, I just happened to have a little more seniority than some of the other, more deserving candidates. I wouldn't find out the results of their decision for another month and a half.

Finally, our turn came to leave for Nha Trang. The last two squads were preparing to attend the last phase of our training. I was in the barracks packing up when Danny Lindsey walked up to me. Considering how much time I had spent hanging out with the 2nd Platoon, we'd gotten to know each other. Then something happened, and we had gotten at cross-purposes. We hadn't spoken to each other in weeks. Now he walked up to me and held out his hand. "Ford, there's no reason you and me can't get along. You're a pretty good guy after all. Good luck in training." We shook hands and parted friends. I felt good about that.

Three days later, on December 5, 1967, Danny became F/51st's first KIA. As I was told by several men who had been present, Danny was acting as point when he'd broken through a wall of brush and encountered several VC. He had immediately taken them under fire and then turned to warn the team. One of the VC had gotten off a few shots before going down. Danny had been hit in the calf of one leg. The team managed to hold their own until the relief force arrived and they had been extracted. Danny had seemed to be hanging on, laughing and cutting up with the others at their good fortune. Then Danny began to slip away. He went into a coma and died of shock and loss of blood before they could get him to the hospital.

Ten days later, we lost another man. Second Platoon's leader, 1st Lt. John H. Lattin, Jr., was on patrol with one of his teams. They had come under heavy enemy fire but were holding on while waiting for the relief force from the 199th to arrive. Told that the reaction force was near, Lieutenant Lattin had stood up to throw a WP grenade to mark their position. The reaction force was a lot closer than anyone realized. Their point man had been alert, and all he saw was a man suddenly jump up from the bushes. He fired off a burst instinctively, hitting the lieutenant in the head. He was killed instantly.

A lot of our guys were quite angry at the 199th for this, but it was not fair. The point man had been doing what he'd been trained to do. His actions were appropriate for the situation and given the information that he had to work with. I could not and would not blame him, nor would I want to be in his shoes. It was simply one of the sadder fortunes of war.

Shortly after this, the camp was renamed, "Camp Lindsey-

Lattin,'' a fitting tribute to two good men. We had now been blooded. I wondered who would be next.

It wasn't long before a concrete podium was constructed in front of the headquarters building and adjacent to the company street where we held our morning formations. A brass plaque was mounted on it with IN MEMORY OF, and then Danny's and Lieutenant Lattin's names were engraved below. The most depressing part was there was plenty of room for many more names.

CHAPTER 10

Recondo School was an absolute bitch! We arrived over the weekend, training scheduled to commence the following Monday morning. There were lengthy calisthenics to loosen up, followed by a two-mile run in platoon formations. Each day another mile was added. But Friday's run was seven miles. I felt like whale shit on the ocean floor and didn't think I would ever recover. But I could not allow myself to quit. An example was being set by an older guy, a corporal from another outfit. We were told that he had been with one of the Ranger companies formed during the Korean War. Time and misfortune had given and taken away his stripes many times over the years. If he, at his age, was going to tough it out, I damned sure wasn't going to quit. He was one tough little rooster, that's for certain.

After sunup and a chance to shower and try to freshen up before the heat of the day arrived, instructions began on the many things we would need to know once we hit the bush, and they would need to be learned until they became second nature. There were numerous lessons in advanced first aid, since we would have to be entirely self-sufficient in that area. We would be carrying our own morphine in case someone was wounded. Many people are just as squeamish about giving shots as they are about getting them. Rather than actually having us give each other injections, we were required to draw blood with a needle and syringe. (We would also carry serum albumin, a blood expander that was injected intravenously. This would also be a part of our field gear.) The man I was teamed up with let me go first, and I must admit, I did a fair job. Then he went to work on me. After five or six tries in which he continually missed the vein, in desperation and pain and when no one was looking, I did it myself. Since he wasn't from our company, I didn't feel badly that he didn't have the skill. It was certainly the most expeditious approach from my point of view.

There were demonstrations in the best ways to rig our field equipment so that it would make the least amount of noise when moving through the brush. Our intention would be to glide through the jungle like a wraith, never giving Charlie a clue that we were around until we chose to let him know the hard way. Camouflage fatigues would be standard, whether these were the U.S. issue woodland style or Vietnamese tiger stripes, but that was only part of the preparations. We were also instructed in the best methods of camouflaging our persons. The military grease stick would be used most of the time, applied to break up the outline of your face and other exposed areas of skin—lighter shades in areas that were usually shadowed, darker patterns on the high points. Some of the people really got extravagant, at times applying the makeup like war paint. For the most part, everyone took this seriously, but as time progressed some, like yours truly, would just put the paint on our faces and then go to the field with our sleeves rolled up, exposing bare arms. It was hard to be totally professional all of the time. At least, few of us spent much time sticking bushes in our hats or belts.

We were also instructed in the finer arts of killing quickly and, when necessary, quietly. And then, what to do if capture seemed inevitable.

It was commonly accepted and discussed that the last thing any infantry soldier wanted was to be taken prisoner. No one had yet heard of any of our guys being taken alive, or at least of surviving. Particularly enlisted men. An officer might have some value, but not a grunt. If you were lucky, they would simply execute you. If you happened to fall into the hands of some sadist . . . I had no tolerance for pain, and knew I had no military information that would be of any use to the enemy. All they would get out of me would be a great deal of screaming and begging. No thank you. I would die free. They told us of one of their Special Forces men who had become separated from his team in a firefight. When they had been able to go back in, they'd found his body, missing its head. Not long afterwards, someone noticed a package in one of the mail rooms, leaking some strange smelling liquid. The package was opened, and a jar was found inside that had cracked, leaking formaldehyde. The jar also contained the head of the dead soldier. The package was addressed to the dead man's family back in the States. I would no longer carry my dog tags, and letters from home were destroyed as soon as they were thoroughly read, not that we usually carried mail to the field anyway. It may have also made me hate Charlie just a little bit more.

We had a number of classes in rappelling and use of the McGuire rig, traveling through the air at dizzying speeds and getting a view of the countryside that I could easily have lived without. One day, we even had classes on rubber-boat operations. These were large, six-man, inflatable boats that we would paddle out into the surf, and then turn them upside down. Of course, we went into the drink. The lesson was to teach us how to secure our equipment in the boat in case we were capsized, as well as how to right our boats again. The surf was a bitch, and just getting the heavily laden boats up and down that forty-to-forty-five-degree angle beach was no picnic. Rubber boats may be a good way to infiltrate enemy territory from the sea, but it isn't much fun unless you've had a lot more practice than we got.

There was more map and compass work, with my hoping no one noticed just how poorly I was doing. Numerous friendly and enemy weapons were demonstrated, so we'd be able to instantly put into use any captured weapons if ours became damaged or we ran out of ammo. I really enjoyed this part of the training, soaking up everything possible.

One day we had a surprise visit from General Westmoreland. He gave a fine pep talk, but since he did not personally recognize the men from F/51, he hurt my feelings.

The first weekend, we were taken to the field for an overnight

patrol and further instructions in a fairly secure area. Weapons
were locked and loaded since there was always the possibility
of contact. This school was advertised, so to speak, as the only
school in the United States Army where a student might well
find himself engaged in actual combat with the enemy. No more
running about with the chamber empty. Those days were gone
forever, also.

Here we had the opportunity to test-fire some of the various
weapons, quite a treat for a fledgling gun nut. There was also
survival instruction, what one could and could not eat if separated from your team and you had to live off the land. Usually
a meal of snake was on the menu, but not enough had been
found to feed the class. We got to try raw fish instead, heads
and all. Sashimi it wasn't.

We were run through an immediate-action fire course, a path
lined with pop-up targets that had to be engaged quickly. It
would take many such lessons to make the instincts true. As
badly as I did initially, I was encouraged by one factor—the new
16 I'd been issued performed without a flaw.

That night, each team was sent off in a different direction so
we could begin learning how to act and react to each other once
the game really began. Instructors did not accompany us. My
team wandered around long after dark but neither saw nor heard
anything of consequence. One thing I did learn; I was no great
shakes at moving in the dark like a cat. That takes a lot of
practice.

The following Monday saw us back at warm-up exercises and
the first endurance road march with full combat equipment. The
instructors put a fifty-pound sandbag in each man's rucksack so
our loads would be identical, and then we began. Two miles the
first day, longer each day until the seven-mile motherfucker on
Friday. These marches were also timed; twenty-four minutes
for the two-mile march, until finally, one and a half hours for
the seven miler. You had to begin and end with your team, each
man supporting the other, as would be absolutely essential in
the field.

Team 4/6 was the twelfth team to leave the gate. We had
trouble from the start; Super Sarge was smaller than the rest of
us, and with his load being equal to mine, he began having
trouble keeping up right away. Tom Santa was broken down
from too many months in the bush. He had also had a recent

attack of malaria that had drained his reserve strength. I had no
idea where it came from, but I discovered a reserve of my own.
Perhaps it was just something in me that made me work harder
if I was giving someone else a hand, no matter how much I felt
like dropping. It just seemed that I was able to do a little better.
Lewis, Tommy, and I supported Lovick and Santa, encouraging
and alternately yelling at them but refusing to let them quit.
Maxwell seemed to be holding up better than the rest of us, but
he didn't seem inclined to assist us. Yes, we were learning more
about each other all the time. Some of it wasn't pretty. We came
in together and in first place. I had to admit that some of our
success could be attributed to the fact that a lot of the other
teams were made up of Orientals: ARVN Rangers, ROKs from
Korea, as well as several teams from Thailand. These guys were
tough in their own rights, but their stature was their biggest
problem. But no one quit.

That last road march pretty well ended our training. Despite
the pain and suffering, I was proud of myself for having completed it. The only sour note from my point of view was not
being able to remain for the last week of training. This was to
be an actual combat patrol in enemy country. Such "training"
patrols often did get into firefights with Charlie. Good training
indeed! Those of us from F/51 had to return to Bien Hoa to
begin our own missions. The rub was that we'd worked hard
those two weeks. By leaving early, we would not be entitled to
wear the MAC/V Recondo Patch on our uniforms. For kids
anxious for fame and glory, every little bauble was a big deal.

Upon returning to Bien Hoa and after learning the details of
the deaths of Danny and Lieutenant Lattin, we set about preparing for our first patrol. This was little more than a practice
run, anyway. We would be inserted into the demilitarized zone
surrounding the base. Our troops generally did not patrol it, and
Charlie wasn't supposed to be out there either. Nor were civilians allowed in the area.

It was late in the evening of December 22, 1967, when we
were set in. We'd barely settled into position when the Stygian
darkness wrapped us in its cloak. There was no indication that
our presence was known to anyone, nor was there any indication
that anyone else was out there either. The choppers returned to
base, and we were really on our own.

The normal night sounds soon returned, having been momentarily stilled by the noise of the helicopters. The different night birds and insects began their bedlam of noise. As long as they kept it up, we knew we were all right. Perhaps that wasn't necessarily true, but I'd believe it if everyone else would. The mosquitos swarmed around my head as mosquitos will do, but were fended off by a good dose of insect repellent mixed in with my camouflage war paint. Funny thing about that bug juice; I'd always thought it smelled a lot like schnapps, but it sure didn't taste like it! And one of my most precious pieces of equipment helped also, my mosquito head net that had come with my bush hat, another of the few times Uncle Sam had a good idea.

The rotting ground vegatation, foxfire, was the only light we had. After my eyes became accustomed to the darkness, this seemed almost too bright. I could easily pick out the forms of the other men and was even able to recognize each individual. The trees above us weren't very tall, but it was triple-canopy jungle. The area had previously been cleared and then allowed to return to nature.

This patrol was to be little more than a shakedown, allowing us to adjust our equipment, as well as to each other. Theoretically, a LRP should sleep with all of his equipment on, in case it became necessary to unass the area in a hurry. The theory is fine if you don't carry much and carry it right. Instead of the hated rucksack, I'd decided to try squeezing everything into a butt pack, tying everything else to it. The butt pack was attached to my pistol belt at the small of my back, and when I tried to sleep, it felt like I was bowed over a boulder. Lewis wouldn't let me shed it. He was a stickler for procedure.

With darkness surrounding us, each man was effectively alone, as if on another planet. We communicated by whispering directly into each other's ears, little more than a breath to convey whatever message. We also learned to touch each other gently to let the next man know it was his turn for guard. In actuality, being with six men like this was a little better than being with a whole company in the 173d. Anything can happen in the dark, so I'd never really felt the comfort of the strength in numbers. There had only been three men on each position back then, and it was hard to feel safe. With the LRPs, I could reach out and touch everyone else in our little world. I felt reassured.

Morning found us still among the living. One thing about

those mosquito head nets; you had to watch them when you went to sleep or they collapsed onto your face. Often I woke up with one side or one spot on my face completely swollen to distortion due to the net settling on my skin and the bugs lighting for a feast.

What courage may have seeped away in the darkness returned with the light. Now was the time to begin a little on-the-job training. We began practicing more map and compass work, then a few efforts to rig jungle antennas (to increase the range of the team radio in case we were too far out, another skill I did not learn with any degree of success). It was really a beautiful day, sunny, warm, and pleasant.

Around noon, we began to hear voices. Everyone remained cool, ready for action, no noise. While there wasn't supposed to be anyone out there, we'd been told to avoid contact. The people could be VC, or they might be civilians going where they were not supposed to be, a not-unheard-of event. We scurried down a short trail, and then cut into the trees to hide. All we had to do was to keep still and quiet until they passed. Then we'd call in our sighting to the TOC and let them decide what they wanted us to do. No sweat.

Once into the trees, we immediately set up in the position we'd practiced so often before; rucksacks in the center, each man facing out to cover the full 360-degree circle. I was facing to just a little to the left of the rear.

I could faintly see several figures moving down the trail but could make nothing out at first. It sounded like a man and at least one woman. Women were known to serve with the VC line units. We waited, listened, and watched.

A rustling to my right made me turn around. Maxwell was sitting up, seemingly more nervous than usual. He was spinning about on the axis of his waist, first one way, then the other. I could see the inevitable about to happen and couldn't do a thing to stop him. As he turned once more, with his rifle held in front of him, he struck a tree. There is nothing natural in the jungle that sounds like an M-16 hitting a tree.

I glanced back towards the trail. I could see that the party walking by had stopped. Someone was bending over and was trying to see through the leaves. At the same instant, I heard Maxwell say, "They seen us!" in more than a stage whisper.

I glanced over at Santa. He'd been facing the trail. He looked at me, shrugged, then raised his rifle to his shoulder. He seemed to hesitate just an instant, as if taking the standard half-breath, and then he fired.

At the sound of the shot, everyone was instantly on their feet, rushing toward the trail. We broke into the clearing and began looking one way and then the other. After a second or two, I saw a man lying face down on a pile of brush about twenty feet away. Santa had gotten one of them. No one else was in sight.

Maxwell and Lovick were still in the trees, covering our backs as we'd been trained. An attack could come from any direction at any time. Lewis was standing at the edge of the trail, his back to the trees. Tommy Thomas had taken up a position to the north, facing up the trail. Tom was standing on the trail, staring at the body. No one was moving, no one seemed inclined to go forward and check him out.

Lewis had not given any orders; in fact, no one was talking at all. Since the inaction seemed to be accomplishing nothing, I took it upon myself to check the man out. I had never touched a dead person before. What would one feel like?

Again, he was lying face down. I approached slowly, watching for any movement, my rifle trained on the small of his back, safety off, my finger resting lightly on the trigger. Every sense was alert.

I noted his light blue shirt and khaki pants. He was wearing a pair of GI issue jungle boots. I briefly wondered how he had acquired those, off some dead American? His arms were folded under his chest. If he had a rifle or anything else, it was hidden by his body.

For several moments, I hesitated, just looking down at this man, alive but a moment ago, now dead. Finally I steeled myself; I had a dread of touching him, as if what had killed him would rub off on me. I took his arm and turned him about halfway over to his right to see if anything was under him. All that he had was a large, woodman's ax, the blade about two feet long and hooked at the end. The handle was perhaps a foot and a half long. He had no rifle.

Quickly I patted him down. There were no other weapons. I recovered the ax and then secured his wallet, something like a biker's wallet, made of leather, long and slim. The wallet was secured to his belt loop by a small chain with links about an inch or so long. It came away easily.

There was a crimson blossom on his left shoulder that was spreading slowly. It seemed that Tom had gotten him solid. I didn't bother to look at his face. All Oriental males looked alike? Or maybe I was just afraid to see his face.

After I stood up and turned around, I found that everyone was staring at me. Still, no one spoke a word. I picked up the ax and the man's wallet that I'd dropped. As I approached the rest of the team, everyone seemed to suddenly come to life. For several minuets, it was as if everyone was frozen in motion, with me being the only one capable of action. Now they returned from wherever they'd been and began reacting as we'd been trained. Tommy was on the radio, calling in that we had been in contact. He'd already made his initial call when Tom had fired his shot. Now he confirmed that we were en route to the LZ, a road not far away.

Along the way, we ran into our reaction force, a squad of men from our platoon. The point man was Robert Green. I noticed that he was carrying his M-16 rifle with one of the latest grenade launchers attached. (This preceded the M-203, and made the combination heavier than the M-16 and the M-79 combined. At least it seemed heavier to me.) Lewis told them where the body was. He had returned to life now, since the deed was done. We soon arrived at the road and set up what was to be our standard security perimeter. It seemed odd; I had not heard the choppers with the reaction force arrive. They'd departed, but with the other men present, there really seemed no need for further alarm. We were simply acting from training-inspired reactions. No one said a word about what had just happened.

Before long, the reaction squad returned, carrying the body. From out of nowhere, two women materialized, running toward the man who had been deposited beside the road. They were wailing and crying. I watched them, feeling nothing at first, then disgust as I watched them rifling his pockets. Then they began to remove his boots. I had almost begun to feel some slight remorse about having taken away their husband and son. The age differences in the two women made that factor obvious. I was not upset at their anguish, I was disgusted.

As we sat waiting for the choppers to come pick us up, I opened the man's wallet and found a South Vietnamese government-issue identification card. The name meant nothing to me, of course. He had been born in Hanoi in 1928. He'd been almost forty years old. The face that looked at me from the ID photo looked as innocuous as any such photo from any ID card anywhere. I wouldn't have recognized him again if I'd seen him alive the following day. His wallet also contained about eight piasters. Not much to show for the ending of a life.

Before long, a chopper arrived to pick up the team and return us to the company area. No one had yet spoken of the shooting.

We were quarantined, each man kept apart from the others until we had been debriefed individually.

It was soon determined that the man had probably been an innocent woodcutter. He had been in an area where he shouldn't have been, and he'd paid for it with his life. The company arranged to pay compensation to his family.

CHAPTER 11

Team 4/6 would now be on stand-down for a few days until our next patrol was planned or a specific mission devised. The last one had only been for practice, and all that it had taken to terminate it was for a man to die.

It was just as well. I believed I was quite justifiably upset with Lewis. He had been prepared to throw me to the wolves. Most of the team seemed to feel he'd just frozen up on us. How was I to resolve this situation? Whatever confidence I'd had in him was gone. But since this was Uncle Sam's army, I could not just tell them I refused to go out with him again. I needed some time to think this out. A few distractions wouldn't hurt, either.

Christmas in Vietnam was not something to bring about any real holiday spirit. It wasn't that I was missing a white Christmas; I'd never had one. Someone had sent us an artificial Christmas tree, and we put this up in the barracks and trimmed it with bright decorations. But the spirit wasn't there. We had just had two men killed. Other teams were continuing to go out, and other men were being wounded.

There was a multitude of packages from the States, many from people we'd never heard of. There was still some support for us that year. There was just too much cynicism within us to appreciate anything. I felt like I was no longer a part of that world I'd left behind.

Probably the only thing that really brought about any laughter from the packages were the hundreds of packages of the earlier presweetened Kool-Aid that had been sent. Someone had sent a letter home complaining about the taste of the water. The powdered concoction soon began arriving in cases. We had footlockers full of the stuff. You couldn't even give it away in town. And it tasted awful. I'd tried it once, dumping it into one of my canteens. I'd ended up throwing the canteen away because the taste would not come out.

The holiday cheer was dampened by an action which happened on December 27. Team 1/4 had been on an ambush patrol under S.Sgt. Bob Edwards, with the second team being nominally under the command of Sgt. Robert Rogers, one of the men I'd come from the 173d with. This was a heavy team and prepared for anything, but sometimes anything can be too much. Early that morning, they had been on trail watch when several VC had walked into the kill zone. The ambush had been sprung in what should have been a textbook ambush attack. Unfortunately, the enemy had not only had an awful lot of friends following, they would seem to have been very well prepared. Before the team knew what had hit them, they were inundated with machine-gun and RPG (rocket propelled grenades) fire. Five men were wounded in the flick of an eyelash: Roger Roberts, Pat Duffield, a Canadian who'd volunteered to serve with the American Army, Shelby Luman, Myron Anderson, and Bill Liggett. Luman and Liggett, in particular, were wounded pretty badly. Liggett ended up being sent home to recover and never came back. Luman would come back to the company after a long recovery period. The team never had any idea what they had hit; for most of them it was their first major contact since the company had been made operational, and in some ways, despite the stories and the reputation of the kinds of actions LRPs would encounter, it was still one hell of a fight. The team did nothing wrong, though there had been a bad feeling that "something" had been about to happen before the first shot was fired. *If* they'd had enough manpower to set a couple of teams well to both flanks, they *might* have had some idea of who was trailing the de facto point element. It didn't work that way. This would have entailed having men scattered up and down the trail from Cambodia to the South China Sea. This was just another of the hard lessons we would have to learn. You take a bite and hope you can swallow the whole thing.

Since my team did have the time off, I was anxious to get back downtown to see Miss Mi. I had visited her again, but it had been on payday. Too many guys standing in line. However, the second trip was almost as nice as the first. I was ready for more.

Arriving in town early, I decided to first treat myself to a nice meal at the American Club. The main course was giant fantail shrimp. I trusted the shrimp; its shape was obvious. Had I asked for beef, I would have been afraid of what, or whom, I was eating.

Next was a trip to one of the bathhouses. Since hot water did not exist at the company, this was always a treat. Just soak your cares and the accumulated dirt away. It made me feel like a new man. I was entertained by a young masseuse who would seem to have known less about the male anatomy than I knew about females.

Eventually, and after a few drinks, I made my way to the East Hotel. There I was informed that Miss Mi had gone to Saigon for the day, but that she was due to return at any time. I decided to wait, availing myself of the other ladies in the meantime.

Afterwards, I returned to the front parlor to watch television with some of the other GI customers. I hardly noticed as they came and went. They were playing a rerun of the series "Lost in Space." In this particular episode Sherri Jackson was a guest star. She was the girl who had been the oldest daughter in "Make Room for Daddy," the television series with Danny Thomas. I'd watched this series frequently while growing up. She'd also appeared in a recent issue of *Playboy* magazine. My, but how she'd grown! I became thoroughly engrossed.

When the show ended, I looked up and noticed that I was the only American in the place. I looked at my watch and discovered that I only had about half an hour until the gates to the base closed. I did not have an overnight pass, and wouldn't have stayed in town anyway. The stories might have been greatly exaggerated, and told to discourage such goings on, but I'd heard too many times of soldiers spending the night in town and never being seen again. I decided it was time to get back, even if I hadn't had a chance to see Miss Mi.

I headed for the stairs and started down the last flight to the front door. A young girl was standing at the grilled glass entrance, looking out. When she heard me coming, she looked up, and for a moment, I thought she was going to swallow her teeth.

Her eyes went wide, almost round, and then she came running up the stairs toward me. She grabbed my hand and began pulling me back up. "No go. MP come. MP come." I followed her, wondering how this was going to set with a board of review. With my reputation being what it was, getting caught in an off-limits section of town would not go over well. I might easily end up back in the 173d or LBJ (Long Binh jail, the military stockade), yet. The girl continued to drag me around the building until she found another woman who spoke a little more English. "No go. MP come," she said. Okay, I get the point.

They both began rushing me around the building from room to room, finally pushing me out onto a covered balcony. I was becoming quite conscious of the time. I was going to be late; there seemed little doubt about it. While waiting, I looked through the lattice trim that overlooked the street. There were no jeeps outside nor any other indications that American MPs were out there. I was beginning to wonder if this really was a runaround.

The girls returned and led me off again to another room. Both began moving a bed aside until they had exposed a wooden grill in the wall behind it. One of them pulled the grill out, revealing a large flue that just happened to be large enough for a man to squeeze through. They would seem to have had experience at hiding people. "Get in. Hide. MP come," they continued to chatter. I had gotten the message already, and I didn't like it. Time still seemed to be my biggest enemy. Soon the gates would be closed and locked, and I would be absent without leave. I was beginning to get real concerned.

Reluctantly I entered the hole, trying all the while to impress upon them my need to get back to the base quickly. They probably understood every word I said. "We be back. You be quiet. MP come." They replaced the grill and then moved the bed back in place. I was alone.

I probably looked at my watch every five seconds for what seemed like hours. I was close enough to the front door to hear the voices of everyone who came in. There were no American voices heard. Perhaps QC (Vietnamese military police)? Falling into their hands would be a lot less fun that being picked up by our guys. There wasn't an awful lot of love lost between them and the American soldiers. Or they might be Viet Cong. We had also heard plenty of stories about the prostitutes servicing the American's during the day and the VC at night. Poor things never got any rest. The possibilities seemed to be getting worse by the moment, and I was completely unarmed. I didn't even have a pocket knife on me. I swore right at that moment that I would never go unarmed again.

I looked at my watch again and had an idea. Not much of one, but it was something. I remembered reading one of the James Bond novels, *On Her Majesty's Secret Service*, where he had been unarmed with nothing but his watch. As he had done, I took my watch off and wrapped it around my fist. Anyone unfriendly coming through that hole was going to get a mouth full of crystal. It wasn't much, but it was all that I had.

I continued to wait. Would my family ever learn what had happened to me? I wondered. My mind was churning with ideas, but nothing seemed to be of any use. Finally, I crawled out onto the ledge beside me and began inching away from the hole. Not far away was a spot overlooking the basement. An old woman was sitting at a table counting something, possibly the night's receipts. "Psst," I whispered. She looked up. "Can you get me out of here?" I asked. She smiled at me as if this was a routine occurrence and then raised her finger to her lips. "Shhh," was all she said, and then she got up and left. I returned to my place beside the grill.

Then I heard the bed being moved. I tensed, poised to strike. The grill was removed. It was the girls. "Come. Come. You go now." I scurried from my hiding place and followed them to the stairs. They dragged me down and outside and then flagged down a Lambretta taxi. The older of the two girls gave the driver several dollars in MPC and piasters and spoke quickly to him in Vietnamese. I yelled at him to get me to the gate. It was obvious he'd already been paid, but he wanted to dicker. "You pay me, too." Son of a bitch was trying to rob me!

"Okay, I'll give you twenty dollars if you get me back in time," I lied. He sped off, greed propelling him along more rapidly than gasoline.

Along the way, we picked up several more men from the company, who were also in a hurry to get back. With the promises of more money from them, I'm certain this driver was thinking of retiring.

We arrived at the gate with less than five minutes to spare. It had only seemed like hours that I had been trapped in the hotel. All of us bailed out of the taxi and ran for the gate, laughing at the driver, who was demanding his payment. I felt like I had been given a new lease on life. I didn't think I would be in any great hurry to go to town again any time soon. I had no idea if the girls were playing a head game with me or there had been some real danger. I was also not anxious to go back and ask, no matter how charming the company of the legendary Miss Mi.

Two days later, we began laying in provisions for a real New Year's Eve bash. I had contributed a few dollars for refreshments and was invited to attend a party that 2nd Platoon was throwing, but I still wandered about from party to party.

As midnight approached, several potheads decided to liven things up by firing off a few pen-gun flares. The flares made bright, colorful stars, but were fairly harmless unless fired directly at someone. Then the alcoholics decided that they could top that. Before long it seemed as if we were in the midst of a battle. Shots were being fired off all over the company area, as well as the rest of the base. There was the continued explosion of hand grenades and even a claymore or two being discharged. And, of course, there were casualties.

Sergeant Butts had imbibed a few already and decided to show the kids just how tough he was. He stepped out of the barracks and jumped up on the chin-up bars out front. In the middle of one repetition, a grenade went off behind him, and he caught several pieces in the back. He was tough though. He didn't need no damned medic! Another guy in the barracks across the way had been lying on his bunk when two large pieces of metal had shot through the tin sheeting beside him, missing him by inches. He was certainly wide-eyed for a while.

We ended up with about sixteen people wounded that night, none seriously, but one man did end up in the hospital when his leg injury became infected. The potheads caught most of the blame, but I had seen the beginning of this miniwar when Sergeant Odom had stepped out and fired off a full magazine from his 16. It just progressed from there. Such goings-on had a tendency to negate the hard efforts at getting looped.

It also seemed that someone decided to assassinate First Sergeant Crabtree. Being the topkick, he was a hard man. It goes with the job. Someone had taken it personally and had rigged a claymore in front of his shack. I do not excuse this act, but I do understand it. Many cases of "fragging" in Vietnam could no doubt be attributed to some slimy piece of worm shit killing or trying to kill a good officer or noncom who was about to press some very deserved criminal charges on the "soldier" in question, and that criminal was just trying to eliminate the key witness or complaining party.

In other cases, I'm just as certain, some petty little demigod would decide that "he" didn't like the lax attitude that we tried to get into between patrols. They wanted things spit and polish, just like garrison Stateside. These men were patently stupid. You do not train men to kill and then pretend they can turn it off just like a light switch. Many of those men had killed a lot; it had become terribly easy, and it was just the easiest way to handle a difficult situation. Not that many men would ever do such things, but the potential was always there, nevertheless. Other than being a hard-ass I don't know what "crimes" Crabtree had committed to bring about this retaliation. I never heard, even by rumor, who had been responsible, and can't say I tried to find out, either.

One of the men working in the TOC that night had gone outside to start up the electrical generator. Usually, whoever did so would simply go out and jerk the starter rope, and that was it. This man just happened to carry a flashlight this time. When he reached for the rope, he noticed a strange wire leading away from the generator. He followed the wire and found the claymore. Had he started the power, the first sergeant and his guests would have had a very unpleasant evening indeed. This tended to make Top a little more subdued until his DEROS (date estimated to return from overseas). It may have also influenced the fact that he didn't extend his tour.

There were many more such cases in later years that I heard about, but was fortunately not witness to any of them on my second tour in '72. By then, many were racially motivated, and often the military seemed unable or unwilling to do anything to the perpetrators, even when they had been positively identified. There were also the cases that stemmed from drug abuse—little wonder when at every morning's police call we picked up hundreds of the little plastic vials intended for one hit of heroin. On that tour, I made a point of obtaining a pistol again, not to serve me in battle but to protect myself from the druggies and other criminals.

Mike Frazier and I placed a mail order for a couple of Gerber MK II Survival knives on January 2, 1968. We received them on January 22, and I was able to send my Vietnamese knife home as a war trophy. Now all that I needed was a chance to use the new knife. That same day that the knives were ordered, heavy Team 4/6 was scheduled to go out. At the debriefing, we were told that a very good trail up north should provide some good hunting. Lieutenant Snyder was going to go with us. My team would be combined with one led by platoon sergeant Richard McCoy, with S.Sgt. James Foreman, a big, redhead, as second in command. I didn't know him well, and since he was a career soldier, he usually ignored me. McCoy was another lifer, who favored a shotgun for combat. He had a tendency to claim any enemy soldiers hit by the buckshot as his kills, even if we only found a pellet in the dead man's earlobe.

In preparing my equipment for that patrol, I decided to go ready for some real hard fighting. I loaded up with forty magazines for my rifle, thirty hand grenades and ten white phosphorus grenades, along with all of the rest of my equipment. I figured I was ready for anything.

I knew I'd made a mistake when I tried to stand up with my loaded rucksack. I thought I was going to die of terminal hernia by the time we'd made the short walk to the choppers. It was too late to unload anything; they would not have tolerated any delay. I would have to carry the whole thing, live or die.

The flight out lasted about thirty minutes. As we flew along, I experienced a strange sensation that would become, in many ways, routine during these flights. Watching the ground passing below, my feet dangling over the edge of the chopper, I felt a strange desire to jump. I didn't feel suicidal, but otherwise could not explain it. Years later, when I finally made a few parachute jumps from a Huey, I found exiting this way much easier than jumping from a plane. Possibly a premonition of that event?

I was to be the point man, despite my limited experience in that position. As the first ship started in, I stepped out on the skid, prepared to jump when the word was given. Our intended LZ was no more than a small piece of ground situated between three large craters. It looked very insubstantial for its purpose. The craters themselves were about eight feet deep.

The first chopper began to lower in, and about three feet above the ground level, I got the pat on my back signifying that I was to jump. Just as I did so, the chopper shifted just enough that I landed halfway down into one of the craters. With the extreme angle of the hole and my extremely heavy load, I rolled headfirst into the bottom, all of my equipment landing on top of me. It could have been worse; at least the hole wasn't full of water.

I was vaguely aware that the rest of the team had made the jump safely and had run on into the tree line, no one bothering to stop and help me out. Finally, I righted myself and crawled out to join them in the woods. Now I would be rear security. I was also completely worn out from the weight of my equipment and knew I would die before we'd gone a hundred meters.

But I had a reprieve. Someone had spotted a couple of VC on the opposite side of the LZ as we'd landed. The mission was compromised right from the start. Without a shot being fired, the choppers returned, and we were extracted. We returned to base to try it again the next day, January 3, 1968. At least it gave me the chance to lighten my load. I didn't really think I would be needing that much ammo.

CHAPTER 12

After the discovery of the Phu Loi Regiment (Prologue), most of the teams were pulled in from the field to allow the ground pounders from the 199th and the 101st Airborne to do their thing. This gave us another short stand-down. No complaints from us this time. We'd found 'em, they could fight 'em.

That did not mean unlimited partying however. The days were spent on never-ending work details, one of the hardest being the filling and placing of sandbags. We filled so many of them, and yet there always seemed to be a need for more. At least that's what the powers that be told us. I wondered where the sandbags were all going, because there never seemed to be that many more around the barracks or anywhere else. I became convinced we were in the business of exporting them to other war zones, or someone was eating them.

On January 12, I was promoted to sergeant, enlisted grade E-5. This meant a slight increase in pay, and theoretically I would no longer have to participate in certain work details. I would now be the man in charge of such chores. Leadership did not come easily to me, especially in garrison. I'd had no formal training in it, and I damned sure wasn't a natural. I felt singularly unqualified for the position. It seemed that most of my subordinates were older than I was, but few of them gave me any hassle. But there's always the 10 percent who don't get the word. What eventually evolved was the only way I knew how to lead—from the front. If the men followed me, that was fine. If not, fuck 'em. Let them find another sergeant.

I was also made assistant team leader of Team 4/4 under Sergeant Odom. He and I did not get along from the start. He was a compact little guy, tough as nails, but with a big chip on his shoulder. He constantly reminded everyone of how tough he was and that when he got back on the "block," he was gonna teach "whitey" a few tricks he'd learned in the Nam. I didn't see that anyone had much to fear, from what I'd observed. He also seemed to make a point of constantly undermining my new authority. I was too uncertain of myself to know how to deal with that.

A lot of time during this period was spent in constant speculation about what special mission F Troop could or would be used for. Having all Airborne personnel evoked images of jumps into North Vietnam or perhaps Laos or Cambodia to monitor or cut the Ho Chi Minh trail. In the meantime, we would continue to learn our craft in our own neighborhood.

The next patrol with Odom was pretty much of a bust. We had radio problems as soon as we landed, being unable to make contact with the C & C, but whatever the gremlin had been, the problem soon corrected itself, and we headed out. It seemed all that we did was wander about, stop, and listen. In fact, that was exactly what our job was, but I'd have preferred trying to pull off an ambush. Odom wasn't interested.

After several days of negative sightings and nothing of significance to report, we set up our last RON to await the morning and extraction. From the small pharmacy that we each carried, I took a dextroamphetamine to keep me awake the last night. Usually this worked without any undue side affects, but sometimes it gave me severe diarrhea. This night was one of those times.

Just after dark, we heard what sounded like a large force of VC moving in the woods about fifty meters from our position. They had stopped at a small stream running near us to fill their canteens; we could hear the metal banging on rocks in the water. It was impossible to estimate how many of them there were, but it was damned sure a bunch. Their laughter and talking could be heard distinctly as they passed on and more men came up to fill their canteens. This went on for a couple of hours. And not long after it began, the cramps came. My guts felt like they were going to explode. I did not fancy the idea of answering the call and having a battle begin while I had my pants down.

The only thing I could figure out later was that one of the VC had dropped his canteen and had been unable to find it in the dark, so he'd just left it. After a while, the voices seemed to fade away, but there was still the sound of a canteen rattling on the rocks. I waited and waited and suffered. It was almost morning before I felt safe in taking care of business, and by then I hurt so badly, I no longer cared. The longest and most miserable night of my life. There do seem to be some things worse than dying.

Things always seemed in a flux. Men were constantly coming in or going home. You would become aware that someone was short because no one ever let you forget it. We'd go out on patrol, and after we'd return, an old face would be gone, and a new one was there to take that man's place. Getting to know new men was a constant hassle. One situation this created was the constant shifting of personnel within teams. It was known and accepted that you worked best with men you had been out with frequently. But there was always at least one new face on every patrol. Yes, this helped us to learn more about different men in the platoon, but the team suffered from it, also. I never went out with the same five men the entire time. We did have a few screwups.

Patrols would continue to go out, and some were meeting with a great deal of success, wrapping up more confirmed kills in one day than many of the larger units could get in a month of hard patrolling. Our reputation was growing, as was the jealousy within other units. We operated in the field with six-man teams and had few if any casualties; the larger units sent out whole platoons or companies and almost got wiped out. My team went out a few times, but ended up having to abort because we were spotted immediately after insertion. Besides, there were just times we didn't feel like arguing property rights. I still wanted more action.

One thing I heard on one of those earlier patrols took some getting used to. These were the sounds made by what we called the "fuck-you" lizard. I'm still not sure if it actually was a lizard or some night bird. We'd be in position and would have total confidence that Charlie had no idea we were in his neighborhood. Then from out of the darkness would come this loud scream, "Fuck you! Fuck you!" Actually, after you heard it a few times, it was more like "Bock you," or sounds that weren't meant to be repeated by humans. Many times, I could only wait until a little time had passed and we weren't hit before I was certain it wasn't Charlie yelling at us.

Much has been made of the racial tensions in Vietnam. It also seems accepted that there was much less of it in the line units, where they quickly learned that they needed each other too much to let seemingly artificial things like color stand in the way of their survival. Garrison troops experienced much more of this than the grunts. F Troop was in the middle; lots of time spent in the brush, but also a lot of time in the rear.

Fortunately, there were few real explosions to make things worse, but we had more than our fair share of bigots, black as well as white. It was just the times we had to endure. I soon realized that it didn't mean anything. An asshole is an asshole, regardless of race, creed, or color. We had just as many as any other segment of the world population. Still, even when I didn't always get along with or care for someone, by and large, we had a bunch of damned good men who cared deeply for the company as a whole and would do anything to help a buddy.

Word came down that there would be a general stand-down in preparation for the upcoming Lunar New Year's celebration. There was also a lot of concern that Charlie would violate the cease-fire. This didn't have any real effect on us. We received a warning order. Another heavy team would be going out on January 29, 1968, for another ambush patrol.

CHAPTER 13

Team 4/0, under Lieutenant Snyder again, was going in as a light heavy team of ten men, somewhere to the northeast of Bien Hoa again. Not having access to maps made it difficult for me to keep track of where we were most of the time. On most of these earlier ambush patrols, the normal duties one had, such as point man, pace man, assistant team leader, etc., were usually dropped, and those lower in the rank structure, such as myself, ended up in positions as little more than rifleman. Sometimes I had a map, other times I didn't.

As we flew out, we'd usually pass over a river or some other distinctive landmark that had been planned as a rallying point, should we have to escape and evade (E & E). The most common feature was the Dong Nai River, but it swung through this area, headed northeast, also. To follow the river, either upstream or downstream, as you would in any other survival situation, would have only led deeper into enemy territory. Often, we flew over an old abandoned triangular fortress, possibly dating from the time of the French, or perhaps from the earlier U.S. advisory days. It seemed a likely spot to head for.

Once on the ground, we went into our normal pattern of listening first, then moving out to our proposed ambush site. This time, we didn't have long to hump before we got there. The target trail itself led along the crest of several large craters, and even at a distance, we could tell that it was well used. It was also situated so that even if Charlie immediately broke and ran, we'd have a clear field of fire for some distance.

The bulk of the team set up in the heavy brush at the south edge of the crater. Lovick, Santa, and I were to make our position closer to the trail, in case there was an opportunity to snatch a prisoner, or to put us closer to check anyone that we hit. I wasn't real sure this was a great idea for many reasons; first, the three of us were much more exposed than the rest of the team. We had a mound of dirt in front of us and a slight rise to our east. There was a huge crater immediately to the west, the bottom full of some milky, greenish liquid that looked like mint Pepto-Bismol. We also had absolutely no overhead cover. If we stayed out for very long, we'd be at the mercy of the sun all day long, not to mention being entirely too visible.

Then there was the factor that Tom was burned out. He was getting entirely too short and really had no further interest in heroics. We all knew a soldier had to do his job right until the last moment, but common practice dictated that you do not put a short-timer on the spot. That's what cherries are for. Lovick was already talking about extending, but not for the company. I wasn't sure what the implications for that were. Me, I was still fairly green, in my own opinion. I'd been shot at more than a few times, but still had a lot to learn. Besides, where we sat, we were too close to the line of fire of our own machine guns. I certainly hoped no one back there was pissed at me for any reason.

The general routine began, watching and listening. The only respite from the sun was when it went down. The three of us took turns spelling each other to sleep both day and night. There was nothing else to do. You can watch a spot until your eyes bug out and find that your best sense will often be your ears in such a situation. If a single VC had come down the trail at a leisurely trot, a man would have had to have his finger not only directly on the trigger but have half the slack taken up if there would be any chance of getting off a good shot. I'd brought a book along to read but quickly finished it, and it wasn't good enough to read again. The only other break in the monotony was to attend to bodily functions and how to do it without exposing ourselves even more. The waterproof bags from the LURP rations provided half the solution. Fill it up and dump it as far to the side as possible. As for the rest, you hope you could wait until after dark. If not, you had to crawl into the crater. In a very short time, the three of us occupied the smelliest piece of real estate in Vietnam.

I had been lucky to that point in having seen some very beautiful country, but this wasn't part of it. The scarred land and blasted foliage had no appeal, and the animal life all seemed to have disappeared. Not a bird or squirrel stirred. In time, we began hearing roosters, and then we'd catch the smell of wood smoke or the sound of an ax striking wood. There would be no friendly civilians in that area. The sounds and smells came from all around us, and it took little imagination for us to figure out that we were much too close to a very sizable enemy base camp. The three of us were too distant from the rest of the team to know if they were picking up on the same things we were, and we were not kept clued in on any radio traffic. It was like we were in exile. Charlie was out there, and I had no doubt that he knew we were in the neighborhood. Why didn't he do something? A trail like the one we watched had been used entirely too much to now see absolutely no traffic at all. I was getting bad feelings about this, but nothing happened.

The days dragged by until finally it was time for us to make arrangements for extraction. Whatever potential this place had for action, Charlie wasn't playing. Snyder beckoned Lovick to come back to his position. After he'd low-crawled there and back, he gave us the news. "Choppers can't come get us. They're tied up with some other business," he said. This didn't make any sense. Those choppers "belonged" to us. They were for our use and not for anyone else.

"What gives? Something going on that they aren't telling us?" Tom asked.

"I don't know, and if the lieutenant knows any more he ain't sayin'. All we know right now is we gotta stay put at least two more days, and then they'll come get us as soon as possible." Being the bearer of bad news is not something anyone wants.

Two more days. Food wasn't a real issue. Each man could carry as much or as little as he wanted. If you spent a lot of time humping, you would need more food over a period of time. Sitting and waiting didn't require as much sustenance. I had two LURPs left; that would easily last me two days. Water was another matter. Eight quarts was about as much as I could handle strapped to my rucksack. The heat had been sapping our strength for days, and most of us were out of water, or damned near. For the rest of the day, I held out, but there was too much heat and too little water left.

Late in the afternoon, I wormed my way down into the crater and sat looking at that sickly looking water, or whatever kind of liquid it was. Possibly some sort of new chemical created by those in the bombs that had made the hole and those in the ground. After some time, I convinced myself that it was merely stagnant water and filled our canteens from the sump, using my handkerchief as a filter. I only hoped it wasn't poisoned. I did use my water purification tablets, but I really didn't think they would do much good. Necessity sometimes requires risks.

I crawled back out and passed the canteens around. "Is it drinkable?" Dennis asked.

"I'll believe it if you will," I answered. There was only one way to find out, and we didn't die.

That day was longer than all of the others. We began hearing a lot of suspicious sounds, but there still was no real indication that Charlie was hunting us. For want of anything better to do, we even discussed the possibilities of an E & E. In effect, we were talking about abandoning our mission and walking back. But there were too few of us, and it was too far to the base or any other friendly location. We would have absolutely no means of support if we got into trouble on the way back. Snyder even asked permission from the rear, but he was told, "Sit tight. We'll get you out as soon as we can."

The fifth night came, and we made efforts to extract more water from the crater. I was wondering just how sick I was going to get from drinking that filth.

Shortly after noon the sixth day and with still no word that we were going to be pulled out, Tom alerted us. He'd seen someone standing in the trees on the other side of the trail, watching us. Tom also advised that this guy didn't seem to care if we saw him or not. I wasn't in a position to see. Some of the other team members began hearing very distinct movement, also. Now I could hear Snyder on the radio advising base of our situation. The time for caution would seem to have passed.

"Three fox, this is 4/0. We have a definite movement and sightings of enemy personnel around us." I could imagine headquarters' reply. "Roger, Three fox. We are certain. Definite enemy sightings, bearing twenty-five degrees azimuth, approximately seventy-five meters. Over."

The waiting seemed to last forever. What is taking so fucking long? Finally, "All right, they're going to scrape up some choppers from somewhere. We've been advised to prepare for a fighting E & E if necessary." This sounded terribly ominous. What the hell was going on? No time to think. Pack up and be ready.

The movement was getting louder, more distinct, closer. No shots had yet been fired, but the bad guys were definitely closing in. "Slicks inbound. Five minutes. Prepare to blow claymores," Snyder told us. It wasn't quite a shout, but after all those days of whispering, who has control of their voices?

Tom was sighting his M-60 in the direction of the VC he'd first spotted. It damned sure wasn't some woodcutter this time. Lovick was going to give cover fire in the opposite direction. I got all three of the clackers for our claymores cradled in my hand and waited for the command. This should be interesting! I thought.

"Blow claymores!" Snyder shouted. I'd scooted down onto my rucksack and had pulled my knees into my chest. Then I hit all three clackers at once, and the world literally exploded. The blast sent Tom flying back on top of me, but he quickly picked himself up and got back into position and began firing while Dennis opened fire in the other direction. I started reeling in the wires and shoved the clackers into my cargo pocket and was ready to go. We always tried to make a point of leaving nothing behind that would aid Charlie in his war efforts. Then we were up and running.

It was about two or three hundred meters to the LZ, a distance it had taken us an hour to cover when we first landed; now we made that in a matter of minutes. There were shots coming in our direction from the surrounding woods, but nothing seemed to come too close. We fired back as we made our withdrawal. Dennis was firing away with the M-79, popping rounds left and right. I happened to glance back and saw one round hit a large tree limb and explode. Bet he couldn't do that again if he tried, I thought in a detached frame of mind. Suddenly gunships appeared and began firing up the woods behind us. I could see their stenciled logos on their sides; they weren't the gunships that were assigned to our company, but they'd do just fine.

In very short order, we were all aboard, and the choppers lifted off. The flight back didn't seem to take all that long. As we flew, the door gunners, and then our buddies when we landed, began telling us about the "big battle," bodies on the wire by the air base and so on. What the hell were they talking about? Yeah, we'd had to shoot our way out, but it really wasn't any big deal. No one had been hit.

The reason, as it finally came out, for our being left out longer than normal was a little thing called the first Tet Offensive. While we were sitting in Charlie's backyard, the whole country was going up in flames. I soon realized my mother probably knew about Tet before I did. Our choppers and personnel had been needed to defend the base. The stories did abound. Colonel Maus had reportedly been directing gunship and fighter plane attacks on the VC who had tried to overwhelm the base. Between their runs, his ship had fired into the ranks of the massed attackers with all of the weapons they'd had aboard until even their pistols were empty. Their last run was made throwing smoke grenades. A lot of the cleanup was already over by the time we got back in. Bulldozers had scooped out huge holes and shoved all of the enemy bodies in for mass burial. A few bodies remained hanging on the wire for months, and the strong smell of the lime used to cover the dead was always in the air whenever we made a trip to the air base. There was also just a light touch of decaying flesh in the air.

If we had E & E'd as we'd planned, we might well have walked into Charlie's retreating forces. One of our teams had been the ones to give the base its first warning that something was up. They had spotted a large contingent of VC moving toward the Long Binh complex and called it in. Later, when Charlie was retreating, this team had to defend itself, and at least one man was seriously wounded. But they'd done their jobs. Company F would receive the Valorous Unit Award for its part in the defense of Bien Hoa. In effect, my team had sat out one of the biggest battles of the war in what would seem to have been one of the safest places in the whole country. We would never know, but maybe Charlie had just sent so many men into the attack that there hadn't been enough of them to deal with us, or they had been under orders not to start any other actions that might alert the base. Who knows? If Charlie had hit us while the attack was going on, we'd have simply been shit out of luck. Close, too fucking close. Maybe a God I did not understand was watching over me after all, or at least someone on that patrol.

CHAPTER 14

Many things changed after Tet. We went on stand-down for a short time, but even if there had been the inclination, it wasn't wise to try to go downtown. "By some macabre, or ironic, twist some of the last of the Tet attackers to hold out were killed or captured in [a] Long Binh graveyard. In other gravesites around the perimeter, Charlie actually had underground positions beneath the graves.''* Quite a bit of Bien Hoa was in ruins, since Charlie had taken cover in many of the buildings while retreating, and those buildings had been destroyed. It is doubtful that many of the remaining civilians would have been happy to see us, and most of the whores had gone into hiding, whether from us or the VC, I didn't know. I couldn't help wondering about Miss Mi's fate. Kid that I was, and marvels that she'd shown me, I thought about her a lot. Hell, she wouldn't recognize me on a bet. But it had been fun.

There was a constant stench in the air from bodies left unburied, or not even found, as they rotted in the sun. The free and easy way of doing a lot of things seemed to have gone forever. While historically the Viet Cong may have been destroyed, there seemed to be an awful lot of nephews who would attend his wake, and they continued to exact their toll.

The month of February saw many things occur. Colonel Maus was reassigned as the commanding officer of Team B-50, with the 5th Special Forces Group. It was good for him that his work with us had been recognized, but most of us were sorry to see him go. The new CO would be Maj., again soon to be lieutenant colonel, Joseph Zummo. He was a small man, not a West Pointer. He would be an unknown factor in the beginning, but from the start, it was easy to see that the man had a severe alcohol problem, not that any of the rest of us had such a problem. It is likely that this had a tremendous effect on many of his decisions in the following months. And perhaps he, too, was bounded by orders he had no control over. We would never know, for the most part.

Lieutenant Snyder had been replaced as platoon leader of 4th Platoon back in December, though he still tried to exercise some control over us. He had been made S-3, operations officer, the new Three Fox. Platoon sergeant Butts had been the de facto platoon leader as well as the platoon sergeant in the interim and did a damned good job. What did we need an officer for? Lieutenant Donald Peter arrived in February to take over the platoon, but it would still be Butts's show for a while. Lieutenant Peter was an ROTC graduate, from California. Tall and quiet, not good-looking by his own admission, but he was a good man and a good officer. I soon learned to appreciate his fairness and honesty.

According to Michael Lee Lanning in his book, *Inside the*

LRRPs-Rangers in Vietnam, "In February and March 1968 . . . F/51 conducted one hundred and seventeen patrols with no friendly casualties. They sighted the enemy on ninety-one occasions and made contact on thirty-three of them, resulting in forty-eight enemy killed, twenty-six more probable kills, and eighteen prisoners captured."† I certainly would not dispute this statement. I was a participant on many of the patrols at this time, few of which stayed out the full four or five days. I spent my twentieth birthday in the bush. We'd either make contact immediately after insertion or pull off an ambush within a day or so. Blasting off claymores and then going out to check for bodies, we soon, despite ourselves, began having some grudging respect for the enemy. Our ambushes were laid out with scientific precision; we'd open fire on men we could see in the kill zone, and then go out and find nothing, or maybe one or two bodies when there had been five or six targets. Sometimes we'd find blood trails, but no bodies. Charlie must have grabbed his wounded in the midst of the rain of lead and steel and fled like a spirit. It was very frustrating.

Our linear ambush positions were seemingly very simple but were laid out in consideration of many hours of practice and, before that, many years of experience by men who had gone before us. A suitable trail would be found that gave us good concealment and would let us set up as close as possible. This was the routine practiced by heavy teams; ambushes pulled by light teams required some slight adaptations and improvisation.

The heavy team leader and RTO would be in the center. The two machine gunners with their assistants would set up a short distance away, on either side of the center, often no more than a few feet away, depending on the site. Flank security would be two men on each end, their purpose being to both close the door on Charlie as he entered and to engage anyone else who tried to come in as the ambush was being sprung. Two other men would be to the rear as security in case anyone tried to sneak in our back door. Variations of this would work out quite well for both near and far ambushes. L-shaped ambushes were designed to set up at the bend of a trail, with the team on the inside to keep us from firing at each other.

Ed Dvorak and Al Markut told me about one particular am-

†Used with permission of the author.

bush that really cracked me up. S.Sgt. Bill Lavender was one of the earlier leaders of Team 1/5. Bill was a tall, gangly hillbilly from Mississippi, with a very distinct southern twang to his speech. The team had been sent out on a heavy ambush patrol well to the east of Long Binh on February 4. The next day they had an interesting incident to report. The area they had set up in was what we called a "bamboo room." You'd find a place as close to a trail as possible to rig an ambush. The team would look for a good thick jumble of brush, bamboo, plaited vines, etc., that appeared impenetrable. The men would worm their way into this thicket until the whole team was inside, then pull more vines in around the entrance. It was felt impossible for anyone to get in to you silently, but it would be just as hard for us to get out in a hurry. You give and you take. Sometimes the accommodations were very short of spectacular. A bamboo room had the advantage of affording some protection if Charlie tried to throw grenades at your position; most of the time they would just bounce back at him. This also meant our rounds being fired out were more easily deflected by the brushes and bamboo.

The team set up so that they could readily take on anyone who came down the trail, but the men also knew they could easily be seen by anyone passing by.

Before long, the sound of equipment rattling around and voices were heard. The team was ready to let loose with everything they had. As the voices came closer, they picked up Yankee twang; the people coming in were Americans.

Shit! A perfect ambush, a clear field of fire, and these targets ain't been legal since the War Between the States, Bill thought. What was a man supposed to do? Lavender and the team knew that their placement was good as long as they intended to hit, but if they just sat and waited for the GIs to pass, someone was bound to spot them. They didn't want to fire up their own people, but they didn't want to be blasted either. A real tragedy was about to take place if someone didn't do something.

Bill must have had either the biggest pair of balls in all of Southeast Asia, or been one of the most laid-back people since God created the first rock. He put his rifle down and stepped out into a clear spot. His camouflaged uniform and war paint certainly wouldn't give him any great advantage. He'd spotted the sergeant who seemed to be in charge of this detail; "Yo! Sarge! Y'all hold up a minute."

The consternation within the American patrol must have been a sight to behold! Bill's southern accent may well have worked to their advantage also. Central Mississippi doesn't sound at all South Vietnam. Those men were a squad from the 199th and were just about as lost as could be imagined. Bill could have been shot down more easily and readily than the team might have been able to blast the Americans. The tension was tremendous as both sides waited, uncertain of the other side's reactions. And certainly, on the part of the 199th, the reaction must have been, What the fuck have we stepped in this time!

There were some very cool heads present that day. No shots were fired, and the lost patrol was ushered into the team's position. Bill took several members of the American squad around and showed them the placement of the team's claymores; the GIs had been dead center in the kill zone. Their green fatigues were no match for the green faces most of them had when they saw how close they had come to being had.

The funniest part was the reaction back at TOC. The RTO may not have gotten the full message out on the radio, or maybe he was another one of those deviants with a weird sense of humor. Headquarters received a report that Team 1/5 had captured a squad. I could just imagine champagne bottles being popped all over the place. "We've captured a whole fucking squad of Viet Cong!" Etc., etc.

"Uh, no, sir, I mean, Three Fox, this is 1/5. Negative. What we got is a bunch of 'Mericans. GIs. These guys is our people. Musta gotten lost or somethin'." There must have been an awful lot of red faces back at the 199th that night. The captured squad had, it turned out, only been about five miles or so out of their area of operations. It could have been worse of course, but I'd still bet there were some very sick GIs that night when they got back to their barracks. Bill should have gotten a medal for the cool he displayed that day.

Not all of our patrols were quite as humorous. Quite often, Charlie did return fire, and we were constantly amazed that so many bullets would be flying through the air and no one was hit. We called these "fun firefights." On one occasion I returned from a firefight to find a large wooden splinter, secondary shrapnel so to speak, imbedded in the rubber heel of my boot. The piece was about an inch and a half long and half an inch in diameter. That would have been a very nasty wound had it hit anywhere else. On another occasion, a pipe I had been affecting was hit. I'd been trying to be cool. When not chewing on the stem, I would tuck it into one of the loops on my ammo pouch that normally held the spoon for a grenade. I returned from the patrol to find that the bowl of the pipe had been shattered by some object's impact, but I had not been hit. Not having anyone wounded was certainly gratifying, but the fact of our having no new fatalities simply amazed me. I wasn't disappointed, but I would probably have found it more believable if we had taken casualties all the time, since that's what I expected war to be like. Every patrol that passed that we didn't lose someone left me with a dread for the next one.

While the major ground units were once again seeking to engage Charlie in a decisive battle, we were once again on a short stand-down. I was beginning to be less impatient about wanting to get into battle. I still chafed at not getting any more kills; my feeling, based upon my training, was that every enemy soldier I killed was one less that I or some other GI would have to face tomorrow. Not being able to see their bodies left me feeling like I wasn't doing my job.

In the meantime, there was partying that had to be attended to. Since we couldn't go to town we went instead to the air base. Granted that we had a great NCO club, but sometimes you have to check out the grass on the other side. There was a Vietnamese officers club that allowed U.S. noncommissioned officers to enter. If someone in our group was not an NCO, someone would just loan them one of their extra shirts with the stripes sewn to the sleeves. No one seemed to notice that in any given group, half of the group usually had the same last names as the other half.

There were some females there, possibly refugees from the town, or they might have worked there full time and had just been allowed to remain after the Tet Offensive. One quickly attached herself to me. After a few drinks, she began to look rather nice; her smile wasn't half bad as long as her lips were together, and I couldn't see that quite a few of her teeth had departed, and most of those that were left were black. As I became more cross-eyed, she became less cross-eyed. Then she began to look almost lovely. I bought many a Saigon Tea that night, not really expecting it to get me any farther than it ever had in my many forays into town. One thing I will say for a prostitute; you get what you pay for. With a "B," or bar girl, the soldier is usually the one who got screwed, but only figuratively.

But there were other matters to attend to. Since we hadn't had a chance to really water up for a while, the beer and liquor soon began taking its toll. We would take turns carrying our "dead" back to the company area and putting them to bed or as close as we could get them. This required two men for each trip, since we were having to hitchhike. Without a doubt these trips helped a few of us last a little longer on this binge. Each group would then return to the club to continue to toast those who had departed, then someone else would fall by the way.

Bob Green was assisting me on the last trip. He and I were the only ones left, since some of the carrier's hadn't made it back either. I bid a fond farewell to my lady friend, with full intentions of returning. Bob and I and our burden made it back without any problems. We deposited our load, and then we started back. We had gotten perhaps fifty feet beyond the front gate when Bob started to sway. I was fortunate that I didn't have to carry him far. I had outlasted all of them. Ford won!

I was entirely too drunk to try to go back alone, and I wasn't ready for bed yet, so I decided to take in a movie. It was *Penelope*, with Natalie Wood. Not something I might have paid to see back in the World, but since the price was right and she had such beautiful eyes, I stayed.

Fourth Platoon was supposed to be on total stand-down, not even having to pull berm guard. Lieutenant Snyder walked up and rudely interrupted Natalie and then announced that 4th Platoon would relieve 3d Platoon on the perimeter. That was ridiculous! They would only need eleven or twelve men for the detail, but we probably only had three or four who were still sober, or at least still on their feet. Whose brainstorm was this?

Butts tried to reason with the powers that be with all of the powers of persuasion he could muster, but to no avail. Despite his many years of service, he wasn't happy. *They* were fucking with *his* kids. Time to fuck back.

He ordered a platoon formation; everyone was going on guard detail no matter what their condition. We didn't bother with standard guard-mount equipment. We just fell out in full field equipment, rucksacks and all.

After forming up, many of the men had to be supported by others who were more sober only by degrees; some never really woke up to what was going on. Then we began to march through the company area, singing every nasty, vile song we could remember or make up. The movie was totally disrupted when we marched across the stage in front of the screen. At any other time, this might have caused a riot, since we were messing with the evening's entertainment, but perhaps the other guys realized we were getting the shaft, so they cheered us on. It took us about half an hour to load aboard the trucks that would take us out. I vaguely wondered if the driver was sober or not.

When we finally reached our spot on the perimeter, one three-man position and four two-man spots, it became a regular cluster fuck trying to sort everyone out and get them placed. Some, who had revived a little, had passed out again. Others did not seem to be long for this world. The march alone had taken its toll. We simply rolled them off the back of the truck.

I was on the bunker that was supposed to have three men. We had about fifteen or sixteen there. Who could count? The only men in the platoon who were sober took up a position as far away from us as possible to distance themselves from the pending disaster. They weren't stupid! We promptly set up our machine guns and claymores, and pointed them into the perimeter. No one had to tell us who the enemy was that night. Then the rations were broken out, the beer and liquor, and I suspect someone had brought along a little loco weed.

Before long, a jeep drove up. It was the officer of the day, some major from another unit, checking the guard. "Who goes there?" someone challenged. "What's the password?" someone else asked. The major identified himself, and then gave what I would guess was supposed to be the password. "No, that's not it. You don't have the password, 'cause we haven't made it up yet." I had no idea who was talking, I was just along for the ride.

The major decided he didn't like what was going on, and he was going to get to the bottom of it! He started forward, and someone pulled back the charging handle on one of the machine guns and "accidently" touched off a couple of rounds in the major's direction. Close, but not too close. This was, after all, an American officer. "You want to die, asshole?" the shooter said.

The major, being no dummy, stopped dead in his tracks and then backed up to his jeep. *He* was going to get to the bottom of this. Redundant asshole.

Everyone had a good laugh as he drove off. Here and there, some of the men might have been begun feeling a little concern about repercussions, but not too many. We remained where we were the rest of the night without being bothered further and returned to the company area the next morning much the worse for wear. It was just fortunate Charlie hadn't decided to try an attack or infiltration that night. Our response might have been nonexistent.

That was not the end of the matter, of course. For some reason, no one pushed to determine who had been on that bunker. Just "maybe," someone had pulled his head out of his ass long enough to realize that he had made a major faux pas in sending out a bunch of drunks in the first place. But someone had to pay. Platoon sergeant Walter P. Butts became their goat.

Zummo had taken personal offense at the platoon's action, so Butts was court-martialed. It cost him some money in fines, but not his stripes. The old fart carried his court-martial papers around like they had been a commendation. Perhaps they were. He'd only been doing what he did best, taking care of his men. No one was going to fuck with us, by God! As a matter of fact, he soon became our first sergeant. Maybe he did know Westy after all.

There was one repercussion; we would no longer be allowed to pull guard in that particular area. What a shame!

CHAPTER 15

The month of March had many highs and lows, startling events as well as trivial bullshit. I finally talked S.Sgt. Norman Taitano into selling me the Browning High Power pistol he carried. I knew beans about stopping power but certainly liked the idea of a thirteen-shot magazine. We could get all of the 9mm ammo we needed from Special Forces supply. Quite a few of the men had acquired their own handguns. At one time, I guesstimated that there were at least fifty handguns being carried by individuals who would not have otherwise been authorized to carry them, and no two were alike. Ammunition was no problem, as long as your pistol used only .45 ACP, or .38 Special that we could get from the chopper people, or 9mm that came from Special Forces. Everything else was in short supply at the country store. Bob DeFer, another buddy in 2d Platoon, had somehow "imported" a couple of pistols; he carried a Spanish Astra, and he'd brought back a Walther P-38 for Mike Frazier. Ron Kaplan carried a Ruger Blackhawk .357 magnum single-action revolver. We had everything from .44 mags to .22 mags, an old German-made single-action.

Until this point, I'd carried a .45 auto I'd gotten in trade from a guy who took it from a VC. Someone had taken an awful lot of trouble to file off the serial number for reasons I could never begin to understand.

I was still wrestling with the dilemma of what unit I was going to extend for. The idea had first struck me, and had grown from there, back in November. At first, I had every intention of extending for the company, but after seeing the way things were shaping up under Zummo, I was having second thoughts. About extending for the company that is. Special Forces or a door gunner's slot crossed my mind. The problem for me was simple; I didn't feel like I'd accomplished enough. I had come to Vietnam to learn something about myself. So far I'd learned zip, other than the fact that getting shot at didn't bother me as long as they kept missing. I tried to appease my mother's concerns by laughing it off, simply stating I was extending because I hadn't had a chance to see Bob Hope's show the last Christmas. Since that didn't wash, I just confessed that I liked the work. Also, I had too much time left in the army, and I didn't want to spend it Stateside going through all of their parade-ground bullshit. War was much easier to deal with. It would be years before it dawned on me what I had put that poor woman through, but I'd long since left the nest; I had to do it my way.

All too soon, it was time to go back to work. Patrols continued making contact, but our luck was holding.

That's not to say there were no fatalities. One day in early March, I was resting in the barracks between patrols. Another team had just returned, but these comings and goings were now such a common occurrence that, unless they brought in a dead VC or some really spectacular booty, no one paid much attention.

Suddenly, there were two shots in rapid succession. "That's one argument that got ended abruptly," I observed. I then stepped out of the barracks to see what was going on. Quite a few men were running toward one of the barracks in the 1st Platoon area. I followed to see what was going on.

It was hard to see over the other rubberneckers, but I could just barely make out the form of a man lying on the floor. His shirt was open, and there were two distinct bullet holes in his chest. Someone was trying to render first aid, but from what I could see, he was beyond help.

An ambulance was called for and soon arrived to take him away. The rest of us filtered out, listening to the witnesses who'd been present.

One of the guys on the team that had just come in walked into the barracks and just plopped down on his bunk, worn out. The other guy had come in and started messing with him in a good-natured way. He had grabbed the muzzle of the other man's rifle and yanked on it. The man from the patrol still had his hands on the grip, his finger on the trigger. His rifle was not on safe. With the hard pull, the weapon was discharged, and the dead man, which we soon had it confirmed that he was, took a round right through his chest. From some instinct, the other man had triggered off another shot that had hit just an inch or so from the first wound. He was probably dead before he hit the floor.

All agreed that they hadn't been fighting, nor had there been any bad blood between them. It had simply been a stupid, avoidable accident. Two friends messing around, and now one was dead, and the other one was quickly hustled off. We were eventually advised that the other man had been court-martialed and sentenced to six months of hard labor. If there was more to it than that, it never came down to me. There was a great effort to put a lid on the whole affair. As it was, I hadn't known either man, and never even noticed them missing from the company.

Another accident occurred in April. Again, I was in the barracks when I heard a muffled explosion. I knew that sound. It was a white phosphorus grenade going off. I rushed to the door in time to see a large plume of white smoke drifting to the north from another of 1st Platoon's barracks. I ran down to see what had happened.

A man came running out of the barracks, looking like some apparition from one of my nightmares. Somehow, I recognized him as a guy I knew by the name of Rennolet. Or was it?

He was moving quickly, and then he'd slow down. He was screaming, ''Put it out! Put it out!'' and then, ''Don't touch me. Don't touch me.''

Most of his hair was gone, as were his eyelids, nose, ears, and most of his lips. Just a blank face with ghostly eyes peering out. The skin of his arms and chest was hanging from him like some tattered and shredded shirt.

Several of his buddies were trying to run him down to help him. I ran into the building to assist with putting out the fire. There wasn't one, just a lot of smoldering equipment and mattresses. Several of us pulled these outside. In the process, I did make one observation—in the midst of the charred debris, I saw a set of LBE. There was the shell of a white phosphorus grenade lying there. It seemed fairly intact, though peeled in one direction like a banana. I could see the head to it; the pin and spoon were still in place. It had not been detonated by anyone pulling the pin.

I went back outside as soon as we made certain the fire threat was over. I ran into Ed Dvorak running from the opposite end of the barracks. As he came up to me, I could see that a spot on his back was smoking. Knowing that WP will continue to burn as long as it is getting oxygen, I ran to one of the rain barrels to fill a bucket to try to help Ed, but someone else got to him first.

Both Ed and Rennolet were taken away. Ed just happened to be in the barracks when the WP had gone off, and he'd caught a piece from it. Once again, there was an inquiry to determine what had happened. It wasn't pretty.

Ed and Rennolet had just returned from another patrol and had been breaking down their gear to return the ordnance to the ammo bunkers. Rennolet had just picked up his LBE to take off the grenades and WP he had strapped on. The white phosphorus grenade just went off in his face.

Some guy from explosive ordnance and demolition came down to inspect the area and dispose of the rest of Rennolet's grenades and ammo. He explained that the WP's casing apparently had a rusty spot on it. The rust had weakened the casing, and it happened to split while Rennolet was holding it. When oxygen hits white phosphorus, the WP begins to burn at an extremely rapid rate and then starts to expand. It explodes. It hadn't been anything that Rennolet had done wrong or anyone's fault. It had simply been a terrible accident that had cost us a good man.

It took Rennolet three days to die from a combination of the terrible burns he'd received as well as having inhaled the poisonous fumes from the burning phosphorus. Ed returned to us after a while, scarred but sound, physically at least.

For some time, we blamed the medical people who had attended Rennolet, but what could they do? I don't doubt that they did everything they could for him, but he never had a chance. And while I hadn't known him that well, would he have wanted to live with such disfiguring scars? I wouldn't have.

And once again there were repercussions. The army seems to have the attitude that there is no such thing as an accident. Someone had been negligent. Rennolet was beyond their reach and they couldn't seem to lay blame on anyone else. Blame was attached by someone to Staff Sergeant Lavender. This had been his team; "Let's fuck him!" seemed to be the reasoning. As stupid as that was to people with any power of reasoning at all, they were going to burn Bill. The only thing that seemed to save his ass was the fact that Bill came down with a bad case of hepatitis and was shipped out of country, far beyond the reach of Zummo and the tight circle that sucked his ass.

Therefore, they attacked the system. Henceforth, ammo and explosives would not be kept in the barracks at all. Equipment would be prepared for the field and broken down in another area.

Further, until this incident, we had been allowed to keep our rifles in the barracks with us. It hadn't actually been allowed, it just hadn't been pushed. This was, after all, a war zone. We were very close to the berm, with nothing between us and any infiltrators. No one wanted their personal defense left in someone else's hands. So to make matters worse, all of our weapons had to be locked up in the supply room, unless an attack was imminent, or for patrol or training.

Our reactions were different. Until this event, many of us carried from one to three WP grenades. They were heavier than frags, but we reasoned that they not only had a startling psychological and physical effect on Charlie, they were also good signaling devices and great for starting a fire if you wanted that effect during an extraction. After this accident, everyone was scared to death of the damned things. Most of us flat refused to carry them any more, for a while at least. But, as we were told in no uncertain terms, you do not refuse to do anything in this man's army. It took general threats of courts-martial to make us begin carrying them again. A few of us circumvented the order by leaving them in their tin-can shipping containers. These had to be opened like a can of Spam; carried this way they were inaccessible, but we felt safer, for whatever that might have been worth.

CHAPTER 16

Not long after this, the company packed up and moved out to do some recon work for another outfit near a place called Tay Ninh, less than ten miles from the Cambodian border. We stayed there ten days before returning to Bien Hoa. A number of teams made some good contact, but not mine. For some reason, we'd been on alert to go out, but the word never came. Just a lot of sitting around, goofing off, to show for the trip.

Staff Sergeant Jones was now my team leader. That suited me just fine; I didn't want anything to do with Odom; Lewis seldom went to the field any more, which was a good idea—better no leader at all than one who freezes up on you in the middle of a firefight. I had faith in Jones.

The next patrol didn't last much longer than many of the previous ones. We'd barely cleared the LZ when we came under heavy fire. Well, our job was to find Charlie so other units could engage him. Being dropped right in his lap certainly fulfills that part of the mission.

We couldn't see a soul during most of the fight, but it was quite obvious that they could see us. We hit the ground firing while the RTO called for the gunships to begin making their runs. In the meantime, we shot and killed a lot of bushes. It seemed really strange to see the muzzle blast of various weapons coming from a bush; you'd fire directly into the bush, and the shooting would stop, only to begin again from another bush somewhere else. It is quite possible that we hit several VC, but there was no way to tell. Either they'd been hit or they had moved away real fast. We had considered putting out claymores, but that would have meant exposing ourselves. And our frags had already set the bone-dry grass that surrounded us on fire. It was reaching a point where I wasn't sure if we'd be shot or roasted.

Finally the slicks were inbound, and we began a fighting retreat. I remembered running past a particular wall of bamboo and brush and feeling an urge to fire into it. I turned to my left, emptied another magazine into it, and ran on. The ships came in hard and fast, and we lost no time piling on. Soon we were airborne and away. It had only been fairly close.

Back at debriefing, we really didn't have much to report. Yes, there had been plenty of VC present but no one had seen any or had said so to this point. We couldn't even guess if we'd gotten any. Fortunately we'd all gotten out without a scratch.

"Ford got one," Tommy Thomas said from the back of the room. I turned to look at him, my mouth hanging open. He'd been quiet since our return, as if he'd been thinking. "One guy came running out of the woods when we was running for the chopper, like maybe he thought he was gonna jump one of us and take a prisoner. I dunno. Anyway, Ford fired him up through this bush, see. Almost cut him in half." Then he shut up and didn't look at me.

This was accepted as a confirmed kill for me and the team. Everyone was well aware that Tommy and I'd had a falling out, and once again I wasn't sure of the reason for it. He'd all but told me in so many words that he didn't like me and didn't want to discuss the matter. I couldn't help but wonder if his quietness upon our return had been his trying to decide whether he would or would not give credit where it was due. It didn't seem to change how he felt about me, though. We never discussed it any further.

Still, I had killed another man. Since I didn't even see him fall, there was no sense of accomplishment. I may have killed several that day; that was what they were paying me for. Taking a man's life is no small thing. But killing without seeing the man die seemed to make it insignificant. It should have counted for something. The only thing I could be pleased about was the fact that my instincts, or plain dumb luck, had saved me. It seemed like I was developing some instinct for battle. Time would tell.

In mid-March I went on R & R to Bangkok, Thailand. I almost missed it because my platoon sergeant sent me to the wrong location to process. Got out one day late and was, thus, one day late getting back. No big deal. It was getting to the point where I needed less time in the field than I'd have thought possible a few months back. Still, I didn't mind the job so much.

Bangkok was a beautiful city, and there was much to do. I signed up for the temple tour and found myself trying to figure out how to get a five-and-a-half-ton, solid gold statue of the Buddha out of the country. Gold will make you do strange things. Failing that, I enjoyed the tour. I had wanted to take the tour to the actual bridge over the River Kwai, but that would have been an overnight trip, and I had other things on my mind.

As far as I was concerned, the whole purpose for going on R & R was *women*. I was impressed with the services but hadn't brought enough money. Fortunately, there were usually as many as half a dozen guys from the company in town at any given moment during that period. I borrowed money from them until my mother wired more to me. Five nights and five different companions, and as luck would have it, the last one was a real honey. Wish I could have stayed another week. Frazier and I spent a day or so running about together and made one trip with our companions to do some swimming in the Gulf of Thailand. I swam into a school of jellyfish. I hadn't realized how painful that could be. We also spent a day or so visiting the ladies at their quarters and were treated quite well. Wonderful country.

Shortly after returning, I was part of another heavy ambush patrol. This time I was directed to watch over Lieutenant Peter, who would be going out for the first time. The patrol was led by Staff Sergeant Foreman. He told me to make sure the new lieutenant didn't get into trouble.

Being an enlisted man, I didn't usually have much use for officers. It seemed like their whole lot in life was to see how much work they could find for us to do. Lieutenant Peter was a quiet man, but I still didn't like playing shepherd.

This insertion was a quiet one, no unfriendlies to welcome us. Besides that, there was no place to hide. The ground itself and what trees remained were charred from a fire that had recently swept through the area. Craters were everywhere. I was reminded of photos I'd seen of World War I battlefields. There were hundreds of 20mm shell casings, from the Vulcan machine guns many of the air force jets were armed with, scattered around on the ground.

We marched single file through the desolation, doubly observant. Dust and ashes were kicked up around us as we walked along. Having a clear field of view up and down the rolling hills did not lessen our concern for an ambush. Charlie was a master at the art of concealment, including his ability to hide where there was no place to hide. Our target trail was on a ridgeline west of where we had dropped in, just a few hundred meters away. The heat and the dust quickly took its toll, and I was real happy this wasn't going to be another long hump. Once we arrived at our intended site, the hard part was finding a place to set up. What few scrawny bushes remained were not encouraging. There would be no protection from the sun, and I had little faith in our being concealed well enough to fool anyone. I was really hoping we could hit something fast and get out of there.

The lieutenant was obviously and understandably nervous. He was fresh from the States and had not yet seen any combat. It was time to break him in right. To add to that, I would doubt that his training had given him much of an insight into the way we did things. Still, he kept quiet and watched me, taking my directions with good grace, speaking only when he had a question. Surprisingly, most of the questions he asked were direct and to the point. Perhaps he wouldn't be so bad after all. He also seemed to try to copy everything I did. I was becoming more impressed with the man all the time. He was no doubt several years older than I, but he did seem to accept the fact that I had more experience.

The rest of the day passed quickly while we steamed in our sweat-soaked fatigues. I was getting ready to give the lieutenant a few more tips about the field and night conditions and conduct when word was passed, "Heads up, company's coming." Someone was moving down the trail.

The lieutenant and I were in position as rear security, so we would not have a chance to take part in the ambush. Without warning, the machine guns began firing, initiating the contact. The firing didn't last long, simply a double string of shots that ripped the silence of the darkness, and then they were quiet. Everyone was up and moving in seconds, headed for their designated positions to provide security while others checked out the results. I was one of those directed to check out the bodies, if there were any.

However many there might have been, there was only one

man lying on the trail. I moved forward carefully, switching my rifle to full auto and placing the muzzle in the center of his chest. Then I began to pat him down for hidden weapons or documents. I noticed that he'd been hit across the hips from what I could see in the gloom. One round had hit him in each hip. His AK-47 was laying at his side where it had fallen.

"Ford, what the hell do you think you're doing?" Staff Sergeant Foreman angrily hissed.

"I'm checking him for any other weapons," I answered.

"Get away from that man. Can't ya see he's wounded?" Foreman continued.

I stepped back and switched my rifle to safe while others stepped forward to minister to the wounded man. "I wasn't going to hurt him unless he fucked up," I said. I felt that I was being rebuked unnecessarily and wanted him to understand. He ignored me.

I watched the others as they began to pat the man down again, then they checked his wounds and gave him a shot of morphine. Someone tried to rig up the serum albumin, but it was too dark to see to find his vein, and no one seemed to have brought a flashlight. We may have been good at seeing in the dark, but no one was quite that good. Lieutenant Peter was standing beside me like a tall shadow, watching everything, especially the wounded VC. It was likely he'd never seen anyone who'd been shot before. A number of the teams I'd been out with had taken wounded VC before, and although I had seldom had anything to do with them, I had quickly become accustomed to seeing bloody men lying about.

Everyone then went about their duties, preparing for extraction. I retrieved my rucksack and returned to the prisoner. The morphine seemed to have begun taking effect. He acted more relaxed. I squatted beside him, lit a cigarette and stuck it between his lips. Without a doubt, he was scared, and maybe he thought the cigarette was poisoned. He just lay there with his eyes open in stark terror, unable to remove the cigarette but refusing to take a puff. I looked at him for a moment and then took the smoke back, took a drag, and held it out to him again. He nodded his head and then took it again, taking a puff and letting out not only the smoke, but it seemed that a lot of tension went into the air also. After one or two puffs, he pulled one arm under his head as a pillow and then drew both legs up, resting one across the knee of the other. I wouldn't have believed he could do something like that with injuries such as he'd received. He just lay there, puffing away on the cigarette, as if he hadn't a care in the world, a man at his leisure. Maybe he was right. His war was over.

By then, everyone was saddled up, and we began to move down the trail to a clearing not far away that would be our extraction LZ. A couple of the other men had rigged up a litter, using a poncho and some poles they'd found nearby. They carried the prisoner to the clearing, and everyone loaded aboard the choppers when they landed. The extraction went off without a hitch. Just a short piece of after-hours violence, one of the things we were learning to do best.

The debriefing didn't last long, and we set about breaking down our gear. Then one of the other men came up and told me the lieutenant wanted to see me. As had been the case so often in my life, I began trying to figure out what I'd done wrong this time.

I walked over to the BOQ, found his room, and knocked on the door. He told me to come in, and I reported in the proper military manner.

"At ease, Sergeant Ford. Have a seat," he began. No, no obvious signs that he was pissed off at me. Usually whenever I was in trouble, they'd keep me standing. Now what? "I wanted to speak to you about a complaint from Staff Sergeant Foreman. He thinks your conduct toward the prisoner was abusive when you were prodding him with the muzzle of your rifle. What do you have to say about your conduct? Understand, this is an informal interview. There have been no formal charges preferred, so you do not need to be concerned about the Uniform Code of Military Justice. Still, if you wish, I can explain to you your rights under the UCMJ."

Bullshit, I thought, and then said, "Sir, it's simple. Dead men don't hurt you. Unless they're booby-trapped. I had no way of knowing how badly he was hurt or if he was gonna get froggy when I started searching him. He was still alive, and that made him a potential threat. I felt like I was just playing it safe. I wasn't going to hurt him unless he fucked up and tried to grab me or something."

We discussed the matter a little longer, and then he said, "There will be no charges preferred, if that's what is bothering you. I do not disagree with your judgment or your conduct. In fact, I would be inclined to think that you acted in a fairly prudent manner. I would simply suggest that you tone it down a bit. I don't think Staff Sergeant Foreman's complaint was intended as a personal attack, you just need to be more cautious in your approach to prisoners."

"Yes, sir," was my only response. I didn't know what Foreman's problem was. It wasn't like we'd had any problems before nor any real personal dealings with each other at all. The lieutenant wrote it off as professional jealousy. End of subject.

CHAPTER 17

Patrols followed, one after another. Not long after this, we pulled off another night ambush. I had elected to carry the M-60 machine gun this time, just for the sake of the firepower. I also knew quite quickly that I wouldn't want to hump the damned thing too far or for very long.

When the team leader initiated the contact, I opened fire and almost immediately had a jammed weapon. The rest of the action was lost on me, as I was forced to assemble a cleaning rod in the dark to use in knocking the empty casing out of the breech. I always liked the 60, but unfortunately, I saw them jam too many times. The team got a couple of VC that time out, but left them where they fell so their friends could bury them.

A few days later, a team returned from another successful ambush bringing one of the dead VC back with them. There were some bad vibrations running through the company that one or two teams may have been faking contacts and reporting enemy dead that they had not dropped. Now we were directed to bring back the bodies whenever possible so the kill could be confirmed and there would be no doubts. This man had caught it from several directions. I noticed a bullet protruding from his left shoulder just below the collarbone. It was obviously a 7.62mm. One of the men on this patrol had been carrying an M-14 rifle, and another one had carried an AK-47, both being 7.62mm, with differences that most of us were not prepared to argue over. The men couldn't really tell which one of them had killed the guy, so they had a short debate, one offering the credit to the other, and the other in turn offering his partner credit. They reminded me of the cartoon characters Heckle and Jeckle. I guess that's what is known as "civilized warfare."

Another body was brought back one day, and the usual crowd of morbid animals gathered around. One of the lieutenants got a wild hair and asked to borrow one man's Randall knife. We watched as he quickly sawed off the dead VC's ear. Everyone, as far as I could tell, thought this was simply hilarious. And maybe not. I didn't see the Lizard around, but it soon became known to him what one of *his* officers had done. He wanted the man court-martialed. The colonel may have realized that the lieutenant was in fact a good man and respected by his subordinates. The lieutenant got an Article 15 instead, entailing a fine, and then he was put to work doing details around the company area, just like any buck-ass private, and seemed genuinely happy to do it. He just smiled and sang a little song as he swung that swing-blade and chopped down half of the weeds in the company area. He knew it could have been worse.

By this time, I had traded for an old M-3 submachine gun, called a "grease gun." These weapons had already seen service in World War II and Korea. They were still carried by some American units, as well as by the ARVNs but were usually considered too heavy for them. In addition, the M-3 didn't have a lot of range compared to most current weapons at our disposal. It was .45 caliber, and this one had a silencer on it. I figured it might work nicely in an ambush situation; dropping someone without his companions knowing they had come under fire appealed to my sense of humor.

In early April, the company took off again for a place called Cu Chi, roughly about twenty miles west of Bien Hoa. We would be pulling a few patrols for the 25th Infantry Division.

This time our team was to be one of the first ones to go in. I accompanied Staff Sergeant Jones on the premission overflight. The area seemed to be gently rolling ground with a lot of jungle and ground cover. The most prominent terrain feature was the Song Vam Co Dong, which flowed through the area from Cambodia, northwest to southeast.

The insertion the following day was routine, but initiated just a short time before darkness. From the beginning, the plan was to move just a short distance and set up for the night and begin patrolling the following day. We moved into the jungle about fifty meters and set up our listening position. Jones decided we'd just go ahead and spend the night there rather than move on. Everyone put out their claymores, and then we settled in again, just to listen as the night approached.

Something else was approaching also. We began hearing voices off to our right, apparently headed directly toward us. There must have been a trail nearby that we hadn't been aware of. It sounded like at least two Vietnamese men, talking and laughing as if they had the whole jungle to themselves. They were not aware of our presence. Jones whispered, "Get ready. If they see us, blow claymores on my command."

I continued watching to my front in the direction of the LZ. The VC were now somewhat to my rear, still approaching. I found it very difficult not to try looking around to see if I couldn't catch a glimpse of them, but there might also be someone to my front. You have to pay attention to your own area of responsibility. The grease gun was at my side, and the clacker for my claymore was held in my hand, waiting. I slipped down on my rucksack and pulled my arms up over my head. By this time I had blown off so many claymores, and at such close range, I was beginning to get just a little tired of being bounced around.

The voices were getting closer, still apparently unaware of the team. They were no more than twenty feet away when the laughter suddenly stopped. They had seen us.

No one reacted for several moments and then we heard the unmistakable sound of the spoon being released from a grenade. "Blow 'em!" Jones shouted. I squeezed my clacker and was instantly engulfed in flames.

For a second, I may have been unconscious. Accompanying the normal smells that always followed the blast of a claymore, the chemical explosive and burned foliage, I could also smell scorched cloth and flesh. My head was ringing like a church bell was in it. I couldn't move.

Then there were feet. I would have sworn that every son of a bitch on the team ran directly across my chest as they shagged ass for the LZ. I lay there for several more moments trying to clear my head and regain my strength. Finally, I got shakily to my feet and began to stumble ahead. I was fortunate that the LZ was directly in front of me. Otherwise, I'm not sure I would have found it. I continued forward, missing most of the trees but running into more than a few until I finally spotted the rest of the team. Their shapes were indistinguishable in the gloom, but I knew it had to be them. As I stumbled forward to join them, a kid named Waters raised his rifle and pointed it at me. It looked like he was getting ready to shoot when, at the last second, he recognized me. He even looked back at the other men to see if I wasn't in fact already there. He must've thought I was just some strange apparition. Suddenly it became obvious to me. Shit! I hadn't even been missed!

I fell into the perimeter and then pulled myself up to lean against a tree for support. Jones was talking a mile a minute on the radio, but my hearing was still too defective to make out the words. I kept shaking my head, trying to clear the fog. I'd never been so shaken by an explosion before. The flames seemed to have sapped my strength completely.

"Choppers inbound. Open fire." Even if the words weren't clear, the message was, as was the routine. There might be bad guys out there, and we wanted to make certain only six of us got onto the choppers.

I raised the grease gun to fire, pointed it back into the jungle and squeezed the trigger. At least I tried to. Nothing happened. I tried again, but still nothing. My finger didn't want to work.

Without knowing what was wrong or taking the time to investigate, I simply shifted the weapon to my left hand and opened fire. The flame from the muzzle leapt into the darkness. Nothing wrong with that hand, I thought.

The chopper had come in and was hovering just off the ground. Everyone leapt to their feet and ran the short distance, piling on board. We continued firing into the trees as the chopper lifted off.

Once we were clear and away, I began to examine myself and soon found a small hole in my right forearm. It was numb at the edges but didn't seem to be bleeding too badly. Son of a bitch! I've been wounded! I said to myself. I also had to explain to myself that it was something I fully expected to happen eventually. It was just surprising that it hadn't happened before this.

We soon reached the base, off-loaded, and piled into the debriefing shack. Our story was short and sweet. There was a good probability that we'd gotten two or three VC, but that could not be confirmed.

"You sons a bitches left me behind, ya know?" I told Jones and the others. "Where the hell did you put your claymore?" I asked Waters. He'd been sitting right beside me when they blew.

He just looked at me for a moment, his eyes getting bigger and wider by the second. "I put it out just like we always do, about ten feet out and behind a tree so the backblast wouldn't get me. Why?"

"I caught your fucking backblast, you dummy!" I said in not quite a shout. It was fairly easy, after the fact, to figure out what had happened. That's the direction the blast had come from. He had been protected by the tree all right, but a claymore also blasts to the sides, and I'd caught it. "You owe me a beer, you fucker!"

"What was it got ya, Ford? The claymore or their grenade?" Jones asked.

I really didn't know, and it didn't seem to make any difference now. I was given a ride to the dispensary to have my wound treated. The hole was a bit larger than the eraser on a pencil. Not much blood was seeping out. I also had scorch marks on both wrists from the blast. Fortunately I'd had my gloves on and my sleeves rolled down. The medic who treated me had me lie down on my back and put my arm across my chest, while he probed around inside the hole for a few minutes. My, but that thing seemed deep! Finally he gave up. "It'll work its way out eventually," he assured me. Twenty-three years later, and it still hasn't.

I returned to the company area and proceeded to get drunk. Since I had a ten-day, no-field-duty profile, I stayed that way most of the time we remained at Cu Chi.

After our time at Cu Chi, Bien Hoa seemed almost civilized, and everyone was glad to be back home again. I still had a love/hate relationship for the company, but in fact, it was the command that I was having trouble dealing with. The deadline was approaching when I was going to have to make up my mind on what outfit I was going to extend for. Special Forces wouldn't accept me because of my lack of education. Being a door gunner might have been fun until it came time to repair the ship. I had about as much mechanical aptitude as a monkey. One of the reasons I'd gone infantry instead of some other job was because I knew maintaining a rifle would be easier than anything else. As for tanks, when the shit hit the fan, I didn't want anything hindering me when I was ready to exit the AO. I should have looked at it in a more reasonable light; I had earned my Combat Infantry Badge; I had been wounded. I had killed a couple of men. Most men would have accepted that as having fully performed their duty to country. I wasn't satisfied. There had to be something more for me to accomplish.

The decision was finally made. I extended my tour and remained with the company. After my recuperation period, I went out on one more patrol before going on my special leave. Nothing of any significance happened. That now made fifteen patrols or, if you will, insertions. Any time I'd gone into a cold LZ and then made it out in one piece, that was a patrol as far as I was concerned. Frazier and Bass extended a short time later, also.

As I was packing up to leave, Lieutenant Peter and Staff Sergeant Jones approached me. "Sergeant Ford, we wanted to let you know that, despite some rough going at times, we do appreciate your performance and your conduct in the field. And to show our appreciation, when you return from your leave, you will be given your own team."

Oh shit! I thought. I hadn't planned on that. It was one thing for me to risk my life, but to have the lives of other men depending on my decisions? Now I was really scared!

CHAPTER 18

Sgt. Jim McElwee went home on the same plane that took me out for my extension leave. We hadn't become good friends in the past seven months since we had been in different platoons and had never worked together, not since that one night outside Dak Siang. Still, I had heard enough about him from others to be fairly impressed with his performance. Jim was too quiet to toot his own horn.

He was one of the men who had successfully used the grease gun with the silencer. His team had spotted several VC coming toward their position. Jim had taken up a spot where he would be able to engage the first man. Despite the clatter made by the weapon's cycling after the first shot, firing as it did from the open-bolt position, the point man had gone down without his comrades being aware that he'd been shot. Number two had stepped forward to assist him, apparently thinking the first man had merely tripped. Jim shot him also, and then the rest of the team opened fire. A very successful ambush.

Another time, Jim had placed a claymore in a sandbag and then laid it on a well-used trail. Eventually, another Viet Cong had come along and spotted the sandbag. He bent over to pick it up and had reached inside to see what the bag contained. Booty and souvenirs are often the demise of soldiers. As the man withdrew the claymore, he must have realized that he'd just committed a major blunder. He was reported to have looked at the detonator wire and then followed it with his eyes. When he made eye contact with Jim at the other end, his last view of anything was of Jim's silly grin and a hand holding the detonator. Curiosity can kill. When McElwee had fired his claymore, so had Dvorak, and the rest of the team opened fire. Bill Lavender was the team leader, and it was later estimated that they had hit what may have been a company of VC, since the point element, which this body turned out to be, consisted of thirteen men. Bill stood up in the middle of the firefight, after the claymores had been blown, and gave Charlie a taste of southern hospitality with his loud rebel yell. Then everyone laid in to Charlie. Charlie gave back some, too. It was hard to tell, but they felt certain they had accounted for about sixteen to twenty dead VC before the VC point element had swung around and tried to envelope the team. It had been a hard fight, and everyone was amazed that their only casualty had been a superficial wound. One of the men had been hit in the chest by a piece of bone from one of the VC who had been blasted to pieces by one of the team's claymores.

Jim had seen enough actions like this and was going home. It was too bad. He had been a good soldier, if just a little bizarre.

My extension leave was great, despite my unfamiliarity with civilization. Hot showers (I left a black ring in the tub for a week), flushing toilets, food whenever I wanted it, women who were dressed in other than green everywhere you looked. Sleeping as late as I pleased and not having to carry a gun. Well, almost. Some habits become so ingrained they can't easily be shaken. Since I wasn't old enough to purchase a handgun, my mother had to do it for me, and I carried that .38 derringer for the remainder of my leave. It wasn't much, but it did give me a sense of not being totally naked.

I also wasn't old enough to enter a bar, legally, but a friend of mine, Jerry Pearson, seemed to know most of the bartenders in Oklahoma City. Once he'd explained where I had been, and was going back to, they seldom offered any resistance to my entry. It was just understood that I'd better not start any trouble. Not me. I was too reserved.

Jerry even loaned me his car to drive until I bought my own. His was a '66 Ford Mustang, a great little automobile. Jerry was a great friend. He didn't have any desire to go into the service, and due to a heart condition wouldn't have been able to pass the physical, anyway. Then when all of his friends started going off to war, it really bugged him to be left behind. I guess, at least in my case, seeing to it that I had a good time on leave was his way of doing something for me in exchange for what I was doing. Jerry died of a heart attack in 1984 at the age of thirty-six.

I traveled back and forth between Oklahoma and Texas in my "new" car, a '63 Plymouth Valiant, fell in love a dozen times, and generally had a ball. I also managed to blow most of the thirteen hundred dollars I had saved, and now had a car payment to contend with.

It was an odd sensation being home. It no longer felt like my home, that I was no longer a part of that world. My home was now the company. The men I worked with seemed more like family than my own mother and brothers. I started to get homesick.

There was one pleasant surprise for me. We had heard a lot about the war protesters and some of our returning men getting a much less than fair or honorable treatment by the population at large. This burned our asses, and the general feeling was, if these idiots wanted to protest, come on over and join us on the line. Then see how long their pacifist bullshit would last. I did not encounter this attitude at all, in either Oklahoma or Texas. If it was out there, I wasn't aware of it. The people of these two states may have just been, if not supportive, at least understanding of our part. I appreciated that a lot.

One thing was accomplished, however. David, the older of my two brothers, was thinking about enlisting. I felt one of us in Vietnam was enough. Not long before I left, I accompanied him to the army recruiting station. With the arrogance of youth, I even went in full uniform. After having successfully corrected and argued with the recruiter on several of his promises to David, the recruiter, a staff sergeant, got pissed off and pulled rank on me. I was ordered out of his office, but David went with me, so I felt I'd accomplished my mission.

Despite being homesick for the company, I was still having fun. My leave was to be for thirty days, but I fudged, staying an additional fifteen days. It was not an uncommon practice for many of the men in the company. My departure was somewhat bittersweet. Grissel Gonzalez, my young ladylove, and I had gotten back together briefly and thought we might try it again. Her family had immigrated from Cuba after Castro had surprised someone in Washington by proclaiming himself a Communist. She was a little doll. We had decided to go steady when

I had left for Vietnam, writing to each other constantly, but somewhere along the way, I began feeling differently and broke it off, for no good reason that I could explain to her. She had gotten married in the interim, but that had ended quickly in an annulment, so we were once again semiofficially engaged.

Bobby Kennedy was assassinated while I was in Alvin, on the Texas Gulf Coast. That was of course the only thing you saw on television until after the funeral. It didn't matter to me. I had gotten out of the TV habit. I also had no desire to see or hear what was going on in Vietnam. However, my uncle Sy, Sylvester Jones, seemed to be glued to his set every day when the news came on. I did see one report about some company that radio contact had been lost with during the night. When another company was sent out to contact them the next day, they had found the company wiped out. Many of the men had been shot to death where they'd slept, but many more were found with their hands tied behind their backs, shot in the back of the head. Charlie had taken no prisoners. I never did learn which outfit that was. That is the only time I watched the news reports about the war, ever, not even when I finally left for good. I had seen it personally; I didn't need to see it from a reporter's point of view.

Going back also presented the dilemma I had been dreading the whole time. I was anxious to return but dreaded having to take over my own team. I actually considered desertion.

Despite several days spent in transit, I was soon headed back. As the *Flying Tiger*, our ship, began its descent the nervousness of most of the other occupants was almost palpable. The pilot tried to lighten the mood by announcing, "We are now approaching Bien Hoa World Airport. The weather is clear and sunny. Ground fire is light to moderate." This did seem to break the chill just a bit. I had gotten friendly with one of the stewardesses on the way over, and as we disembarked, I even got a kiss. Quite a treat for the bashful kid that I was.

It was one sad, sorry group that stepped onto the tarmac. Many of these men no doubt realized that quite a few of them were not going to be going back home in the same condition they were in that day. As we stood there, another mob was seen approaching; they were going home.

"Short. We're short." "Next! I'm goin' home, ya bunch of pitiful cherries," the other group shouted at us. I looked around at their sad faces and just had to add my own two cents to the bedlam. "Short, cherries!" After all, they had a year to pull, and I only had nine months to go. Besides, I already knew what lay ahead.

I slipped away from the group, dodging customs, and hitched a ride back to the company. First Sergeant Butts welcomed me back. "Where've ya been, Ford? You're late."

"Got held up, Top. I tried to call to let ya know, but none of the operators could get me through." It was only half a lie, but he could have cared less.

"Okay, report back to your platoon." No sweat. I had not asked the question that was uppermost on my mind; how many men had we lost while I was gone?

My welcome by my platoon sergeant was not quite as cordial. "Where the fuck you been, Ford?" a senior NCO shouted at me. "You were fucking AWOL!" The nerve of this asshole, I thought. I remembered that he'd recently gone on his own extension leave and had been gone over two months. A rumor had come back that he'd been killed in an accident while on leave, and they were getting ready to remove his name from the company roster when he finally dragged in. His threats of courtmartial, reduction in rank, KP, emasculation, etc., continued for several more days until he found something else to bitch about. Yeah, welcome home, Ford.

At least there was one pleasant surprise. We'd had a few more men wounded, but no one else had been killed. I was truly amazed. Through normal rotation, there were of course a few new faces, and many of the old faces were no longer there. Every day, it seemed like there were only a few of the old timers left.

There were many new war stories to listen to. One in particular cracked me up, told by another man who had been on the patrol. The "victim" refused to discuss it.

The team had moved into a new AO and set up a listening post. There had been no signs of enemy activity. One night, one of the men was on guard when he felt someone tapping or patting him on the butt. Thinking it was the team leader checking to make certain he was still awake, he just said, "Yeah, I'm awake, Sarge," without turning to look around.

A few minutes later the patting began again, a bit more insistent this time. Still without looking, the man hissed, "I told ya, Sarge, I'm awake."

Finally the man felt his ass being squeezed. Indignantly he had jerked around, saying, "Who's the faggot?" much too loudly for their location. He caught a slight movement of a long arm going back into the branches overhead. He had fallen into the clutches of a lonely orangutan.

Shortly after my return, the company packed up again and moved north to a place called Phuoc Vinh. Of course, that was the name of the nearest village, and the base would usually take the same name, not that we would often have a chance to get into the town.

Our living quarters were almost as nice as Bien Hoa, except that there were no bunks. We slept on our air mattresses on the concrete floor. But as I had learned while on leave, there are bunks, and there are beds. In the field I had become accustomed to sleeping on bare ground, and the bunks in the garrison weren't much softer. I wasn't able to sleep in a bed while home; it hurt my back since it was too soft.

Just a matter of waiting a few days until my team was to go out. One night, I experienced the closest I would ever come to a mortar attack. I was wandering about, looking for a drink. Liquor was either in terribly short supply or safely hidden away. Guess the legs (non-Airborne personnel) had heard of our coming and knew our reputation for putting the stuff away.

Charlie must have been using little 60mm mortars that night, since the flash and explosions were far from being spectacular. The rounds were being walked up and down the dirt runway, causing about as much damage as a child would with a shovel and sand pail. I decided to watch the show and climbed up on a nearby mound of dirt. The attack didn't last very long. When I stood up to leave, I turned slightly to brush off my pants and glanced behind me. I almost shit! The mound I was sitting on was part of the revetment to protect a huge rubber bladder of JP-4 jet fuel. One round in the wrong place, and I'd have been nothing more than a crispy-critter memory!

The next day, I was relaxing in the barracks in the middle of the day. That was one thing about being away from the company area on these little expeditions; there was a lot more time to ghost if you weren't actually involved in patrol activities.

Some guy from another outfit stuck his head in the door and casually advised us, "We'll be blowing up some old ammo and ordnance in a few minutes; just wanted to let ya know.'' We waved a thanks and returned to our pursuits.

About four hours later, the loudest and most horrendous explosion I'd ever heard literally shook the building to its foundations. Rafters and walls creaked and shuddered, and dust descended like a cloud. My immediate thought was that we were under a rocket attack. Everyone was up and moving instantly for the two doors, with the predictable bottleneck happening. Thirty men trying to get through two doors at the same time is a mess.

Once we'd cleared the building, everyone looked about for the expected carnage, but there wasn't any. Everyone else was walking about in the same state of confusion that we were in. There were no bodies or fires, and all of the buildings seemed intact.

After a while, someone noticed and pointed out a huge mushroom-shaped cloud about half a mile to our southwest. We soon learned that this was from the old ammo that had been blown up. Someone needed a new watch. There was no telling how many tons of that stuff they'd blown up.

However, all good things must come to an end. I'd been drawing a sergeant's pay for six months; now it was time to start earning it. Team 4/4, my team, was advised to prepare for the field. We had our warning order.

Having been through the process of getting ready for a patrol several times as an assistant might have lessened the impact somewhat, but I was still operating in a fog. There was the overflight before we went out to get a bird's-eye view of the area where my team would operate, preparation of map overlays with predetermined artillery markers for fire adjustment, drawing of codebooks, maps, and supplies, etc. I didn't want to forget anything, but knew I would. I did have one piece of luck, though. My assistant would be Ron Kaplan. Ron was a couple of years older than I was and had a lot more experience than I did. He would have made a great team leader, but he didn't have the rank and I'm not certain he wanted it. Ron was a good-looking Jewish guy from Dallas. If the age difference or lack of experience on my part mattered to him, he didn't let on. Whatever I forgot, he remembered; whatever I didn't know, he did and told me about it, and seemed generally happy to do so. Perhaps he was just one of those men who never wanted to be in charge.

The only thing of significance about this patrol was that it rained for the entire three days we were out, after having been so nice, dry, and sunny during the days before. And I forgot my insect repellent. I was forced to resort to covering my skin with mud to try to keep the mosquitos off, not a very healthy or practical solution. We saw very little of any real significance, and while it may not have been a very auspicious beginning for the fledgling team leader, it suited me just fine.

Once again, this expedition had lasted for ten days, and we were soon back home in Bien Hoa. (We were fairly certain that we knew that area better, no matter how wrong we might have been. It was, after all, Charlie's land, and he knew it well.)

It seemed as if the turnaround time between patrols was getting shorter all of the time. Lieutenant Colonel Zummo had decided he did not like the previous practice of a patrol being terminated "only" because we'd gotten into a little firefight. From then on, if a patrol was terminated for any reason, whether in the first few hours or on the last day, you would be extracted, resupplied if necessary and sent back out until the mission was completed. This also meant less downtime between patrols. Zummo was not a popular man.

Without it really being discussed by anyone, an attitude attack occurred. "Fuck with us, will you? Well fuck you, too!" The war effort was no longer important, nor was our own survival. Leave the men alone, and they would fight, hunt the enemy out, play the game. Mess with them, and they'd just goof off. Since neither Zummo nor most of the other officers usually went to the field with us, their operational control, once we were on the ground, became a very iffy affair.

On my next patrol, even if I'd wanted to fight, I couldn't have. We'd been dropped into an area in which, after we'd cleared the LZ, we ran straight into a wall of thickets where Brer Rabbit would have been quite at home. It was chock-full of brambles and briars, and the trees seemed to be interlocked as far as we could see into the gloom. And I wasn't about to take my team out into the clearing to try to find another place to start.

This time out, Ralph Fox was my assistant. He had just been promoted to specialist fourth class, and was going home soon. Someone decided he needed a little experience in command before he went home. Certainly, this was logical; lots of call for an assistant LRP team leader back on the block!

Fox was a nice guy, quiet to the point where you might not think he was too bright. Perhaps he just subscribed to the theory that it's better to be silent and be thought a fool than to speak and take away all doubt.

It rained most of that mission. Our main concerns became keeping dry (impossible) and warm (not even close—I was always amazed at how cold it could get in the jungle). At least we didn't have to worry about running out of water.

Finally, it was the last night of the patrol. I had the last watch before morning. To relieve the boredom and give myself something to do, I walked out to the edge of the LZ to scan the clearing with the Metascope, a small, single-lens, infrared, night-vision device. Despite my resolve to take it easy, I would not have missed an opportunity to ruin some unsuspecting Viet Cong soldier's day. But I saw nothing.

I heard some rustling behind me. Looking back into the gloom I saw nothing out of order. Mark Eastman was lying off to one side; Bill Walsh, a new man from Chicago, was lying beside Fox and another kid, all of them covered with their ponchos, trying to keep warm. My eyes had adjusted enough to the darkness that I could see everything almost as clearly as in daylight. "Just an animal," I thought.

At first light, I began heating some water for my breakfast of beef and rice. I noticed Fox slowly raise up and peek out from under his poncho. His eyes were as big as saucers. "We're still here?" he asked.

"What'ya mean?" I asked in return.

"I seen a VC walk into the perimeter last night," he said.

I could feel the hair begin to rise on the back of my neck. "What?" I said very slowly, "what did you do about it?"

"I hid." Obviously, I was the VC he had seen. And he'd hidden under his blanket like I'd done as a child, hiding from the bogeyman. All I could do was shake my head. It could have been worse I guess; he could have just shot me. I was just thankful he was going home, and none too soon.

CHAPTER 19

I'd often theorized that war would be nice if you could go off to battle on Monday morning, fight all week, and then take off on Friday afternoon to spend the weekend at rest or play.

It reached a point where that is almost how things had become. There didn't seem to be that much going on, and who knew one day from the next anyway? In a very short time, we were once again on patrol. There were a few new faces as usual. It was getting harder all the time to keep track of the men.

Once a team received a warning order, there was much to do, all of the gear to draw from supply and pack up, etc. Then there would be the briefing before we went out, the time we learned what our mission was and what was expected of us. We could also ask any questions pertinent to our mission. In one of these sessions, we were informed that the so-and-so Viet Cong Sapper Company was believed to be operating in our area. "What's a sapper?" "Oh, they're just a bunch of VC, kinda like our engineers." Was that all? No sweat. We could handle a bunch of REMFs with one hand tied behind our backs.

Much later, when I did find out what a sapper was, the elite of the elite when it came to sneaking up on the most alert American soldier, I almost shit! Those guys were considered fanatics, slipping into our bases to plot targets for rockets and mortars, slicing the throats of unwary sentries, or worse, as frequently reported, finding several men sleeping in a bunker, the sapper would go in and cut the throats of every other man. Imagine waking up in the morning and finding the men on both sides of you dead! This was psychological warfare at its highest form.

At the very least, the sapper would go in and make off with the American weapons, just to let you know he'd come calling. I'm just glad I never had to meet any of those dudes the hard way.

The area of our next patrol was well to the east of the Bien Hoa-Long Binh complex. Often we would follow Highway 1 out while flying to our AO. Along the way, there was an old quarry site. Months before, I had noticed what looked like a body lying in the clear. On another lower pass, I had been able to confirm that it was, in fact, a dead man, probably a Viet Cong killed during or shortly after Tet. Now, six months later, he still lay there, though much the worse for wear.

It had been raining during the insertion and continued to do so for some time. We moved to the side of a well-used trail, looking for a likely ambush spot. There were quite a few expended ammo casings around with a good mix of 5.56mm, 7.62mm, as well as the Chicom 7.62mm medium. Someone had been doing some heavy fighting around there. Before long, Bill Walsh noticed a sign nailed to a tree, the printing in Vietnamese. We paused and called the TOC, spelling out the words for them to have translated by one of the interpreters. It's a good thing it wasn't in Sanskrit or Chinese. How would I have spelled that back by radio?

In a very short time, word came back; "Don't move another step! The sign says 'Danger. You are in a minefield.' " Another oh-shit day, I could tell. We spent quite a bit of time carefully backing out of there. Blind luck.

Later that day, we caught a young boy about sixteen or so coming from the direction of the highway, headed north. That was VC territory, so it was logical for me to presume that he was in some way allied with them. Bill Trenum was my assistant this time out. He and I bushwhacked the kid by jumping out onto the trail and taking him prisoner without firing a shot. He didn't appear to be armed, but one never knew. We also obviously scared the shit out of him. He had no ID on him, so we contacted headquarters, and they sent a chopper out to pick him up. Later we were told he had simply been an innocent civilian who'd gotten lost. Yeah, and I've got a bridge to sell.

Another couple of nights with little relevant to report, Trenum and George Gentry began trying to persuade me to fake a contact so we could go back in early. This was Gentry's last patrol before he went home, and he just didn't feel like playing any more. He and I had never really gotten along. I saw nothing to be gained by faking anything, so I declined. I thought that was the end of the matter.

Then Trenum and Gentry began seeing things, reporting that they had sighted a couple of men standing in the trees on the other side of a clearing. I didn't buy it, but duly reported what they had seen to the rear. As darkness descended, nothing else seemed to be going on, so I settled down for a little sleep after I had posted the guard.

Not long after I had gotten to sleep, I was awakened by an explosion, with another one in rapid succession. "Sarge, we're under attack!" Gentry whispered. "They threw a couple of grenades at us. Everyone's okay but we gotta get outa here." I didn't believe him for a moment, but . . . ?

"Walsh, get on the horn and get some help. The rest of you, grenades only. No shooting unless you actually see something close enough to take down. Surround this place with frags." It would keep Charlie, if he was out there at all, from pinpointing our exact location, and besides, I didn't feel like cleaning my rifle once we got back in.

While they were scrambling back at the base, I had a ball. By this time, I was carrying at least twenty frags, and I didn't mind playing with them at all.

Our little grenade battlement went on like this for several minutes. I was on my knees, poised to pull the pin on yet another grenade, when I saw Gentry throw one. It may be that he lurched forward at the last second, but in the light of another couple of flashes from the other men's grenades, I could see that Gentry's frag only went out about five feet and landed. I shouted, "Grenade!" and immediately dropped flat, just as it went off.

I hadn't been hit, but Gentry immediately began screaming, "They got me! They got me!" He seemed to go mad and grabbed the M-60 and let loose in a wild arc, barely missing some of the other men.

After he'd ripped off about twenty or thirty rounds, I managed to get the gun away from him and pushed him down. "Be still, you're hurt. Trenum, see what you can do for him." Another new man named Hackley had also been hit by the fragments, but he didn't seem to be hurt too badly.

"Well, that cat's out of the bag," I muttered to myself. "May as well play." I stood up and started pumping out rounds from the machine gun. If Charlie was, in fact, out there, may as well give him a real show. Besides, I didn't have to clean the gun anyway.

Very quickly the chopper arrived and was on its way in. Night extractions are so much fun. We used trip flares to illuminate our position. This gave us plenty of light, but it would also be a beacon to the enemy. However, the extraction went off without a hitch. Hackley and Gentry were dropped off at the dispensary, and the rest of us were flown back to the company for debriefing. Along the way, I figured out I was going to have to clean the 60 after all. It had been Gentry's weapon.

After the debriefing, the rest of the team wandered off to put away their equipment. Lieutenant Peter stopped me as I was leaving. "Sergeant Ford, you seemed troubled about something. Would you like to get it off of your chest?" Jones was there also.

I stood there for a few moments and then began, "Sir, I don't know if Charlie hit us, or maybe some of my guys faked that contact." I went on to explain everything, including Gentry's wound.

The lieutenant was quiet for a while, and then he asked, "All right, Sergeant, it's your call. What do you want to do about it, officially, that is?"

"Sir, Gentry's going home soon. Let him have his Purple Heart and his war stories. It won't help anything to drag this through the mud. Besides, I couldn't prove the contact was faked anyway." I'd already thought it out and decided that this was the only way to handle it. Just a judgment call.

So that's the way we handled it. Gentry went home not long afterwards. About a month later, one of his buddies got a letter from Gentry's family. He had been killed in a car accident while on his DEROS leave.

I had five missions within my first thirty-three days back in country. It got old fast and began to feel like there wasn't any other life going on. On the next patrol, I got a wild hair and went hunting for a contact. This was made easier with the assistance of the L-19 observation plane, call sign: Aloft. These were nothing more than Piper Cubs flown by men from the 74th Recon Airplane Company out of Phu Loi. We also called them "Little Brother," or "Bird Dog." They would often fly around our AO as long as their fuel held out, a really boring job I'm certain, but they were always on hand to relay radio messages or give a lost team leader his location, based on spotting either our signal panels or mirrors. They were damned nice to have around.

Some of the light teams had gotten into the habit of pulling off ambushes themselves rather than leaving all of the fun to the heavy teams. (Okay, so maybe not all of "us" did it, but some did. It may not have been the best idea, looking for trouble with only six, sometimes five men, but it was a lot more fun than strictly recon work. No one stopped us either.) The area I was operating in that time was fairly open, and I won't say I was really comfortable moving around as much as I did, but I wanted some action. If Charlie wouldn't come to me, I'd see if I couldn't find him. No luck whatsoever. The only conflict that came about was from a couple of my subordinates, who became incensed that I moved around so much and, in their humble opinions, took so many chances, and I'd done all of this without consulting with them. Maybe I was getting paid back for all of the lip I'd always given my superiors in the past.

One brief little outing showed me how silly things could really be at times. My team was sent out to relieve a company of Australians who had been patrolling an area up north. From all that I ever heard about the Aussies, they were some damned hard-fighting SOBs. So there we were, all six of us, going in to relieve a force of well over one hundred men, and we were going to "secure" the area until the arrival of an element of Mike Force people, Special Forces advisors leading a band of specially trained Vietnamese, though sometimes they might be Montagnards, or other Orientals from who knew where. That day passed uneventfully; we were not attacked, nor did we even hear a shot fired, but it didn't seem like we held much of anything.

Another of our routines was to pull off stay-behind ambushes. A team would be assigned to spend the day humping with one of the line companies operating in a given area. When the company would move out the following day, the team would remain hidden in the brush, waiting to see if Charlie came scrounging for any goodies left by the wasteful Americans. Sometimes teams would have success, other times they just came back nervous wrecks. I listened to more than one LRP complaining about

Author Gary Ford, F/51 LRP, 12 October 1968.

F Company, 51st Infantry, company street seen from the north. Bien Hoa, 1968.

Our house, Cu Chi, 03 October 1968. Note fifty-gallon barrel mounted as shower above and to the left of door. In the background, without shirt, is John Plunkett. From left to right are Bill Trenum (back to camera), George Christiansen, Gary Ford, Bill Walsh, and Danny Arvo.

A fairly typical load for the field, just a little light in magazines and grenades! Bien Hoa, November 1968.

Before a mission September 1968. (Left to right) top row: Ralph Sutterfield, Jim Berry, Keith "Lurch" Morris, Paul Martin. Middle row: Bill Trenum, John McFoley, Bill Walsh. Bottom row: Gary Ford, Mike Frazier of 2nd Platoon, Charles Drew.

Team 4/4, Cu Chi, 03 October 1968. (From left) Bill Trenum, Bill Walsh, Gary Ford, Danny Arvo, Keith Morris.

Team 4/4 in the field, 12 October 1968, after insertion into the area where the team was hit on 14 October. (From left) Bill Walsh on radio, Danny Arvo, unidentified ARVN, Mark Eastman. Author is behind the camera.

Author making commo check west of Vam Co Dong River, October 1968.

Author and Danny Arvo prior to moving out to check area of oasis, west of Vam Co Dong River, October 1968.

Author and Danny Arvo moving out, October 1968.

Author hefting toady's Long Range Surveillance Unit (LRSU) rucksack
at a demonstration in Ft. Carson, Colorado, July 1990.

Our first get-together, 75th Ranger Regiment Reunion, Colorado Springs, July 1990. (Left to right, back) Charlie Mundo, Mari Eastman, Gary Ford, Bill Walsh, Mark Eastman. (Foreground) Jan Ford, Speedy Gonzalez, Dennis Lovick.

Author Gary Ford with Congressional Medal of Honor winner, retired Master Sergeant Roy Benevitez. June 1991.

The Gathering, Austin, Texas, 14 June 1991. (Left to right, back) Myron Anderson, George Heckman, William Maus, Jack Meli, Gene Slyzuik, ???, Jim Beake behind Roy Benevitez (center, in beret), Al Souza, Pat Duffield behind, Speedy Gonzalez, Dave Fowler, Tom Grzybowski, Bob Edwards behind, George Christiansen, Joe Havrila. (Front row) Bill Mortenson in white hat, Dave Hillard behind Mike Akins, Bill Houser, Gary Ford, John Witherspoon, Al Markut, Don Hall. Jim Fenner was unable to attend but was present in spirit.

Our insignia. The unauthorized Ranger scroll is at top, the authorized Airborne tab at bottom.

how much noise the line doggies made on the move and in their
perimeter after dark. For us, absolute silence was the rule; having spent my time with the Herd, I could only sympathize with
those who'd never spent any time with a line unit. I was fortunate
not to have to pull one of those details.

I was proving my worth and grace in other areas. I was running for the barracks one day in the rain and hit the metal grate
in front of the door at a bad angle. I slipped and went flying into
the bay, doing a couple of back flips and double gainers, and hit
a foot locker. It took about five stitches to close up my chin.

On July 22, I had written to my mother, grousing about the
company and complaining in general. I also made a remark that
I would live to regret. I had not as of then received my first
Purple Heart, figuring the paperwork had gotten lost in the shuf-
fle. I merely said that I guessed I was going to have to go out
and get another one.

It was July 31, just a little after 0400 hours, when we were
hit. The area we were operating in seemed totally devoid of life.
No trails to monitor and no indications that anyone had been in
this area, ever. Don Crowe had joined me this time as my assistant. He asked if he could take out a couple of men for a short
recon around the area. It seemed harmless enough, so I let him
go. They found nothing else either.

Perhaps there was a trail nearby that we missed, or maybe
Charlie was just wandering cross-country. I had no way of
knowing if Crowe's team had been spotted or, as we felt more
likely, the VC had heard Hackley snoring. He had a snore that
would rival a freight train, and it made no difference if he was
on his back, his side, or standing on his head.

I was asleep when the explosion went off and was told that I
came off the ground firing my grease gun. All I knew was coming to and finding myself standing there with an empty weapon
and a pain in my head and back. Hackley was screaming in pain
for all he was worth. He had been lying between me and the
blast and had caught a lot of shrapnel in his leg, and his scalp
was peeled back. Bailey Stauffer had been sitting up on guard
and had caught shrapnel in his ribs. He never heard a thing until
the explosion went off. Bill Walsh had taken some metal in his
leg but didn't seem too badly injured. Crowe and the other man
hadn't been hit.

We called in the contact and then set about bandaging the

wounded. I simply wrapped a bandanna around my head. The choppers soon arrived, and we were extracted. Hackley and Stauffer would be down for a while; Walsh and I returned to the company on light-duty status. I had caught a small piece of shrapnel in my head just under the scalp on the left side and another piece in my back. I'd been sleeping on my right side when the grenade came in, and had my bush hat on. For some time, I had been smarting off about how a LRP's bush hat was better than a helmet—it didn't deflect shrapnel, it absorbed it. Now I'd had the case proven. Once again, I was told that the pieces would eventually work their way out. Later, I was also told that another of our teams, not far away, had heard the explosion and then the unmistakable sound of my grease gun. I'd removed the silencer this time out). A few minutes later, they heard the sounds of two men running like bats out of hell from the direction of our contact, right past their position. Seemingly two VC had spent all night crawling up on us to throw one grenade, and then they had beat feet.

I also decided I had carried that damned grease gun one time too many. This had only been the second time I'd carried it out, and I'd been wounded again. I believe in such a thing as a jinx.

Not long after this contact, Don Crowe approached me and told me that a couple of the men decided I should get the Army Commendation Medal for the way I'd handled myself and the team during this action, especially since I'd been wounded myself.

"If you write it up, Sarge, we'll all sign it." Thanks, but no thanks. I couldn't see that my conduct had been all that commendable, and I just didn't have the time to bother with it. What I didn't take into consideration was the fact that, in a left-handed manner, my team had tried to recognize me for something they thought was important. I had not accepted it with the good grace that I should have. The medal wasn't the issue; the respect was. That issue would arise again before long.

Another matter had to be addressed. Hackley was a real problem child. He'd seemed like a good man when he joined us, ready and willing for a fight. We'd gotten along well, other than his snoring, which, perhaps, he couldn't do anything about. But he had another bad problem, his inability or perhaps unwillingness to stay awake on guard duty. It may have been some form of narcolepsy, but whatever it was, I had watched him too many times. He would be awakened for his guard, sit up, look around, and then lie back down and go to sleep. I did everything I could to take care of the matter myself, and when this failed I took it to Staff Sergeant Jones. He was on my side, but told me others thought I was just prejudiced against Hackley because of his race. Nothing was done about it. Sometimes you must take desperate action if you want to get anywhere.

On a later patrol and after Hackley had been returned to duty, I decided to just watch him. The first night the routine began. I had set the guard and went to sleep. I had already developed a habit of waking up about every hour to make certain everything was kosher. I could hear the unmistakable sound of Hackley's snoring; I looked at my watch and saw that it was the time he was supposed to be on duty. Quietly I got up and walked over to his sleeping form and straddled his body. I held in my hand a small sap or blackjack I had purchased while on leave for who knows what reason. I was in a cold, quiet rage when I reached down and grabbed him by the shirt. I jerked him up off the ground and was getting ready to beat the living hell out of him when, "No! Sarge, don't. I'm on duty. Me and Hackley switched guard. You was asleep, and we didn't see no harm in it." It was Woodson, one of Hackley's "brothers." Maybe they had, or maybe he was covering up for Hackley. I just stood there poised to strike, shaking just a little from my anger. Hackley was wide-awake now, his eyes as big as dinner plates. I tossed the sap down and pulled out my Browning, cocked it, and stuck it in his face. "Motherfucker," I hissed, "you ever go to sleep on me again and I'll blow your fucking head off!" Then I lowered the hammer one-handed, something I'd never been able to do before, returned to my bed and went back to sleep.

Poor Hackley. We had another two nights left on that patrol, and he never slept at all, not even when it was his turn. Every time I looked at him, he was just sitting and staring at me, pensive, possibly afraid. I think he had believed me. Hackley left the company shortly after this. Oddly enough, I had recently requested a transfer out of the company, but that had been denied. Maybe they decided to punish me for my treatment of Hackley by keeping me where they thought I didn't want to be. It had just been a passing thing anyway, in response to my last wound. I didn't want to leave. Too much of me was invested in F/51.

CHAPTER 20

Once again, I had a little downtime due to the new wound. I ended up pulling CQ (charge of quarters, something of a H.M.F.I.I.C. job: head motherfucker indirectly in charge) more than would have been my normal share, but guess someone decided they couldn't have me being a total ghost. The nights I wasn't on duty, I was enjoying my newest passion, Cutty Sark Scotch. Some time back, I had returned from a patrol and wanted a drink badly. All they had was beer and scotch. The beer seemed to have been cycled through a stable, so I settled for the scotch. I was amazed at how quickly I learned to love the taste.

One interesting visual display was observed during this downtime. There was a small village or hamlet several miles north of the Bien Hoa complex that frequently had VC slip in and take up positions where they could fire on passing aircraft from the base. Such things were decidedly unneighborly, so the matter had to be addressed. The solution was often handled by Spooky or Puff the Magic Dragon, a converted C-47 cargo plane armed with several 7.62mm, and at least one 20mm, Gatling guns. They could put out an awesome rain of bullets that literally flattened anything in their path. Many nights I would stand and watch the fireworks display; you couldn't see the plane in the night sky, but you could easily see the steady red stream, originating somewhere in the heavens, directed toward the ground. It was like watching some futuristic laser beam controlled by aliens from another planet. Even from a distance, the noise was impressive. Many times we would fly over this village and see it blasted to ruins, only to return a few days later and find that the locals had pretty well built it back up, only to have the same play repeated a while later when Charlie moved back in. Our guys were certainly rough on the place, but the enemy seemed quite unconcerned about the consequences for them. Who was the more coldhearted?

On August 11, we received word to prepare for another extended expedition to Cu Chi. There were six teams scheduled to go in the first day, and one of them was 4/4. That suited me just fine. I'd decided, if you have to go anyway, it's better to be one of the first ones through the door. Less time spent thinking about it then.

Come the morning of the 12th, everyone was up early, so we could wait. Each platoon would be ferried out one by one until everyone had arrived. Those scheduled to go out first would be inserted just as soon as they arrived.

I was sitting in the barracks playing blackjack with some of the other guys. This game had been going on for most of the last three days. I'd won about thirty-five dollars over that time, and then lost it all in about two hours. I never could lay the cards down without seeing what came up next. A guy I knew casually as Henrickson, from 1st Platoon, walked in and watched us for a while. I had been aware that he was to go home soon and asked him why he was going with us. He said, "Yeah, I was supposed to leave tomorrow but decided to go out one more time. I might miss this place, ya know. Besides, Sergeant Diers is sick." When he said that, I thought his voice had an odd ring to it, but it didn't really sink in. He continued, "The team would only have four guys if I didn't go. It's no big deal."

I had noted before that Henrickson carried a British .45 Webley revolver in a shoulder holster designed for a U.S. .45 auto. "What will you take for your shoulder rig when ya leave?" I asked. I could never make up my mind how I wanted to carry my Browning, wearing it on the right hip one patrol and on the left in reverse draw the next time out. A shoulder rig might work better and would keep my pistol out of the mud and water, maybe.

"You can have it free," he said. "I'm just taking the pistol home with me."

In a fairly short time, we had arrived in Cu Chi, put away the rest of our gear and were ready for our liftoff to begin. On the way out, I was monitoring the radio traffic as the other teams were being inserted, switching frequencies back and forth. I heard Team 1/5, Henrickson's team, report that they'd spotted some bunkers and were going to check them out.

Very quickly, things began to get quite confused. Someone, who didn't know which team he was on, was reporting three of their men were dead and that one was badly wounded. It took a while for "higher" to eliminate all other possibilities to determine that this man was on Henrickson's team. Our men had walked into a meat grinder.

This did not seem real. After so many months of our luck holding tight, it had run out. Teams not already on the ground were advised that their missions were scratched and we'd be flown back to base. Air resources were needed to extricate what was left of Henrickson's team. Bill Houser from TOC was one of the men who had gone in to retrieve the bodies, the wounded, and the gear. The sight he walked into had a very profound effect on him that would last a lifetime. As he said, we were just not used to seeing our own men dead or dying. It really hurt.

Back at base camp, we waited, hoping against hope, but this time the news was all bad. Henrickson and two other guys had walked right into several bunkers that were manned and contained several machine guns. First reports indicated that they might have been captured and mutilated with knives. Later we learned that, in reality, they had just literally been shot to pieces. One other man had been hit pretty badly and ended up being sent back to the States. The only man not hit had been on his first patrol. Other than Henrickson, I hadn't known any of them.

There was a lot of criticism and complaints; why was Henrickson, who was "merely" a Specialist Fourth Class, leading the team? One of the men, Whitfield, had been with the company for several months, but the others were really all fairly new. Henrickson had been with us from the beginning and had quite a bit of experience, but with three, maybe three-and-a-half cherries, the odds had been stacked against them from the get go.

Some of the really bigmouthed SOBs blamed the new man for the whole debacle, saying he didn't do enough, and why hadn't he been killed or wounded? This was blatantly stupid. Experience in combat is achieved over a long period of time. It's not God-given at birth. He did okay.

Few, if any, of us would ever know the truth about what

happened or if there was really blame to be placed. Countless hours of reflection gave me one answer; Henrickson, as were many of us, had been guilty of too many carefully developed bad habits. We were not accustomed to finding enemy bunkers that were actually manned. This was a new AO for all practical purposes. Any one of us might have made the same mistake. It was Team 1/5's misfortune to have to break the new ground.

Everyone was in a pretty somber mood. The bodies were taken away to graves registration. Their equipment had been recovered and dumped in a trailer, left for us to view for a few days. All of it was covered with blood, tissue, and bone, and most of it was beyond further use, having been so shot up. One thing was obvious; someone had put up one hell of a fight. If, as we were told, the three dead men had been killed so quickly that they had never had a chance to fight, and the wounded man had been hit as badly as reported, then the new man had emptied an awful lot of magazines. I picked up one of the blood-spattered mags, intending to clean it up and use it in seeking revenge, but I couldn't bring myself to touch it again. It just lay on the floor beside my bunk, a constant reminder.

Later that night, I cried for the first time since I was twelve years old. It wasn't important that I hadn't known any of the men well; some I hadn't known at all. Still these were our people, fellow Americans. We had almost come to believe that death would not visit us again. We had become too cocksure of our own abilities and experiences, been too lucky for too long. Now the war had become personal once again. Don Crowe tried to comfort me, but nothing seemed to help.

My team was inserted early the next day, not far from where Henrickson and the others had died. I was filled with a desire to get even, but for the first time, once we hit the ground, I ran into a solid wall—my own fears and doubts. I had temporarily lost my nerve.

We found some very skimpy cover about twenty yards or so from the riverbank where we should have set up our position. Instead, I halted the team, and we just sat. All I could do was just stare at the tree line bordering the bank and see images of thousands of Viet Cong waiting for us. If the other men wondered at my inaction, no one said anything. I was, after all, the team leader. I was supposed to know what the hell I was doing.

Finally, an hour or so before dark, I picked up and began moving toward the bank; the rest of the team followed, wordlessly. We discovered an old VC fighting position, actually little more than a firing shelf. This seemed as good a place as any to set up. Shortly after we moved in, we received a radio relay that Team 3/5, Sully O'Sullivan's team, had spotted six VC in a motorized sampan headed north, right toward us.

About the same time, I began hearing slight noises just to the north of us. I couldn't be certain, but it seemed like I could see movement and indications of VC in a bunker about fifteen or twenty meters away. The descending darkness may or may not have been playing with my imagination.

My imagination had nothing to do with the sounds coming from the south. Crowe had taken up a spot at that end of our tiny perimeter and was straining to see down the river. We could all hear the distinct sounds of an outboard motor coming toward us.

I cursed my luck. I was not in a spot where I would be able to see, let alone engage, the sampan, and I desperately wanted them for myself. Six enemy soldiers were not nearly enough as far as I was concerned to begin getting revenge for Team 1/5, but it would be a start. But I would have had to crawl over the rest of the team and probably make too much noise in doing so, and that might alert the spectral enemy to our north. I could reason that they weren't really there; they would have already known of our presence from earlier in the day and been able to act against us. But they may also have just arrived by a hidden trail, and they still didn't know we were there. What to do?

I signalled for Crowe to draw closer so I could whisper, "Don, you get to take out the sampan. Don't miss. When you open fire, I'll start blasting those guys back there," I said and indicated with my thumb to my rear.

Crowe just grinned and then slowly picked up the M-60 and placed it in a position on a small rise in front of him. Walsh and the others really weren't in place to do more than support one or the other of us, and then they'd have to wait until we were either dropped or stand up and shoot over our heads. There was just no room to maneuver.

"Headquarters 4/4. Be advised, have sampan sighted. Will engage when it gets closer. Also believe I have movement; two to three Victor Charlies in a bunker within fifteen meters of my position. Will engage them also when sampan is engaged," I reported.

The sampan continued to draw closer, unseen by me but very distinct. Damn, Crowe, you going to let them land here with us? I wondered. Too much impatience.

Finally, almost catching me by surprise, the machine gun opened fire. I was vaguely aware of Crowe running out a long string of shots as I opened fire to my front. There was too much brush to use grenades. I ran through several magazines as quickly as I could recharge and blast them off.

Then, almost as if we'd rehearsed it, Crowe and I stopped firing almost at the same instant. "Got all six, Sarge. Sank their boat and a RPG they had mounted on the front," Crowe said.

"Yeah, man. They tried to swim in, but he just kept the water boilin' around them," one of the other men said. Guess that makes it confirmed, I thought.

. My own sorry showing was less easily determined. There had been no return fire from my front. I couldn't tell if I'd hit anyone or if they'd gone to ground, or hadn't been there in the first place.

Walsh nudged me and held out the handset for the radio, "It's Six [the company commander] on the line."

"Four/four, this is Six. What do you have?" I told him briefly, again adding my uncertainty about the enemy to my front. "Four/four, this is Six. Be advised, have gunships standing by. They will be making a run in about one mike to suppress your front and rear. Display your strobe lights now."

I could hear the chopper to our west, and when I looked up through the trees could just barely make out the silhouette in the darkening sky. He was coming in broadside of us. I held my strobe high while Crowe did the same at the other end.

Watching the red tracers coming in, I reflected that they seemed kinda close together. When they began to impact in front of me, I knew I'd been right. They were really chewing up the ground less than a foot in front of me. Now that is close support! I wondered to myself.

The gunship made several more close passes and somehow, miraculously, we survived. "Four/four, this is Six. Prepare for extraction. Slicks are inbound."

We hadn't had time to unpack. I grabbed up my empty magazines and shoved them in my cargo pocket and ran. We didn't have far to go. I dropped to my knees and thrust out my hand to support myself, and dropped flat on my face.

"Punji pit!" I screamed in my head. I lay there, waiting for the expected pain to hit me, but all I felt was cold water. Slowly, I pulled myself up. It was just a hole filled with water. As I straightened myself, I saw Walsh looking at me, a big shit-eating grin on his face. "Not one fucking word outta you, mister!" I said through clenched teeth.

He pretended like he didn't hear that. "I just overheard Team three/seven advise Six they just had about six VC run past their position, and they think they're headed for us."

"Seems as good a time to leave as any. Don't want to wear out our welcome," I said. Nope, I'd rather hit them than wait for them to show up when they were prepared for us.

Extraction went off without a hitch, and our debriefing was almost joyous. Killing people may not be just cause for celebration, but when that's what they pay you for, what would you expect? On top of that, we were advised that Team 2/2, Bob DeFer's team, had some very good hunting just after midnight that same day. DeFer was, unfortunately for him, on R & R at the time, and Dave Deshazo was leading the team. They'd spotted a bunch of sampans moving on the river and had engaged them with grenades and small-arms fire. Gunships and artillery were also called in. The fight had seemed almost one-sided, but it resulted in at least forty VC killed, with many more wounded who got away. All of this was confirmed several days later by one of the survivors, who was captured during a sweep of the area by the reaction force. Their docking site had been destroyed along with numerous sampans. None of our men had gotten a scratch, though they had expended just about all of their ammo during the massacre. Bob just about died when he got back and found out what he'd missed out on.

It had been a long time since we'd had any really significant contact. However, if Cu Chi was going to exact its price from us, at least we could get in our own licks.

I learned something else shortly after returning to the rear. Sometime during that day we had gotten in a new group of gunships, and they were flying AH-1 Cobras. This team was called the Playboys, an element of the 334th Aerial Weapons Company, and was one of the first Cobra gunship teams in country. I had thought our covering fire was being delivered by door gunners from the Charlie model gunships, the Mad Dogs, part of the 240th Assault Helicopter Company out of Bear Cat, using their side-mounted M-60s. While perhaps not scientifically precise, those guns could be manipulated to allow the gunner some play when firing. As long as the pilot kept the ship steady, the gunners could deliver their fire just about as close as you could ask for it. That is what I thought was covering us. Instead, I found out that covering fire was coming from fixed machine guns. It just so happened in this case that the Cobra was the same width as our perimeter had been. I almost could have died.

Not long after this, I learned of one incident that demonstrated the skill of the Cobra pilots, this case supposedly witnessed by another ship in the area. One particular Cobra was patrolling around, actually hunting, when they spotted a VC in the open. They immediately went into the attack. This VC was carrying a Chicom Type 56 light machine gun, copied from the Soviet RPD. This weapon had a drum magazine mounted horizontally on top that held one hundred rounds of ammo. Charlie immediately began firing at the Cobra, but it just dodged about like a mosquito, circling the man until he ran out of ammo. They circled one more time, and then went in for a quick kill. Too easy. The pilot may have realized his skills hadn't really been tested, so he flew in low, turned the dead VC's body over with his skid, then picked up the RPD by its sling, hooking it onto the skid to bring back to the company to prove the kill. I saw them bring the weapon in, hanging there. It was a good story, and I wanted to believe it, but sometimes those fly-boys could be bigger liars than LRPs.

CHAPTER 21

The next day we went back out, setting in less than fifty meters from where we'd landed the day before. We didn't find anything to indicate our previous victory. The tide may have washed away the bodies, or their friends had recovered them. Charlie was pretty efficient about cleaning up our mess.

I had gotten my nerve back and was feeling froggy once again. I was also convinced we'd get another sampan, so I had brought along a LAW (light antitank weapon) for that purpose. I extended the tube immediately after we got into our position overlooking the river.

That first night I was on guard duty when I spotted a sampan moving quickly to the north, headed right for our spot. They had come in with hardly a sound, so I'd almost missed them. I brought the LAW up into firing position and was getting ready to squeeze the trigger when something hit me; I lowered the weapon and looked back over my shoulder.

The whole team was lying there asleep, directly behind me. The backblast of the LAW might not have harmed them, going instead over their sleeping bodies, but it certainly would have been a rude awakening. "Shoulda had your rifle, dummy," I reflected. It was too late to act, so I watched helplessly as the sampan slipped by and was gone. Damn it!

I decided then to disarm the LAW and then realized that I couldn't remember how to do it. Shit!

It began to rain the next day and continued for each day that followed. All that I had brought for protection from the rain was half of a VC poncho. I was fairly used to being wet by now, so hadn't considered that as really important. Now I found this thin piece of material was barely large enough for me to be able to protect myself and the LAW from getting wet. I had to sleep with that thing, armed and ready to fire, huddled against my chest for the next few nights. Not the warmest companion I've ever had and I wasn't about to admit to the other men that I'd forgotten how to disarm it. My training with LAWs had been very limited. I had a reputation of sorts to uphold. I was supposed to know what the hell I was doing at all times. Hell of a burden.

We remained in that position for five nights. I had thought that first day's successful ambush would count toward our patrol time, but this was not to be. We were ordered to remain out one night longer than I'd planned on. Guess they really did have their own way of figuring things in the rear. We didn't see or hear anything of significance the entire time, other than that first night.

One night it rained so hard, the drops felt like hail, and the lightning was like an artillery barrage. It was pitch-black, except for the occasional flashes of lightning, so I told everyone to just get some sleep and forget about guard duty. Number one, I figured Charlie was too smart to be moving about in that weather without good reason. And number two, you could not see your hand in front of your face. Five days wasted.

As the team was preparing for extraction, I was still stuck with that LAW and still unwilling to admit I couldn't collapse it without being certain I wouldn't fire it in the process. Therefore, I took the simple approach; I just told the men I wasn't sure if it had gotten wet or not, so rather than take back a potentially defective piece of equipment, I was just going to fire it across the river. Damn, but those things are loud!

We were picked up early on the morning of the 18th and returned to base. Debriefing didn't last long, and we set about putting away our gear. Other teams were continuing to have some successes, but one thing I did pick up on was that there were a lot more VC operating around this AO than we'd expected.

Later that afternoon, I happened to be in the TOC and overheard a report of Jerry Brock's team being in contact. Jerry was a good friend of mine, as well as Frazier's and DeFer's, one in whom I truly felt that the difference in our skin color made absolutely no difference.

Jerry's team had been out for a few days and had been inserted and extracted several times. Their last drop-off found them in an area with a lot of bunkers in the tree line and indications of a lot of VC. The decision was made to extract them once again.

The pickup slick was inbound when it was hit by machine-gun fire. The pilot, copilot, and one gunner had been wounded, but they had managed to fly their ship out.

Gunships immediately began making firing passes at the bunkers as another slick started in to pick up the team. Just as the slick touched down, it, too, came under heavy enemy fire. The team was in the process of boarding when the pilot was killed, hit in the head by two .51 caliber rounds. The copilot was wounded, as was the starboard door gunner and two members of the team. The port door gunner was killed.

Everyone on the TOC was mesmerized as the reports came over the radio. "Those guys are in deep shit!" someone said. I just stared at the radio, almost believing I could see the action.

Apparently the copilot was able to lift the ship out of the LZ. We waited for Jerry to radio in that everyone was on board and accounted for, but the call didn't come.

Then one of the gunship pilots reported spotting a body on the LZ. It had to be Jerry, or he'd have called in. We didn't know if he was dead or alive, but we had to do something.

"Those sons a bitches aren't going to leave one of my men out there. Get a chopper ready," Lieutenant Colonel Zummo shouted. "I want four of our men to go with it. I want that man out of there!" His logic and perception of the situation may have been off, but this was one time I wasn't going to argue with him.

I was out the door in a flash, as was every other swinging dick who'd been within earshot of the TOC. My hootch was in a direct line to the chopper pad, so it was simple for me to run in, grab my rifle, a couple of bandoliers, and my pistol belt, and keep on running for the chopper without having to really break my stride. I was the third man to make it to the ship and pile on.

As the last of the four jumped on, I looked back and saw at least half of the company still running toward us. We'd beaten them by seconds. It had been an odd sort of race. "That's all. No more," the copilot told the rest. The ship was already winding up. Every face in the crowd of those left behind had a singular look of disappointment. That was our man, by God! They all wanted to help. Being denied the chance to go to his rescue, they began tossing us bandoliers and belts of ammo for the two extra machine guns two of the other men had brought.

It seemed like we had turned that ship into a veritable flying fortress. There were four M-60s, six M-16s, and two M-79s had even found their way on board. We had ammo out the ass. But as we all looked at each other, the crew included, we had no illusions. This was a suicide mission, pure and simple. Everyone shook hands all around, and we took off. I felt a new sense of pride in the men of the Greyhounds, the part of the 240th Assault Helicopter Company who flew our slicks. They had always been there when we needed them, and while their job may not have seemed as glorious as that of the gunship pilots, they were indispensable to us, and this day they were giving their all and more.

As we flew out, we were able to monitor some of the radio traffic from other ships still out there. Efforts were still being made to get Jerry out, or at least to protect him. It was costing a lot though. Another pilot had been wounded and another gunner killed. That ship flew away, and another went in. This pilot had not even been involved in this operation but had been flying an "ash and trash," a resupply run, when he'd heard of the action and had volunteered to assist. The pilot was killed and another gunner wounded. What chance did we have? "But we gotta try," I thought.

Our ship had banked and was starting into that field of death when the call came, "Abort! Abort rescue mission! Missing team leader is safe and on board the ship with the rest of his team. Repeat, abort rescue mission." The damaged slick had managed to limp out and away and had landed at a runway near a Special Forces compound not far away. Jerry and all of the team members were accounted for. The body on the LZ was a dead VC; it was surmised that he might have been trying to run out to capture a prisoner, but as the ship had lifted off the ground, it had spun about, and the VC had been hit by the tail rotor. Jerry had been attempting to render first aid to the pilot; he had pulled back the pilot's seat only to discover that the man was beyond help. His head had all but been shot away.

The wounded copilot had asked Jerry to assist him in flying the ship. Jerry may or may not have known any more about flying than I did, but he could certainly take instructions. Their radios had been damaged, and there'd been just too much going on to get the mandatory call out. We'd lost a lot of good people for nothing other than the love for a fellow soldier everyone thought was in trouble. "Greater love hath no man than this, that a man lay down his life for his friends." A fitting tribute if ever there was one.

Our ship was directed to fly to the site where the death ship had landed in order to secure it. The team, the dead, and wounded had already been taken away. Most of the equipment on the chopper had either been removed or was being removed at that point. The ship was a disaster.

Knowing very little about aircraft, I could only wonder how it had made it at all. I noted two large holes in the Plexiglas windshield, one directly in front of the pilot's seat; the other round that hit him had entered to the right of the copilot and had obviously passed directly in front of that man's face to hit the pilot, also. These were estimated to be .51-caliber rounds. There were pieces of bone and brain matter scattered all over the interior of the ship. Almost the entire port side looked like it had been painted with port wine. I didn't try to count all of the bullet holes, including several that had come up through the floor of the ship. I could only be amazed that more of the team hadn't been wounded or killed. There were even holes in the rotor blades.

We secured the ship until almost dark. A large number of civilians from the two adjoining villages passed by, the airstrip also serving as a road. I noticed two young, military-age Vietnamese males passing by on a motor scooter. They were laughing and pointing at the helicopter as they went by. A homicidal mood came over me, but I held myself in check. Granted that we didn't often see the enemy, but I still hoped some day one or both of those bastards would walk into my gunsights.

We had no idea until the last moment whether we'd have to stay with the ship all night or not. There seemed little point. Other than the hull, all items of military value had already been removed. Finally, the SF camp commander invited us to spend the night with them. We were preparing to move our gear into their compound when one of our choppers came to pick us up and return us to the company area.

I felt singularly drained when we got back. All of that death and so many hurt. We had come so close to joining the dead, the other would-be rescuers and myself. To still be alive seemed almost anticlimactic. When would my time come?

The pilot who had voluntarily flown the last rescue ship in and was subsequently killed, WO1 James Doyle Eisenhour, of La Crosse, Kansas, was later recommended for the Medal of Honor. This was later reduced to the Distinguished Service Cross. Why I don't know, but the fact of the matter is, all of those men, officers as well as enlisted personnel, had been heroes as far as I was concerned.

CHAPTER 22

Over the next few weeks, it seemed like every patrol 4/4 went out on drew a dry hole. It's not that Charlie had gone to ground. Many of the teams were making good contact, in some cases almost biting off more than they could chew. One day a team would hit several VC and get one or two, while the rest would run away. The next day they'd hit two and find out that they had brought along a bunch of friends, and the team would have to bug out. This was a very frustrating time for me. I wanted revenge.

Still, the net results were encouraging. We only had ten men wounded in approximately four weeks of operations, and only a couple of those were serious. There were also several snake-bite victims. Don't know what kind they were, but I didn't hear of any of the men dying. In return, we killed over one hundred enemy soldiers, with another twenty-eight probable, and took three prisoners. Our forte became the ambush. Taking prisoners was not easy, and all too often you couldn't recover either the bodies or their weapons. It was very obvious that the local variety of VC were a lot more aggressive than the ones we'd encountered before. Charlie was getting in the habit of reconning by fire, shooting into every bush to try to hit us or get us to respond on his terms. If they weren't sure where you were, they would throw rocks, apparently hoping we'd think it was a grenade and react. He wasn't missing a trick. Still the odds seemed in our favor.

What we were doing was making an impact on people outside of the company, however. In late August, I had to make a trip to the dispensary one day due to "fever of unknown origin," which is medicalese for "We don't know what the fuck he's got." I heard one of the medics refer to me as being one of the men from Delta company. "That's Foxtrot company," I corrected him.

"No, it's Delta. *D* for death. You guys are a walking advertisement for a mortuary. We patch you up and send you back with a no-field profile. Two days later, we get the same man back in, wounded again. It ain't right."

And he was right. It shouldn't have been happening that way, but he may have been exaggerating just a little. We didn't have that many wounded, though I wouldn't doubt that we had a few who were hit lightly and didn't report it for fear that they would miss the next patrol. Since the deaths on Team 1/5, as well as the men who had been killed trying to rescue Jerry, there was a new attitude within the company. A few men had extended who could have gone home. Not many, but enough to make you wonder about their sanity for having done so at a time and place when we were seeing a lot more action than in all the previous months. And it wasn't always on our terms. Many of us still harbored grudges against the colonel, feeling he was sending us into shit we weren't prepared to handle. But still, the men kept at it. They kept seeking out the enemy when that was not always our primary mission. They wanted to close with and kill or destroy the sons of bitches.

As previously stated by our superiors, our job was intended more for reconnaissance purposes than combat. There seemed little danger or glory in going out on a purely recon patrol with only five or six men. That wasn't any fun. Ambushing the enemy did a number of things; it made him realize that the area he thought belonged to him was now suspect. He could no longer be sure what lay in wait down the next trail, or if we were listening to his conversations, preparing to wax his ass when he got ready to move out with artillery, or simply shooting a hole in his head when he least expected it. Recon work provided higher authorities with the ability to send out large bodies of troops to strike him, always trying to engage the enemy in a decisive battle or to pummel him with the lethal rain of destruction that we had at our disposal. Sending a team out to listen would tell them if an area was worth the effort or not. What we heard and saw, or did not hear and see, did have its importance. We didn't have to attack, but we often chose to, regardless of the consequences. The funny thing about all of this is, in retrospect, most of the time I felt like it was totally my decision whether or not I would recon or try to attempt an ambush. Even having been hit a few times when I wasn't expecting it, I still thought of the option as being mine.

Having done it so many times, the fact of our being in such small groups many miles from any friendly units and linked to them by such a fragile piece of equipment as a radio had become routine. It would have been nice, and safer, had we carried two PRC-25s, but they weren't available. The danger was not forgotten but no longer held in awe. We had become accustomed to sitting quietly while the enemy might be passing by in staggering numbers, even stopping within mere feet to take a crap. One night, I was again monitoring the radio when Jerry Brock had called in to report a large number of the enemy passing by his position. His transmission was a bit garbled, and it took a while for everyone to realize that what they were hearing next was Jerry counting the passing enemy while he had his handset keyed. The numbers ran well over three hundred. Nope, sometimes you let them go by, regretfully, but that was too many for the best of us to handle.

We had learned to live in such a way that we became a part of the jungle or forest. After we lay still for so long, the animals would begin to treat us like part of the landscape. I had squirrels run across my body while I watched a trail, and saw the same thing happen to others. It might have helped that we didn't smell like people any more. What would have been a totally impossible situation for many grunts became, for us, home.

Going out on patrol seemed to be just about the only activity there was for us at Cu Chi. We couldn't go to town, and females, for the most part, were not allowed on base. There were a couple of steam bath and massage parlors. The masseuse would often strip to bare nothing, but she still wouldn't let you touch her. At least they wouldn't let me. Which is not to say nothing happened. They were cautious; perhaps they'd been busted too many times already. But what wonderful things they could do with baby oil!

Many things were much more relaxed at Cu Chi than had been the case at Bien Hoa. No morning formations, and once again, we were allowed to keep our weapons in the barracks. You could stand and look out over the countryside for miles. This also meant Charlie could see you and, thus, shoot at you whenever he took the notion. The general attitude seemed to be, though, don't worry about it until it happens.

Having lost so many good pilots and crew members, we needed replacements so we could continue our missions. Most of the time they were good and dependable men, but other times . . .

A team brought in a dead VC so the kill could be positively confirmed. This was the trophy. Everyone gathered around the chopper to take a look. This may not have shown us in our best light, but it did serve a purpose. Exposure to death, particularly a dead enemy soldier helped all of us to lessen our fear of it. Most of the bravado was false.

One of the old timers jumped aboard the chopper and grabbed the body by the hair and the seat of his pants to off-load him. Someone else told him to hold that pose for a minute while he took a photograph. It soon turned into a macabre sideshow. Our man turned out to be quite a ham. In genteel company this would have gone over like a lead balloon, but we were in a war zone, after all.

Soon the sideshow was over, and the body was carted off. Then the platoon leaders were called to the CO's office. When Lieutenant Peter returned to our barracks, he was one serious dude. "A couple of the new pilots were offended by the abuse of the dead Viet Cong soldier. They have filed a formal protest and are requesting a board of review over desecration of the dead."

We were stunned. What kind of chickenshit pilots were these guys anyway? The corpse hadn't been mutilated or otherwise mistreated, he'd been simply put on display. What was the deal?

"Colonel Zummo," the lieutenant continued, "feels the only

way to quash this thing is to confiscate all film used to take those photographs. You will now surrender to me everything that you have. Believe me, the colonel doesn't want any of our people burned, but he has also stated that if anyone holds back any film and is found out, he will personally burn that man himself.''

Well I'll be damned! I thought. First time old Zummo had stood up for us as far as I knew. I didn't have any film or a camera, but others did and handed over the evidence with a great deal of reluctance.

That was pretty much the end of the matter. All evidence was destroyed, and not many people would care to rebut the testimony of about a hundred LRPs. None of us had seen a thing! This also did not endear us to these new pilots, but fortunately they were transferred out soon after the nonincident, probably for their own good.

September 11, time to go back out. Since our arrival in Cu Chi, most of our operations had been either on or damned close to the Oriental River. This time my team would be going north into the Hobo Woods. I'd heard about that place and a lot of hard fighting that had gone on there in the past. It turned out that I didn't get to see very much of it. There weren't enough trees around to really call it "woods," in my opinion. There was a lot of rolling ground with a few hedgerows and stands of trees. Most of the area I observed, you could see in all directions for miles.

It began to rain shortly after we were inserted, so we moved up a slight incline and into the dubious shelter of one of the hedgerows to wait out the storm. We had a good trail, and while this wasn't planned to be an ambush patrol, that is what I intended to do. I had no desire to recon in the open. That was a job I was quite willing to leave to the line troops.

Everyone was packed fairly close together, and a couple of the men were napping. I was sitting on the trail itself, with my poncho pulled up over my shoulders, simply resting and waiting. Then I had a very strange sensation come over me, as if I was being watched.

I slowly looked up and found myself staring into the face of a young Viet Cong soldier. He was no more than twenty feet away. I hadn't heard a sound as he'd approached, and it seemed that he hadn't been aware of our presence either. He and I were in direct eye contact, and it would have been hard to tell which one of us was the most surprised.

He was anywhere from twenty to twenty-five years old, clean shaven, wearing khaki pants and shirt, with a black-and-white checkered scarf wrapped around his neck. He was also holding a very impressive looking AK-47 diagonally across his chest. His right hand was on the pistol grip; his finger was on the trigger.

I had been had! My rifle was laying at my side, and my pistol was in its full-flap holster on my left hip in reverse draw. I would never have time to reach either one before he would be able to sweep his weapon down. I was dead, and worse, by my fuck-up, I had just gotten my team killed.

Neither of us moved. Our eyes remained locked together. Okay, go ahead and shoot. What are you waiting for? I said to myself. One thing I did know with a full certainty; I was not about to raise my hands and surrender.

After what seemed like a lifetime, and probably was, I decided I'd had enough of this Mexican standoff. One of us had to do something. I grabbed for my rifle, fully expecting to hear his weapon begin to hammer away and to feel the impact of his bullets thumping into my body. Okay, let's get it over.

As I swung my rifle up, I saw the most incredible sight. The son of a bitch had turned around and was running away as fast as his legs could carry him! In fact he'd run right out of his Ho Chi Minh sandals. They were lying there in the mud, with a spacing of his stride.

I yelled at the other men and jumped up. As he ran, I sighted down the middle of his back and slowly began to squeeze the trigger. The rifle bucked, and I saw dirt flying up, but it was about three feet to the right of the running man.

I knew instantly what had happened. We'd recently received some "silencers," or sonic sound suppressors. They were fairly easily fitted over the muzzle of our rifles, after the original flash suppressor had been removed. You then had to rezero your rifle since this added an additional six to eight inches to the barrel. I had not been allowed to rezero because the company no longer had a firing range. It hadn't been "authorized" for a company such as ours.

While the thought was instantaneous, Charlie had been moving right along, my stray shots no doubt giving him an additional burst of speed. I brought my rifle back up to try again, using a little Tennessee windage, but by then he had covered about seventy-five to eighty meters of ground and had dodged behind another tree line. I dropped my rifle and grabbed the M-79, throwing a few shots in the general direction, but finally gave it up as a lost cause.

When I turned back to the team, they were already scrambling. Walsh was once again on the radio, "Four/four contact! four/four contact!" We'd hardly had time or cause to unpack, so we were already prepared for extraction. I then took the radio and reported what had happened.

However, Colonel Zummo had other ideas. "Do you have a prisoner or a body, four/four?"

"Negative, he got away."

"Wait one, four/four." I knew what was coming and didn't like it one bit.

Someone else came on the radio, "Six advises, move out seventy-five meters, set up and see what develops." I tried to argue the point; we were compromised. Charlie knew we were in the area. Besides, there was hardly any cover around there to speak of. Logic did not prevail. We stayed.

The clouds had gone from a threatening gray to broken and scattered as the rain slowed, and the sun made its appearance. We loaded up and began to move out, but not too far. Nearby was a large crater, probably from an artillery round. Some tall trees that looked like some type of evergreen were standing at the edges and all but surrounded the crater. The hole was about five or six feet deep, with several inches of green ooze at the bottom. I decided that might be a fairly good location, good being an extremely relative term. Under our current circumstances, it still sucked.

We set up in what cover there was, the idea being that we could use the crater for shelter if, no, when the shooting started. There was no doubt in my nonmilitary mind that Charlie was going to come back. Then it was just a matter of sitting and waiting.

An hour passed, then two. I was lying on my rucksack when I heard voices and then detected movement off to my left. There were two VC standing out there, about twenty meters away, and one of them was the man who'd walked up on me. He was pointing in the direction of our first encounter. Due to our being flat to the ground, with there being a dip off to the right, these men had been able to approach without being detected.

The second VC was also armed with an AK and was wearing khaki pants and a dark blue shirt.

Slowly sitting up, I again reached for my rifle. This would be an easy shot, even with the faulty silencer. A long sweeping burst, and I'd have both of them. They had no idea they were being watched.

Just as I raised my rifle there were shots to my right. Trenum had fired first. I wasn't so startled so much as pissed. I felt like his shots might have been too hurried.

The VC had gone down. I couldn't tell if they'd been hit or not, or had just taken cover. Bill was on the radio again, reporting another contact. I threw out a couple of grenades just to make sure no one was playing possum. By now I had developed the technique of pulling the pin on my grenade, releasing the spoon, and counting to at least three before throwing it out. This was of course done only when Charlie was believed to be close, to prevent him from throwing my grenade back at me. I had long since made up my mind that American technology was second to none and a four-and-a-half-second delay meant exactly that. And hopefully, if I was ever wrong, I wouldn't be around to know the difference. The explosions came one and a half seconds later, right on schedule.

I stood and assumed a crouch and began moving forward slowly, signaling for Trenum to follow me. We split up and moved out so we would be approaching from different angles.

There was only one of them. Trenum's shots had been too hurried after all. The first VC had gotten away again. I would have bet he was praising Buddha, or Uncle Ho, or whoever he worshipped that day! There wasn't even a blood trail or any other indication that he'd been wounded.

The one who'd been left behind was lying on his back, a few feet away from the edge of another large crater. His AK-47 lay just a little to his right where it had fallen.

I directed Trenum to continue his sweep around the crater, to make certain the other one wasn't hiding and waiting for a shot at us. Then I moved forward and secured the AK.

"Six says slick is inbound. Asks if we have a prisoner?" Bill said.

"No, he's dead."

"Also advise Six, we have recovered a weapon and documents. That should make him happy." The man had been wearing a long blue sash tied diagonally across his chest from his left shoulder. I had taken it. Before I put my pistol belt on, I wrapped it around my waist. Perhaps a memento from his family or just a personal affectation? Now it was mine. I figured it had to be luckier for me than it had been for him.

We prepared for the extraction. The clouds had returned, and it began to rain again. We swept the area one more time, and then the slick came in, and we loaded on board. I watched the body as we flew off until the waves of rain and the distance blotted it out. I felt nothing.

CHAPTER 23

The next day Colonel Zummo decided to send the reaction platoon back into that area to sweep for whatever they might find. I was ordered to go with them. In other words I got to hump with the grunts for a day. Maybe he was punishing me, reminding me of what could happen if he chose to dump me from the company. The team remained behind.

I should have left my rucksack behind for this operation. As it was, we actually carried a lot more gear than most line troops. I had, by then, readjusted my LBE again; I was wearing three ammo pouches and three canteen pouches, but one canteen pouch was full of magazines, and the other two were empty, hanging at my back in case we ever had to E & E. There were also seven to eight grenades on my belt at any given time. I didn't normally carry a canteen on my belt any more, but I did carry about twice as much ammo on my person as most grunts, that being twenty mags on my belt, and I almost always wore one seven-mag bandolier across my chest. But one never knew when a day's march might turn into something else. Besides, there was still the matter that I was so used to carrying my rucksack, I felt naked without it. Helped me keep my balance.

We found the dead man where I'd left him. No one cared to approach him in case his buddies had booby-trapped him. We also found another dead VC. I had no idea who had gotten him. He was fairly fresh, but . . . Other than those observations, we just had a long day of walking.

Upon returning to base that evening, I was advised that my team would be going back out the next day. May as well, I reasoned. Garrison sucks.

While I was readjusting my gear that evening, Bill Walsh walked over and sat down on my bunk. I liked Bill. He seemed like a streetwise kid, prone to be a smart ass at times, but very good-natured, and he never bucked me. He wasn't a pain in the ass like a lot of draftees who didn't want to be there. Despite the rank difference, I felt like we were friends.

"That guy yesterday had a letter on him," Bill began. "We were there when Nghia [one of the interpreters] translated it. It was from the guy's wife. She told him how happy she was that his time in the South was almost over and he would be coming home." He didn't say it accusingly, he'd just made a statement. We had killed a short-timer. I felt a slight chill, but it passed. Life was a bitch, wasn't it? Nothing more was said about it. It did seem odd, though. As far as anyone knew, those who'd come down from the North were there for the duration. Perhaps that guy had been some high-ranking politico's son or nephew. Guess that power hadn't done him any good after all.

But I did think about it a lot more, after all.

The rains had stopped when we inserted the next day. I didn't like this area from the get-go. It was even worse than the last one. There was even less cover and concealment than before and absolutely no place to move without being under observation from any lurking VC from miles away. I also had a very bad feeling about this place almost immediately.

I tried to convey my apprehension to Three Fox, Lieutenant Snyder. I wasn't trying to get out of a patrol, I just didn't like this spot. I was told to get on with my mission and let them worry about the rest. Fine! I thought, They'll worry about it from the safety of a sandbagged bunker at base camp!

We moved into a spot with cover, little more than would be found on a parking lot. I watched and listened and thought about it for a long time. I could do it their way, and there was always the chance that I was wrong. Yes, we all took our chances every time we went on patrol. But you do not discount gut instinct. At least I wasn't going to.

The decision was made. I gathered the team around me even more tightly than usual and told them what I intended to do. "We're going to fake a contact." Trenum looked at me with a big shit-eating grin on his face. He probably remembered when I had been so adamant in refusing to fake a contact a few months back. Fuck you. This is different, I thought, but said, "Just about dusk we'll begin reporting movement, indicating we're surrounded. Then we'll report rocks are being thrown at us. Finally, while I'm on the radio, one of you will throw out a grenade just over that hump," pointing to my right. "Everyone will get real close to the ground. The explosion will be heard at their end. It should be close enough so they don't question it."

"Snyder will," Walsh said. While he hadn't been with us very long, he'd already figured out the ways things flew.

"We'll handle that when we have to." I was hoping this would work out the way I planned. It was risky in many ways; it could get me a court-martial, and it certainly left me at the mercy of my subordinates if they ever tried to hold it over my head. I was really beginning to wonder what it felt like to be brought up on charges, and then to find myself in LBJ? Oh well, better jail than dead. I knew I was right.

There was no need to push it too fast. We began with reports of sounds near our location just before dark, and then progressed from there through the evening. We reported movement here and there, until those listening in the rear couldn't help but realize we were being surrounded; then we'd spotted three VC at such and such. As darkness came on, we had something thrown close to the perimeter, but there was no explosion. Must have been a rock. This went on for several more minutes. Then there was another rock.

I was on the radio with Three Fox the whole time. He wasn't buying it. The sarcasm dripped from each word as he responded to my reports. Fucking asshole, I thought. You know what it's

like to be out here. You've been here before. Have you forgotten
so quickly?

About five minutes later, I was on the horn again, just reporting another rock, but I was flat on my belly when the explosion came. Damn! They really do want it to sound good. I looked
at Trenum. He had that same shit-eating grin on his face. He
was having a good time. That one had only been about six feet
away, with nothing between us and the grenade but a ten-inch
mound of dirt. I could have slapped him.

"Four/four contact! Four/four contact!" I shouted into the
handset. Now, shithead, I thought, think what you will, but you
don't dare ignore that, will you? I wasn't so sure.

There was a noticeable pause, then Snyder came back on the
radio. "Slicks have already been scrambled, four/four, and are
en route. Prepare for extraction. Be ready to give gunships co-
ordinates so they can give cover fire." He sounded distracted.
Maybe he was already drawing up my court-martial papers?

The choppers arrived in short order, and the gunships fired
up the scenery, based on my directions. Then the slicks were
headed in. We were crouched below a low dike, waiting. Aerial
flares had been thrown from an accompanying slick to illuminate the LZ. I was nervous. Even if I had faked this contact, I
was still positive Charlie was out there somewhere, and very
close. We sure did make good targets sitting there in the light.

The slick swept in, and I climbed aboard on the starboard
side, being the last man to board. We were probably no more
than fifty feet off the ground when green tracers came out of the
darkness from a number of different directions, headed right at
the ship. I'd been right; Charlie had been close, and he'd brought
along a lot of friends. That was the first time I could remember
smiling while I was being shot at.

At the debriefing, I could see that Lieutenant Snyder was
prepared to light into me. "Sergeant Ford, you lied. There were
no VC out there. You faked that contact."

One of my men must have told the chopper crew that something like this would happen. They did not normally attend our
debriefings. I hadn't even noticed them come in. One pilot
stepped forward. "Lieutenant," he said, "I don't know what
happened out there on the ground, or what you think your sergeant did. But I'll tell you this, there were VC out there, a lot

of them. And they were shooting at us. I saw it. My men saw it. We may even have bullet holes in my ship.''

Snyder didn't say another word. Not one. He glared at me for a moment, and then stormed out of the room. We made a point of not telling this story too widely, bet on that. I had no idea what the statute of limitations would be on such an offense, but there was no doubt in my mind that Snyder would be waiting to pounce on my ass if he ever got wind of what we'd done. I didn't care. We'd gotten out alive and in one piece. Once again, I'd been vindicated. I was later told that Snyder was, in fact, a good man, very sharp, that he was hamstrung by Zummo in most of his decisions. That is possible, but I still felt like the man had a personal grudge against me. Even paranoid people have enemies.

Trenum was pissed. During the extraction he'd lost his bowie knife. He had the AK as a trophy, but, of course, wouldn't be able to take that home. His knife had been a tangible trophy. Now Charlie no doubt had it. Shit happens.

Of course, we had to go back out again the next day. If this continued, all day out then back in, only to be sent out again the following day, with the colonel's attitude on such things, I began to think I'd spend the rest of my tour on patrol.

The hedgerows in this new area were thicker and wider. I hadn't noticed any trails that looked promising during the insertion. But I was learning very slowly not to worry about trouble. I didn't have to look for it; it would find me in its own time. All I had to do was just sit and wait for it.

On the first night, I was on guard after midnight and was getting bored and sleepy. I began running over various things in my head to keep myself awake and then started trying to remember all of the signs of the Zodiac. Not being able to remember them all, I called up one of the guys on one of the radio-relay stations and asked him. He couldn't remember either, so another man in the bush, also quite bored, chimed in with his opinion. This was a hell of a conversation. Radio relay could speak in a normal tone of voice, while we in the field had to whisper, with the sound being no more perceptible than the beating of a hummingbird's wings. The man sitting beside us usually couldn't hear what we were saying. No wonder the first thing we would do upon extraction would be to yell, just to loosen up taut vocal cords. We never did remember all of the signs.

The next night, I was again monitoring the radio when I heard Mike Fuson report trouble. Mike had recently joined the company, having also been with me in Alaska. He had gone to the 173d and had been seriously wounded at Hill 875. To add insult to injury, he'd been wounded again when one of our own jets had mistakenly bombed the field hospital Mike was being treated in. He'd been lucky, though. A lot of the other men in that tent had been killed. He had volunteered to return to Vietnam after he'd recovered.

Mike was reporting heavy movement on all sides. "They're throwing rocks at us, trying to find our position." Was he really in trouble, or was he pulling my stunt, I wondered?

Then, "one/five to Three Fox, they are getting too close. Am preparing to blow claymores." Obviously Mike felt things were getting out of hand, and I could appreciate his concern.

Something didn't seem right. This probing had gone on too long, and Charlie was acting more weird than usual. I got a mental tic. I clicked my handset and said, "Four/four to one/ five. Do not blow claymores. Repeat. Do not blow claymores. Use grenades." Mike and I were not the best of friends, but maybe something in the tone of my voice struck a chord. "Roger," was his only response.

His team wasn't terribly far away from mine. I couldn't see the flashes, but the explosions were clearly audible off to the northwest. They had a regular grenade battle going on throughout most of the night. After a while, it stopped. Mike reported that all was quiet, and since he was due to go in the next day, he would sit it out. And I'd have to wait until I got back in to find out the results.

The next day we had a VC stumble onto our position, but he got away before we could react. Later we started getting a whiff of tear gas. We didn't have our masks with us, but fortunately the wind was strong enough, it didn't get too uncomfortable.

Later that afternoon, I had to stand up to stretch my legs and did so at the edge of the bushes. Suddenly a sniper opened fire on me. I straightened up a little more to get a better look. The rounds were coming from a small grove of trees, down a slope to the south. I wasn't unduly alarmed; this guy was a really bad shot. The rounds were hardly coming close enough to be considered hostile.

His position had two large trees and a lot of brush surrounding them. I couldn't see him or his muzzle flash, but it was certain he was there.

I stepped back into the bushes and picked up the radio. "Four/four to Three Fox. Have sniper fire being directed at my position. Request artillery mission." Wanna play, asshole? I said to myself. Okay, let's play big time.

A 105mm battery was contacted, and clearance was quickly given for the mission. Must be a slow day, I thought. I'd had a theory that we'd call for artillery, they would have to get clearance from the ARVNs, the ARVNs would call Charlie up and make sure he wouldn't be endangered, and then we would get the mission. Unless of course, for reasons that were never explained to my satisfaction, the ARVNs just refused to give clearance, period. This happened all too frequently and made no sense. We were told repeatedly that the areas we operated in were completely free of any friendlies other than our own teams. What else was I supposed to think but that our "allies" were in collusion with the enemy?

The radio began to squawk, "Shocker to four/four. Range and distance." Now I was speaking directly to the artillery liaison attached to the company.

"Four/four to Shocker. In some trees, bearing 210 degrees azimuth, approximately 300 meters. Request two rounds, HE [High explosives.]" Within moments, the rounds arrived, blowing a lot of dirt and bushes into the sky. That had been a good shot, probably no more than fifty meters to the left. I unintentionally overcorrected, and the next two rounds were about fifty meters to the right. Unintentional or not, I'd done a good job of bracketing the bastard.

"Correct fifty meters left and give me eight rounds of HE and fire for effect." It might have been a case of overkill, but I was having fun. It wasn't often I had the opportunity to see my artillery rounds strike the target.

The rounds were soon on their way, and I had a perfect front-row seat. Almost too perfect. The sniper's rounds hadn't worried me much, but within moments I heard large pieces of shrapnel shredding the bushes to my right. I decided this show would be better watched from a prone position.

It really was a spectacular view. A beautiful sunny day, hardly a cloud in the sky, a nice gentle breeze blowing softly through the leaves. The brown grassy field sloped down to the sniper's location, which was hidden behind the dark green brush. The artillery rounds arrived unseen, announcing themselves with a flash of fire and thunder, followed by a geyser of dirt and debris. Other than the fact that I was trying to kill someone, it really was glorious, but he'd started it.

In short order, the trees and bushes had been thoroughly shredded, and the fire mission was over. If the man had been real fast and alert, he might have gotten away. I did not feel inclined to walk that distance in the open to check it out, so wouldn't be able to confirm a kill. But he didn't start shooting at us any more. That was good enough.

The next day, we were pulled out for a little time in the rear. I didn't figure it would last very long. Fuson was waiting at the chopper pad when we landed.

"Ford, how'd ya know?" he asked. "We had our claymores out, no more than ten feet from our position, like always. When we went out the next morning to get 'em and look for bodies, we found they had stolen three claymores, just cut the wires, and turned the other three around on us. We'd have blown our own asses away if we'd fired 'em. How'd ya know?" I couldn't answer him logically; it had just been a feeling, and I told him so.

"Get any of them?" I asked.

"Just a lot of blood, but no bodies." Well, it was better than our guys getting hit. I was learning to pay attention to that little tic.

CHAPTER 24

During one of these downtimes, we met several men from Company F, 50th Infantry LRPs, who worked for the 25th Infantry Division. We exchanged stories and tidbits of information on ways we had each operated. I don't know what they got from us, information wise, but we learned a few things from them. At least one point was that they had cut the barrels and stocks off of some of their M-79s and carried them in canteen pouches. Few grunts ever used the sights on the 79 anyway, so this seemed like a good way to lighten the load. Not that we'd be allowed to get away with it.

One thing they did get from us were our "toe-poppers," the little M-14 antipersonnel mines. They were quite small, and the blast radius was one foot, literally and figuratively. For our part, we usually wanted to get more bang for the package. Several teams had deployed these, but they had also planted them on top of two to four pounds of TNT. Field adaptation.

A couple of their men later told us about a real fuck-up on the part of one of their team leaders. It seemed that he'd decided the toe-poppers were a great way to let his team get some sleep and not have to pull guard duty. They had planted the mines around their position before dark. The next morning, when they went out to retrieve them, they found them the hard way. Ended up wiping out the whole team. At least with injuries. It seemed ludicrous, but stranger things have happened.

As an indication of the diversity of personnel who came and went in the company, F Troop had developed quite a reputation within certain circles of the military establishment in Vietnam. Officers from other units were always stopping by to question

us about our tactics; their men would occasionally come to run
a patrol with us and to watch our men in action. At other times,
whole groups would come in to either work with or learn from
us. For a short time, we had a number of representatives from
the Thai Queen's Cobras, considered a very badassed bunch of
people. Another time, they sent us a squad or so of Navy UDT
(Underwater Demolition Team, later absorbed into the SEALs).
They were supposed to assist us in setting up a really elaborate
river ambush, using explosives strung across the Song Vam Co
Dong. I never heard how that one came off, or if it did.

I was right about our not being in too long. It seemed like
we'd hardly had time to break down our gear when we received
another warning order. Guess it really didn't matter though. Cu
Chi base had so little to offer in the way of the proper entertainment. Besides, it was just easier in the field.

Lieutenant Peter decided to go out with us this time. This
suited me fine. He had a good reputation with the platoon by
now. For one thing, he went out more often than some of the
other officers, and for another, he didn't fuck with the team
leader. He let the man who knew the men do his job. He generally went along just as an observer.

Someone certainly had a knack for picking out the really ideal
spots. This time we were dropped off on what amounted to little
more than a wider-than-usual dike that separated the river from
a swamp. The dike was perhaps ten meters wide. There wasn't
enough brush along the river's edge to hide us, so we had to take
shelter in the swamp. The only reason for our being there in the
first place was because of a well-used trail that ran down the
dike. This time we had permission to try an ambush, not that
most of us would have ever let authorization or lack thereof stop
us from taking a shot at Charlie.

However, it rained, and it rained. It didn't stop or even seem
to let up for three days. And for those three days, I knelt on the
slope that fell from the top of the dike into the swamp, with my
feet "almost" out of the water. There was only about four feet
of bank for us to set up on, so there was no real room to stretch
out without getting even more wet. For the most part, I found
myself kneeling on the slope of the dike, as my primary mission
soon became just trying to keep my rifle and pistol dry, and as
much of my body as possible. That amounted to a small spot

on my chest and little more. Spend sixteen to twenty hours a day in a kneeling position, and see if you ever fully recover!

I did try to ready myself for an ambush, crawling out of the swamp after dark and sitting closer still to the trail, hoping someone would come along. I had decided to carry out a Remington Model 870 shotgun this time, thinking it would work great in an ambush. They were too slow to reload and too limited in their range for my taste, so I still had my rifle for more serious social encounters. Hours spent waiting beside that damned trail, and Charlie didn't have the decency to come calling even once.

Late on the third day, they pulled us out without our having to ask. They may have decided that that trail was a bust. We were given one day to dry out, and then they put us back in. The lieutenant chose not to go along on that one. I guess it's nice to have the option.

Another couple of days wasted and wet, and we were pulled back in again. The monsoon was in its full fury, and for the first time that I could remember, the war was being called on account of the weather. All of the teams were being pulled in, the men too soaked to function. And I'd thought Zummo didn't have a heart.

When it's raining, even garrison time sucks, more so than usual. You'd try to stay dry after so many days of being soaked and then get soaked again going to the mess hall. We'd gotten a new mess sergeant, Sergeant First Class Mortenson, and he was doing a pretty good job with the chow, as well as getting it to us, considering what he had to work with. Still, quite often, we would forgo a good hot meal and simply opt to stay in the relatively dry hootches and dine on LURP rations. Food had become a necessary routine, not nearly the obsession it had been in the Herd. I'd have killed for a Stateside meal.

And there was always the letter writing to catch up on. My true love, Grissel, and I were on the outs again. She didn't exactly send me a "Dear John," but the effect was the same. I couldn't blame her; I just didn't care any more, again. The war wasn't ever going to end, and DEROS was just something too far away to think about. One of the strangest novels I'd ever read at that time had the war still in full progress in 1992. I could have believed it. And I was pissed at my brother, David. He had, behind my back I felt, gone ahead and enlisted in the army.

I cursed him and the war and the system, for all the good it did. I wondered if Charlie, the little brother that I'd spent the most time fighting with, would have the sense God gave a rock and stay home where he belonged? No, he later enlisted, also, as a medic. In the final analysis, at least neither of them had to come over here.

The latter part of September, I had to run up to the headquarters building to pick up some papers. Bill Schmidt, one of the company clerks, was on duty. "Hey, Ford. Here ya go." He handed me a long, slim black box that said, PURPLE HEART on the outside. I opened it and there it was, all nice and shiny, the purple ribbon looking like silk.

"Sure is pretty," I said. "Where's my other one?"

"Don't know, but it'll probably be in soon." It only took another seven years until I got that one, but at least then the Coast Guard, during my hitch with that service later on, had the decency to pin it on me in a proper ceremony instead of handing it to me like a package from home.

Finally, it was time to go back to the field. We were sent in on October 3, for what was supposed to be a routine river ambush on the west side of the Oriental. This time, according to my acting platoon sergeant, Staff Sergeant Jones, these men would now represent my permanent team members. No more shifting people around from team to team every time we went out. Trenum was to be my assistant; Bill Walsh was my RTO; Keith Morris, the gentle giant from Indiana whom we'd taken to calling "Lurch" after the butler on the TV series "The Addams Family," was considered a natural for the position of machine gunner because of his size. Taking a machine gun was often something that just depended on my mood. The last man was a brand-spanking-new guy from Virginia by the name of Danny Arvo. We soon began to call him "Danny the Kid." He seemed so small and helpless, and I'd have bet a paycheck he was only sixteen. It turned out later that he was a full month older than I was. I was also advised that the slot for the sixth man would in the future be reserved for either a *Chieu Hoi* or an ARVN soldier. This time we'd just go out with five. That was fine with me, considering the alternatives.

For some time the company had been working with a number of *Chieu Hoi*s, or *Hoi Chanh*s, Viet Cong soldiers who had surrendered and were now working for the South Vietnamese government. They had been properly processed and had gone through a reindoctrination program and were now considered worthy of our trust. They did, after all, know an awful lot of the tricks of the VC: how to recognize Charlie's markers on trails that indicated booby traps ahead and how far away they were. If Charlie stopped close enough to a team's position and started talking, the *Chieu Hoi*s could listen in and report back anything of military value or, if nothing else, just let us in on the enemy's gossip. A number of the team leader's swore by their *Chieu Hoi*s and really treated them like one of the family.

One day, several of them had gone to town for a little R & R; they could do that even if we couldn't. Naturally they were not allowed to go armed. It was against the rules. After getting into town, they had run into a very aggressive band of QC, the Vietnamese National Police, who hated the ex-VC more than they seemed to hate everyone else. Maybe they were afraid some of their former cohorts might expose some of them as the traitors and collaborators we suspected them of being? The QC started fucking with our *Chieu Hoi*s, and the inevitable fight broke out. One of the *Chieu Hoi*s that I, even as cynical as I was, knew to be a damned good man was gunned down in the street by one of the QC. Another *Chieu Hoi*, a scrawny little twerp with cross-eyes, jumped on his back and deftly cut the cop's throat. One other QC was dropped by another one of our *Chieu Hoi*s wielding a pen-gun flare. At close range, the flares could be as deadly as a .45.

The rest of our people beat feet for the company and told the rest of the men in 1st Platoon what had happened. The dead man had been one of theirs. Almost the entire platoon fell out in full combat equipment. They commandeered a truck and were headed to town to settle things. I loaded up with them to go along, thinking that the action should prove interesting. The only thing that prevented the pending massacre from happening was the intervention of Captain Meyer, the operations officer and one of the more respected officers in the company. He made us understand in no uncertain terms that we would proceed over his dead body. I don't think Zummo could have gotten away with that.

Whatever the final outcome was, and we were seldom apprised of such details, there were no repercussions against our *Chieu Hoi*s. The matter was closed, but not forgotten.

Still, I'd been prepared to go downtown and take my chances for the sake of the fight and for my friends in 1st Platoon, not for the *Chieu Hoi*s. As far as I was concerned, once a traitor, always a traitor. I might have to work with them on occasion, but I didn't have to like it. Going out shorthanded suited me just fine if there weren't any other Americans handy.

Around that time, we had an incident occur that tended to prove my feelings for the *Chieu Hoi*s. One of them deserted, taking his M-16 with him. We often theorized that Charlie would surrender when he got hungry enough. Once well fed, and his mind full of all the things he had seen in the meantime, he would go back to his comrades. Bringing back an American weapon was his bona fides of his good intentions all along.

One day, one of our choppers was en route back to Bien Hoa when they spotted a VC in the open. They decided to try for a prisoner. They flew in, fired a few shots to get his attention, and then swept in to pick him up. Guess what? It was our missing *Chieu Hoi*, now carrying an AK-47. He explained to the interpreter that he had been captured and then escaped and was simply bringing in the AK to show his good intentions. I guess that story can work both ways. Something went wrong on the flight back. Maybe the guy changed his mind again. We were told that he tried to escape. Poor boy. They were flying at fifteen hundred feet when he made his successful attempt to get away. I figured he wouldn't do that again.

After we set in, there was nothing significant going on to report. We watched the river traffic, everything nice and legal as long as everyone stayed in the middle of the river. If they had engine problems or whatever they could put in on the east bank. Anything, and I do mean anything, that put in on the west bank at any time was fair game. That was Indian country.

Actually, I couldn't see that it made that much difference. Our guys were getting into just as much shit on both sides. But all traffic on the river after dark was to be considered enemy. Good enough.

We did monitor the radio traffic, as usual. There was a report that Team 1/4, a heavy team, had run into some booby traps and had several men wounded, two seriously. Once again, we would have to wait for details until we got back in. I didn't know at the time that both Bass and Fuson had been on that team.

Charlie had been in that neighborhood before us, of course. As we cleared the LZ, we found four bunkers. We figured each of them would accommodate two to three men. They weren't too old, but not recently occupied either. Maybe the bad guys would come back, so we had to remain on alert. I decided to blow them up when we left, just for something to do.

The days passed with none of the expected activity, and things got downright boring. One night I climbed into a tall tree near our position to see what I might be able to spot in the distance. There was a beautiful full moon that lit up the whole world. I could have almost read a book by it, and tried, but my eyes weren't quite that good. There was still nothing to be seen. Later that night after the moon had gone down I heard sounds of what I took to be trucks in the distance. I called for an artillery mission and gave the distance (estimated) and azimuth. The first two rounds came in fine, so I gave additional instructions to really lay it on them with the next two and then have them fire for effect. The next two rounds were about fifty meters farther away, so I doubled the correction. This went on for about eight rounds until something clicked; I had been trying to look at it from a forward observer's point of view. As far as I understood the concept, they would look at a map, and based upon the overlays we had prepared before a mission, they would reverse whatever we told them, right to left, left to right, up was down, etc. I had been trying to be too efficient and was calling in right when I intended left. When all else fails and you've fucked up, just call in "end of mission." Who'll ever know?

I enjoyed playing with the artillery, and most of the time I did fairly well, based strictly on the fact that we were operating on sound alone. We'd move into a position in any given locale, and all I'd have to do was to drop my rucksack, make sure it was nestled good and solid to the ground, and then pull out my compass. I would determine exactly which direction I faced with my back pressed against the rucksack and if something came up, day or night, all I had to do was face forward and visualize the compass in my mind to give an almost perfect bearing. Other than the temporary FUBAR (fucked up beyond all recognition, long before the movie *Tango and Cash*), that was one of our sayings of switching right to left from time to time, this method always worked fine. The worst part was hearing some really distinct sounds that you knew were enemy activity, and calling in a mission and not being able to see the results.

On the fourth day, with absolutely nothing of significance to report, we were prepared for another long day of hoping against hope for some excitement. Just after 1000 hours, we heard voices, female voices, to our north. I grabbed my rifle and ran to the river's edge and looked upstream. Before long, I had spotted them, two women in two sampans, both boats about the size of a canoe. The women were paddling carefully toward us while trying to keep their boats under the tree branches that hung over the water. I couldn't see any weapons or equipment in their boat. The woman in the lead appeared to be much older, and I just took it for granted that she was the mother of the two.

Technically speaking, they were fair game. If they were innocent civilians, they would have been out in the middle of the river, or at least on the east side. What was more likely was that they were headed for a pickup point to take on supplies for Charlie for delivery somewhere else.

I didn't have any reservations about shooting a woman. To my certain knowledge, it had not happened yet, but I had also long before decided that if they wanted to play the man's game, they could pay the man's price. These two didn't seem to be armed, though, so I decided to try to take them alive. I stepped into a clear spot and pointed my rifle at mamma-san. *"Lai day. Lai day!"* I shouted. I thought I was telling them "come here," but for all I knew, I was telling them I lusted for their asses. I tried to put on my fiercest face and manner.

I guess it worked. Mamma-san flat put the wood to the water and took off like a shot out of a cannon, and daughter wasn't wasting time either.

They moved so fast, I didn't have time to deal with mama; she was away and gone before I could spit. Daughter didn't have a chance though. She obviously wasn't going to land, so I acted without thinking.

There was a tree at that spot that grew out from the bank at about a twenty-degree angle until it began its ascent into the sky. I ran out on the trunk where it swept over the river and jumped into the front of the sampan, rifle and all. And to my surprise, the boat immediately sank. Daughter went into the water, and I grabbed her around the waist.

Cold water does have a tendency to make one suddenly realize certain factors of life. There I was in the water, with a rifle in one hand and a thrashing woman in the other, and despite having earned the swimming merit badge in Boy Scouts, I'd always done well just to keep myself afloat. But all of that was academic; I wasn't about to let her go.

Fortunately, the bank wasn't that far away, and despite the struggling woman, I made it to shore. Bill and Danny waded in to help me with my burden. Danny took the woman over to sit on one of the bunkers and then covered her with his rifle. Walsh helped me up the bank, just shaking his head at me. "Ford does it again," was all he said. I gave him my best go-to-hell look, as if it would really affect him.

Shaking the water out of my rifle, I walked over to the woman, our prisoner. Then the farce began. Of course, we spoke no Vietnamese, and if she spoke any English, she wasn't about to admit it. I began to shake her down for weapons, documents, or anything else she might have been carrying. She in turn responded like any woman would, and took my actions as a sexual assault upon her person. She'd try to push my hand away, and I'd slap hers back. After several moments of this nonsense, I recovered the grand total of half a pack of Vietnamese cigarettes and a pack of C-ration matches.

She seemed quite apprehensive. I don't know why. Just because a female suddenly finds herself alone in the wilderness and surrounded by five Americans, dressed more like brigands than soldiers, all armed to the teeth, and smelling none too sweet, I might add. What did she think she had to worry about?

"She goes back," I said. "Walsh, call base and tell them we have a prisoner."

Despite her seeming lack of knowledge of English, the woman seemed to relax a little after that brief conversation. While we waited for the chopper to come pick her up, I gave her one of the cereal bars from one of my LURP packs. These had always been favorite treats for me. She indicated that she would save it for her baby-san.

A chopper soon arrived to pick her up. She waved at us as she flew away. I never found out what happened to her, but there wasn't much doubt in my mind. That country was just chockfull of innocent civilians.

We stayed in another day and night after the woman was

picked up. When the choppers came in, I sent the rest of the team to the LZ. I had already prepared charges to blow the bunkers. It wasn't that I had any great expectations of doing the enemy any serious harm or inflicting a great deal of damage. It was just something to do.

Each one-pound block of TNT had an eight-second-delay fuse. I simply pulled the pin on the first one and then began running down the line from bunker to bunker pulling the rest of the pins as I came to them. Being the cautious type, I stopped behind the last bunker until the other three blew; hell, there might have been hidden explosives in one of them, and I don't like surprises. I then armed the last fuse and ran for the chopper. It blew up just as we lifted off. The damage I did probably didn't amount to half the cost of the explosives and detonators, and that even took into consideration the manual labor involved in building them.

Once we returned to base, we learned a little more about Team 1/4's casualties. They had apparently assaulted a village after being fired on from several of the hootches. This was not something we normally did. We stayed the hell away from villages in the first place. The team had discovered nothing of significance in the vill except for some empty AK brass, and no one was talking, so they had retreated to the nearest LZ. One of the men had left his LBE behind, so they had gone back to get it, using the same trail they had just traveled. Minutes later, and following the same trail for the third time to get away, they had hit the booby trap, described as no more than trip wires attached to some of our own M-26 hand grenades captured from Americans or sold by or captured from the ARVNs. Of the four men hit, Bass and another man went home for good, but at least breathing. Fuson had been hit bad but would come back. Purple Heart number two for him. He would get one more before Uncle Sam decided he'd had enough. As will happen, I couldn't sympathize too much for Bass. It was unfortunate for the other men on the team who'd been hit, but they had been fucked up by their team leader's error. You just do not run down a trail and expect to get away with it. In all of those months of activity, other than one man finding a punji stake the hard way, we never had anyone else hit a booby trap. Bass should have known better.

CHAPTER 25

Shortly after we returned from the last patrol, I was able to make a quick trip back to Camp Lindsey-Lattin. The place was as dead as a ghost town with so many of our people being at Cu Chi. Still we had a damned nice club, and I spent several happy hours enjoying a new song they had just put in the jukebox, "Classical Gas" by Mason Williams. I almost wore that record out in one night. I also had a chance to visit with Norman Taitano, our original operations (S-3) sergeant, who had left the company several months before to work with the South Vietnamese National Police. Tai was from Guam and was a real bullshit artist. He told some wonderful stories that you sometimes had to take with a half pound of salt. What always amazed me later was just how gullible I was back then. What did impress me was Tai's personal protection, a beautiful German Luger pistol with rosewood grips. The Luger may not have been the best combat pistol to ever see service, but it certainly had class. Tai couldn't or wouldn't talk too much about what he actually did, but he implied enough that you could imagine that he was either in close contact with James Bond, or was just full of shit.

Returning to Cu Chi, I had a couple of days off before time to get ready for the next patrol, scheduled for October 12. I really wasn't at all surprised to be told that, after having been promised that my team members were all permanent, we had a last-minute change. Trenum was going on R & R, so Mark Eastman was assigned to be my assistant. Mark had done the artwork for our company yearbook, creating a character drawn on many pages that he'd called the "Lerplin," a cute little cross

between a LRP and elf or goblin. I'd been asked to autograph
one particular cartoon a couple of times because that one had
shown the Lerplin holding his fingers in his ears while a frag
came in behind his back. Guess they remembered a couple of
my patrols. Mark had been with us since the previous January.
He was a real quiet guy and stayed to himself a lot, leading some
people to believe he had a chip on his shoulder. We'd been out
together a few times and usually got along in the field, but we
had a difference or two at times in the rear, so our socializing
was kept to a minimum.

I was also assigned an ARVN Ranger to accompany us. I
didn't like it one bit. I tried to do some checking up on him to
find out just what I'd been handed. I went to the interpreters,
sergeants Mot and Nghia, separately, and asked a few questions.
Sergeant Nghia was not impressive when you first met him. He
was short and dumpy and had cross-eyes. But I had learned to
have a little more faith in what he said than I did in Sergeant
Mot. Nghia told me the ARVN had been in the army for about
a year and had not seen any real combat yet.

Mot on the other hand assured me this man had "boo-coo"
combat experience and had been in the army for about eight
years. This did not indicate a minor difference in opinion, not
even to a stupid American. Mot was a real Dapper Dan, charming and polite, much more impressive physically than Nghia. I
didn't trust him. Even with the ARVN along, I still considered
it a five-man team. To top it off, the guy spoke not one word of
English. Fucking fine!

Our AO was not far from the abandoned village of Tra Cu,
just a dot on the map, a few hundred meters west of the Song
Vam Co Dong. The map indicated that Cambodia wasn't all that
far away. Considering a few things that happened, it was a long
time before I would be certain that we hadn't been in Cambodia
after all.

We made a routine insertion just before noon on the 12th.
The first obstacle that we encountered was an almost solid wall
of bamboo and brush at the south edge of the oasis, as I called
it, that had been selected as our target area. It took some time
to pick our way through the wall and drag our equipment with
us, only to learn, after the fact, that by going to our left another
ten or fifteen meters, we could have just walked around the
damned thing.

The oasis was about fifty to sixty meters long and perhaps twenty-five meters wide, a rough rectangle, oriented toward the north. The place had apparently been a small farmstead at one time. We discovered the remains of a building situated in the middle of the area. It was hard for me to believe it could have been a habitation, considering how small it was, the general outline being no more than fifteen by twenty feet.

The surrounding area was little more than an old dried-up rice paddy, extending for miles to the north and west. A tree line was visible several hundred yards to the south, with another tree line extending from the southeast. What we had was several square miles of nothing.

The south and east side were made up of the already encountered bamboo wall. The west side was fairly open. We also found a lot of brush and trees along the north side that extended halfway down the west side. Weeds covered most of the inner perimeter of the oasis, growing to about chest level. One large tree dominated the center.

There were a number of trails that intersected in the oasis, however. This gave indications of being a very lucrative spot for staging an ambush. There were numerous old campfire spots noted, and this could only mean a lot of transient activity.

After our usual wait-and-see period following insertion, I took Danny with me on a short recon of the area to get a better look. It was time to teach the boy a little about soldiering. Bill continued to monitor the radio while, at the same time, taking a number of photographs of the back of my head and my ass as I moved out, using an old Polaroid camera that had been sold and resold around the company for some time. This was the only patrol I went on when I had something of a photographic and panoramic view of the place. The rest of the team maintained the normal security watch.

The recon revealed that there would be more concealment at the northwest edge of the area, but there was very little cover to speak of anywhere. We discovered a couple of cone-shaped mounds at the northeast corner, hidden in the brush, about five feet high and wide at the base. Never did figure out what they were intended for. There was also no place that we could really set up to watch for Charlie's approach without either being exposed or having us ignore other approaches. We'd just have to

fall back on our listening abilities to warn us of the approach of
any unfriendlies.

We also found some expended U.S. ordnance in the form of
warheads from butterfly bombs lying about. These, I'd been told
previously, had been dropped by the thousands all over the country. By design, they didn't explode upon landing, but would
become hypersensitive to vibration or touch. In effect, they became booby traps for unwary enemy personnel. Charlie, of
course, was ignorant of this fact and would seem to have run
about grabbing the things up in bushel baskets for reuse, no
doubt thanking the stupid Americans for his generosity. There
may have been many of the inevitable casualties, but at the same
time, we did provide the enemy with a lot of material that could
be returned to us, the hard way. I had seen several captured VC
mortar rounds made from the warhead of these bombs, their
size being just about perfect in circumference to fit an 81mm
mortar tube, once the fin had been manufactured. There were
also a lot of Vietnamese "Indigenous Ration" wrappers, and I
wondered if the ARVNs had been active there lately. Headquarters assured me that no friendlies had been in the area for quite
some time.

Everything was duly noted and reported to headquarters. After a while, we moved to a spot that I'd selected at the north end
of the oasis. We would be right beside a trail where it entered
the area, and I was playing with the idea of jumping anyone who
wandered in, in an attempt to take them without firing a shot.
Sometimes I would get a wild hair when really bored.

The remainder of the day passed quickly. We heard some
sounds off to the northwest that sounded quite suspicious, so I
called for an artillery mission, but the results were undeter-
mined. A heavy rain squall came in not long before dark and
lasted well into the night, but this was not unusual.

The next day, we settled into our normal routine of listening
and watching. Other than that, the only thing to do was to sleep
or catch up on some reading. Despite the possibilities, I just
didn't have any great expectations of contact. There had been
entirely too many such missions that brought a negative return
for our efforts. I'd recently had a dream about a really bad contact, but since nightmares were a normal part of my sleep pattern, I'd discounted it.

I'd brought along a book, the last of the trilogy by Tolkien,

The Return of the King. Frazier had gotten me hooked on them in Alaska, but it had taken a while to get through the series. There'd been too many other books to read. The day passed with little to report.

Just before 1800 hours, we heard voices coming from the southwest. Then Lurch spotted two VC coming in from that direction. At least one was carrying an AK-47. We made our hasty preparations for an ambush. This wasn't the time to try to jump someone, since they were armed, and there would be no spot to leap from that would be close enough and not leave us exposed. I directed Mark to take the second man in line while I took number one.

I slipped into a spot beside the trail and squatted down, so that my head was just below the top of the weeds. Mark was to my right. I knew without looking that the others would be covering the backdoor as well as our flanks. I switched my rifle to full auto and waited. The men were still coming, laughing and talking, obviously unaware of our presence. I waited until, judging by sound alone, they were about twenty yards out.

Then I stood up quickly, shouldered my rifle, and began firing at the first man. Once again, I experienced that strange sensation of time seeming to slow down. I was looking over the top of my rifle, not even bothering with the sights, both eyes wide open. I could almost see each of my individual rounds striking the man as he convulsed with the impact of each bullet. His arms flopped about spasmodically, and his head jerked violently back and forth. His movements reminded me of a puppet on a string. When my last round hit him, he dropped as would a puppet whose strings had been suddenly cut.

I had been vaguely aware that Mark had only fired a few shots and then jumped out of the way. Where he had stood, I could see the flashes of at least two rifles firing toward the second VC, but the shooters were hidden from my view by the large tree. Mark's rifle had jammed, but the other VC had gone down. Hit? I wasn't sure.

I dropped into a crouch to reload, and then tossed out a couple of grenades, just for luck. I looked over at Mark. He indicated that he had cleared his jam, so we stood up and began moving cautiously forward to check the results.

Despite my full certainty that I had gotten my man, I was actually surprised to see him lying there. All too often, we'd fire at the enemy and then wouldn't be able to find them. But he was alone. There was no sign of the second man, not even a blood trail. I had Mark sweep the area just in case he was hunkered down, waiting for a shot at us.

Then it was time to consider my victim. He was barefooted and wearing dark blue shorts and a dark blue shirt, now covered with blood. He had been wearing a canvas bandolier across his chest, the kind designed for AK magazines. One of the pouches was split, as was the magazine it contained. One of my rounds had hit the mag and obviously exploded several rounds, adding even more injuries to the man. I also noted that he was wearing what looked like a locally made cammie bush hat that was still nestled on his head, one side pinned up like the Aussie's wore theirs. He hadn't been carrying a rifle or any other weapon that I could see at first glance.

He was still alive but in bad shape. I had hit him at least eight times, plus the additional damage done by his own exploding ammo. I could see into his chest cavity, and that's just what it was, a dark hole with no organs showing. I was always amazed at the smell of Vietnamese blood. Due to their diet, often consisting of fish, heads and all, as well as their flavoring sauce, *nuoc mam*, fermented fish, etc., their blood just smelled bad, much different from that of an American.

As I pulled his hat off, I could see that the back of the hat and the back of his head were gone. Perhaps one of my rounds had gone up through his body, or the grenades I'd thrown out may have done this damage. Still, the hat had remained in place.

I had begun pulling his equipment off when I heard an explosion behind me. Thinking the other VC might have snuck around behind us and was attacking, I spun about, ready to engage the threat. Bill and the ARVN were standing there, Bill holding the ARVN by the arm. Bill waved to indicate everything was okay, so I returned to the business at hand.

There were two good magazines left in the ammo pouch as well as cellophane bags of loose rounds. He also had a couple of hand grenades that looked like they had been made in some jungle workshop out of Budweiser beer cans. You have to give Charlie credit for having balls. I'd hate to have to depend on ordnance like that. There was nothing else of interest on him other than a handmade cigarette lighter, with the numbers 555 roughly engraved on the side. I stuck this in my pocket, another souvenir.

I looked at the mess I'd made. Company policy had been changed again. They felt they were getting entirely too few prisoners in lately, so we'd been told that if we'd bring them back alive, the team would get a free in-country R & R to Vung Tau. It didn't matter if the prisoner died shortly after we got him back in, as long as someone in authority would see that the effort had been made. This man didn't have much time left, but at least it was worth a try.

Bill had already called in our contact and reported the situation. Six and the gunships were on the way. "Tell Six we have a prisoner, and we'll be ready for extraction by the time they get here." That was stretching the point a little. They wanted a prisoner to interrogate; I just wanted an R & R for my team.

While we waited for the choppers to arrive, Bill told me what had been the cause of the explosion. "I was on the horn to base after the shooting started. I happened to look up and see the ARVN stalking you. Guess he froze during the fight. He had pulled the pin on a grenade, and it looked like he was going out to kill Charlie. I didn't think you'd appreciate it, since you were with the guy, so I took the grenade and threw it away." He grinned at me, and I grinned back. There was a good probability that he'd just saved my ass. Then I turned to glare at the ARVN. The idea of making him Airborne qualified on the chopper flight back to base seemed to have a lot of appeal, despite the fact that we had no parachutes handy. Mot and I were going to have a few words when we got back.

I was loading my gear up when Bill walked up and handed me the radio. "Six," was all he said.

"Four/four, this is Six. What do you have?" Zummo asked. His voice sounded strange, garbled.

I told him and concluded with, "We'll be ready for extraction in five minutes. One VC got away."

Zummo then replied, "Negative, four/four. We will send a chopper in to pick up your prisoner. You will remain in. I want you and your team to move seventy-five meters, set up, and see what develops."

No matter how many times I'd heard that same line, I was still surprised. I was well aware that some team leaders did frequently volunteer to remain in an area after they had been compromised. Maybe they had more balls than I did, or perhaps a greater sense of adventure. I could admire them on one hand and still figure the best bet for my team, the men I was supposed to be responsible for, was to get our asses out of there and start over somewhere else with a clean slate. "Six, this is four/four. Look around. There is no place to move to. This spot has the best cover, and it is now compromised. Request extraction, and you can insert us someplace else." I don't know why I bothered or thought I could reason with him but I had to try.

"Four/four, this is Six. Negative. I repeat, we will send in a chopper for your prisoner. You will remain on the ground. Move seventy-five . . ." Ad nauseam.

I stood up and looked around at the men. They knew what was going on without my having to tell them. Then I looked down at the prisoner. Fate had decided.

I handed the radio back to Bill. "Tell Six the prisoner just died."

I had considered letting the chopper come in, and we'd just all pile on board, and I could take my chances with a board of review later. It always seemed like I was just inches away from a court-martial anyway. In a good cause, wouldn't it be worth it? I guess I was just too conventional in those days. I really wasn't in the habit of disobeying orders, no matter what else I might do.

"I told him," Bill said. "But he didn't like it."

"So fucking what! Let him bring his bony ass down here and do something about it," I replied. I really didn't care.

After Zummo's ship left the area, one of the gunships remained for a while in case we needed any assistance. At least someone cared. "Four/four, what do you want me to do?"

"Four/four to Playboy One. Fire up the tree lines around here in case that other guy is still hanging around, in particular those on a bearing of approximately two hundred degrees. Maybe you'll get lucky."

"Will do, four/four. Good luck." He stuck around for a while and continued to fire up the area until he started to run low on ammo. Then he made a wide circle prior to his departure. The afternoon rain squall was coming in, and it wouldn't be wise for him to get caught in that.

"Playboy One to four/four. Be advised. Spotted an estimated VC company about three clicks north of your location, and they seem to be headed your way. I will go back and rearm but don't know if I can make it back before the rains hit, and I won't be of any use to you then. Watch yourself.''

And then we were alone. Minutes later the storm hit. We heard shots being fired off to the northwest as the gunship left. I ran to the edge of the oasis to have a look. Off in the distance and just ahead of a major portion of the squall as it swept in, it appeared as if a line of VC wearing ponchos were advancing toward us. I yelled at Bill to relay the information but soon realized the ''VC'' were merely trees blowing in the wind. The firing we'd heard was not my imagination though.

That storm was a real toad-strangler and lasted off and on throughout the night. I don't know which kind of night feels the longest, one that passes peacefully or one like that one, when your heart is in your throat. It was not my imagination that we could distinctly hear the sounds of equipment rattling as men moved around us. Logically they should have entered the oasis if they were just passing through the area. And just as logically, if they knew we were in there, they were going to hit us. What chance would we stand?

I called for an artillery mission to discourage visitors. Either they were anticipating the call, or they had just finished a mission for someone else and were still in the gun pits. Within moments of my request for fire, the first round had landed just to our east. I thought it was an incoming grenade and almost panicked, but Bill was on the radio and got assurances that this was indeed the stuff we'd requested. The fire was coming from a 4.2-inch mortar, working out of a place called the Sugar Mill, not far away. Those guys must have had us plotted perfectly. They walked rounds around our position through half of the night. When the mission finally ended, all was quiet. I requested the mortar crew remain on alert and thanked them for the fireworks display. They may well have saved our bacon. Then it was time to see what the rest of that night would bring.

CHAPTER 26

That night of terror finally ended, and morning found us alive and safe, if a little worse for wear in the nerve department. With the light of day, I felt a great wave of relief and decided it was safe for us to try to get a little sleep. No one had been able to sleep during the night except the ARVN, and even he had stayed awake after someone had fired off a shot not far away. We were bushed.

After my brief nap, I called in my sitrep for the morning and tried to figure out what to do with the rest of the day. It was October 14, 1968, just another Monday in the bush. I always figured that any week that started off with a Monday was going to be a lot of trouble. Still, I hoped the day would be peaceful.

Later in the morning, I went out to check on our kill from the day before. Yep, he was still dead. Danny went out with me to take a look but decided he'd seen enough when he saw what ants and night creatures had done to the man. There was no doubt that, once we left the area, Charlie would come back and retrieve the body. Why not leave them a little surprise? I rigged up a little package, four pounds of TNT with a hand grenade wired to the top. I buried it under the man's body and, despite what rigor mortis had done, was finally able to get him flat against the grenade's spoon. I pulled the pin from a safe distance with a trip wire and was pleasantly surprised when the bomb didn't explode. That would have been a mess.

As a final touch, I rigged up a signpost with a few sticks, and then wired on one of the propaganda leaflets we had for such an occasion. The leaflet said, in effect, "If this man had surrendered yesterday, he would be alive today." It was intended for us to leave behind on our victims and hopefully persuade some other poor sap to give himself up. Then I stuck the sign up by placing the stick in one of the bullet holes in his chest. I figured that would get a response.

The day progressed with little of importance to report, so we settled into our routine of watching and listening, sleeping and reading. I decided to move our position away from the northernmost trail entrance. If someone walked in, it might be a little too close to play, and I wasn't feeling quite as froggy as I had the day before. Eastman thought we were too exposed and moved off a little to the side, around another tree. To each his own, I thought.

Shortly after 1600 hours, Lurch heard voices again, this time from north of our location, but it was hard to tell. That boy sure had ears.

I got to my knees and began scanning to the west, then sweeping back to the north. I detected some movement off to my right and turned in time to see at least three VC walk into the oasis, just at the point where we had previously set up. I raised my rifle and began a firing sweep across the three men, who walked just parallel to me, perhaps ten to fifteen meters away. The three I could see immediately went down, and I dropped to reload. Then the shit really hit the fan.

Firing began to come in from several directions at once. We picked out the distinct crack-pop of AK-47s as well as at least one M-60. Then I heard an M-79 thumping out there, and we began to receive explosions all around us. Grenades were coming in rapid succession. The air was literally alive with bullets and shrapnel.

Everyone rolled behind their rucksacks and began pouring fire outward. I got to my knees again so I could direct my fire to various points as the threat indicated. While changing magazines at one point, I glanced over and saw Mark rolling over a thick bamboo pole that had separated him from the rest of us. Moments after he cleared the pole, bark began to fly as it was zipped by at least a half dozen rounds. Mark had lucked out that time. There was another explosion, and Mark grabbed for the back of his head. When he pulled his hand away, it was covered with blood and some kind of gore. I thought his brains were spilling out. He looked at the mess in his hands for a second, and then turned over and began firing again.

I looked at Bill and saw that he was firing out to the north. "Bill, damn it. Get on the fucking radio and get us some help!"

"It's dead," he said. "79 round got it. It also got one of the claymores, and I can't get the other ones to fire." Shit! It looked like the grenades were shredding our wires. Bill turned back over and continued to fire and then stopped for a moment. Another grenade had gone off beside him, and as I looked, it was almost as if a giant, invisible claw had shredded Bill's pants and his legs just below his butt. He grabbed at the wound, stared at the bloody hand he pulled away, and simply turned back over and continued firing.

Keith screamed. He'd taken several hits from shrapnel, and a bullet had torn into his right leg below his cheek. He, like Bill, stared at the wound and just turned back to the business at hand. This wasn't the time to worry about non-life-threatening injuries. Everything else could wait.

I looked around and saw Danny firing toward the southeast with his .38 revolver. "What the fuck are you doing? Use your rifle!" I screamed at him.

"I can't, Sarge. They shot it," he replied weakly. He had an exploded round in the chamber and the hand guard had taken a couple of hits while he was firing it. I had to admit, he was shooting and reloading that wheel gun pretty fast.

Several grenades had gone off close to me, the concussion knocking me over each time. I'd get up and try to resume my position, only to get knocked down again. It didn't occur to me to stay down. I felt the shrapnel peppering my chest, back, arms, and legs, but like the other men, I didn't spend too much time checking it out. It briefly crossed my mind that I was going to look like a piece of Swiss cheese when this was all over. I was continuing to fire as fast as I could put out the rounds and alternately throwing grenades out as far possible. At one point, I was trying to do both things at once. I grabbed another grenade with my left hand and, without thinking, tried to pull the pin with my teeth. The cotter pin had been straightened earlier in anticipation of action, but that was still a dumb stunt best left to the movies. The pain from my abused tooth reminded me real fast, and I went back to using my fingers to pull the pins, as I should have done all along.

Firing began to come in from the southwest. "Shit, that does it," I thought. "We're completely surrounded." The bad guys' firing was becoming more intense by the moment, and we were returning everything we had. It didn't seem to be making any difference. I grabbed my pistol and shoved it into the back of my waistband. I wanted my "insurance" handy when the final moments came, not stuffed in a holster and inaccessible.

I was digging into my rucksack for the emergency radio, the URC-10, when the ARVN crawled over to me. He was holding out his arm and trying to hand me a field dressing. He'd gotten a small wound in his arm. I took the dressing mechanically and started to wrap it around his arm. Then it hit me; I looked at his arm and then his face. He wasn't hit nearly as badly as the other men, but you could see it in his face; there was no fight left in him. He'd given up. I slapped him down in a rage and threw the dressing in his face. He crawled over to the side, clutching his rifle to his chest but not using it. I should have taken it away from him and given it to Danny, but this didn't occur to me.

I turned my rifle on the ARVN, and for a moment, I was prepared to shoot him, worthless piece of shit, but then realized there was a good possibility I might need that bullet. I had an instant flash photo appear in my mind; now I knew how the men at the Alamo must have felt. I turned and continued to fire.

Another grenade came in from the north. At least one of those first three VC was still active. I threw out a couple of my own grenades in reply, and there were no more from him for a moment or so.

I was twisting and turning about, trying to cover all points of attack when I saw Danny toss a grenade out. I could see it land no more than three or four feet out and explode. I was peppered again, and Danny winced as more shrapnel hit him. "Watch it, damn you! You'll kill us all!" I yelled at him.

Keith had rolled over to change magazines again. That blast had missed him. "But, Sarge, that was one of their grenades. Danny picked it up and got rid of it. It had landed between us." Shut the fuck up, Ford, I warned myself. These men are doing just fine without you running your damned mouth.

The men were really hurting. Danny kept passing out, only to rouse himself and try to rejoin the fight. Keith's fire was growing slack also. Mark and Bill were doing okay, but they were immobile. Their groans of pain were about to kill me. With the radio dead, I knew we were on our own, and the prospects of getting out of this alive were very slim. I had to do something.

I pulled out the URC-10 and extended the antenna. We'd been told that if we had to use one of these radios, we were not to activate them for more than five minutes at a stretch. If your transmission lasted longer than that, the radio was considered compromised, and a B-52 strike would be sent in to wipe out the place. We would be considered overrun. Now my hope was that after we were all dead, Charlie would hang around, dancing over our bodies just long enough to receive that bomb load. I wasn't real certain that was what would happen, but it was worth a try. Postmortem revenge, I guess. I dropped the radio to return to the fight.

Something had to give somewhere. I directed the men to put on their gas masks and throw out their canisters of tear gas. I could only hope the noxious cloud might help us, but it certainly wouldn't hurt to try. We had eight tear gas grenades and threw out six of them before there was even a slight let up in the enemy fire. Maybe they were closing in for the kill?

Now seemed to be the time to act. I threw off my mask, grabbed a couple of bandoliers each of magazines and grenades, and charged from our perimeter. My first order of business was to clear out that son of a bitch to our north. We'd gotten entirely too many grenades from him. I tossed out a couple of grenades and then followed them, firing as I ran.

There wasn't anyone there, or they had moved out real fast after the explosions. I refused to believe I had missed those first three; one of them must have been sound enough to drag the others away, or someone else had come to help them. There was a lot of blood on the leaves, though.

Turning around to return to the perimeter, I saw the trees and bushes shaking down by the southeast corner; someone was trying to get through there and was stuck. I again charged forward, throwing more grenades, and firing as I ran.

My ''tactics'' were simply to charge about, firing up and fragging every bush as I became aware of firing coming from that direction. Not being able to see the enemy, though, it seemed certain some of them could see us, or at least me. I had no way of knowing how much success I was having, except for one factor; their fire seemed to be slacking off more every second. I didn't know if I was hitting meat or if they were just losing interest. At that moment, one was as good as the other.

This mad run probably only lasted a few minutes, but it seemed like a lifetime. It almost was.

I returned to the perimeter for more ammo and grenades and to check on the men. Mark and Bill were helping each other with bandages; Danny appeared unconscious. Keith was down but not out. He seemed to be in the most pain. There didn't seem to be any immediate threat for the moment, so I felt it was safe to start giving the men a little first aid. I pulled out one of my morphine Syrettes to give Keith an injection.

I had jabbed him in the leg several times, forgetting that you're supposed to give it in the shoulder, or at least closer to the heart so it'll work faster. The stuff wasn't coming out, and I was feeling guilty about the additional pain I was causing Keith. Then I remembered what I had done wrong. When I'd removed the plastic covering from the syringe, I had dropped the smaller needle that was needed to break the inner seal. I dropped down and began to dig through the litter and debris until I found it. In another moment Keith got his shot.

I was trying to bandage Danny when I heard an aircraft engine. I looked up through the trees and just barely saw the outline of a Piper Cub, one of our radio-relay planes, as it came in from the east. I grabbed a signal panel and my rifle and ran into the clearing. I waved the international red side at him, to indicate the enemy was close. This man had to get the word back to base that we were in deep shit, and I didn't want him getting shot down. Besides, they were known for shooting their sidearms at the enemy, and occasionally connecting. He waggled his wings that he'd seen me, and then he banked to the north and flew away. I yelled at Bill to get on the URC-10 and try to make contact with him. Perhaps the VC had also observed the plane and they figured out help was on the way. Their firing had slacked off quite a bit before; now it seemed to stop almost completely.

Returning to the perimeter, I continued to bandage Danny and Keith, then I took the radio. I wouldn't be able to talk directly to the C & C ship because of the URCs ultrahigh frequency channel, and the C & C didn't have that. But I did have direct radio contact with the gunships, and that was even better.

The gunships arrived soon after that, and I found myself speaking to Playboy One again. "Where do you want it, four/four?"

"Anywhere you please, Playboy. They have us surrounded."
We tossed out a smoke grenade to mark our position and waited
for the fireworks to begin. The two-ship team began to suppress
the countryside with a withering fire.

"Playboy One to four/four. A slick is inbound to pick you
up, and a reaction force is on the way. Can you move to the
LZ?"

"Roger, Playboy One. We're hurt pretty bad, but I think we
can make it. Advise reaction force, do not touch the dead VC
in the middle of the clearing. He is booby-trapped. Repeat, do
not touch the dead VC in the clear." I didn't want our own
people getting killed by my toy.

The gunships continued to fire up the area, and I could hear
the slicks approaching. I looked at my team. There was blood
everywhere, and all of the men were in bad shape. Empty magazines covered the ground, and our gear was literally shot to
rags. At least the rucksacks had served a very useful purpose;
they had absorbed a lot of shrapnel and not a few bullets for us.

"Grab your rifles and what ammo you have left. Leave everything else behind. The reaction force can pick up this junk," I
told them. They weren't in any shape to try to carry anything. I
was afraid for them, they were all hit so badly. I was trying not
to think about my own injuries. At least I was able to move.

The slick set in near the northwest corner of the oasis. "Let's
go!" I shouted. Mark and Bill were helping each other to their
feet. Danny had awakened and was helping me with Keith. They
all looked like hell; no false heroics, no time for pats on the
back. But each man had his rifle or, in Danny's case, his pistol,
and none of them seemed the least inclined to quit. Damn, but
I was proud of those men!

The ARVN of course wasn't sticking around to help anyone.
He jumped to his feet and ran for the chopper. Looked like I
had missed my chance to kill the little bastard after all.

We had just gotten Keith to his feet and were starting to move
out when I glanced down and saw my book lying in the debris.
For some reason I reached down and picked it up, shoving it
into my right cargo pocket.

It was a very long walk and everyone was moving very slowly.
We had to break through some brush before we were into the
clearing. Just as we broke through the last bush, we all fell into
a deep ditch that we hadn't noticed before. It was about three

feet deep and full of water. All of the men cried out as they fell. I looked toward the chopper; the ARVN was sitting on board, and it was obvious that he wasn't going to come help us. The starboard door gunner looked back and forth between us and the ARVN in guilt. I wasn't blaming him; his duty was to be on the gun. We weren't out of this yet.

We crawled out of the ditch and began to inch our way across the ground to the chopper until we made it. We helped each other on board and just fell across the deck. Those last few yards seemed like the longest I'd ever crawled. The chopper lifted off, and we were airborne.

I climbed up between the pilots' seats, "Take us directly to the hospital. Tell them to stand by to receive six badly wounded men." Then I fell back into the pile of bodies. For a moment I considered kicking the ARVN out of the door, but I just didn't have any energy left.

CHAPTER 27

The flight to the hospital was quiet, as each man considered his own injuries. I still hadn't figured out how badly I'd been hit. I saw the faces of the door gunners; it was obvious that they wanted to help, but they had no idea where to begin. But we were all still alive. That had to count for something.

Once the chopper landed at the 12th Evac Hospital at Cu Chi, an army of men and women in white charged out to help off-load us. The door gunners were now able to help at last.

After the last man was off, another corpsman pulled a gurney up for me. With several sets of hands assisting, I gingerly stepped to the ground. I knew what it felt like to be wounded, but the sensation wasn't there. Only exhaustion and a lot of aches and some dull pains. I waved away the gurney; I thought I might well be laid up for a while so I wanted to walk while I could. Staff Sergeant Maggart, our platoon sergeant, was there, and he walked along beside me, in case I fell, I imagine.

By the time we'd entered the emergency room, it was already in pandemonium. Medics and orderlies were cutting away the men's fatigues while others carried their rifles away to be locked up. There were five tables lined up against the wall. My team was shot up so badly that I was afraid some of them might die, yet. I just wanted to cry for them. I had never felt that helpless before.

A nurse walked over to me. "Where are you hit?" she asked.

"All over," was all I could say. I was covered with blood, so it seemed obvious to me that I'd been hit, even if I didn't know where.

She had me take off my shirt and then began to check me over. Nothing. Then I dropped my pants. On the outside of my right thigh was a small red-rimmed hole with hardly a drop of blood seeping from it. As many times as I'd been hit, that was all there was? I couldn't understand it. All of that blood belonged to the other men. I began to shake violently but was able to contain it. Just nerves?

The nurse gave me an injection to prevent infection, then slapped a Band-Aid on my leg, a very small one. I just stood there, overcome with waves of guilt. That hurt me more than any physical pain I could imagine. I just looked at the other men, wanting to cry but too numb to do so.

Maggart helped me put my shirt back on and then led me from the emergency room. We loaded into his jeep for the ride back to the company area. There was nothing more I could do for the men.

As we rode along I looked at my right hand and noticed a small burn mark on the back. It was in the shape of the birdcage pattern of the muzzle of my rifle. Concussion from one of the grenades must have knocked me over onto the weapon at some point. It had been blistering hot from the heavy firing. I just stared at this insignificant injury as we drove. The sky was gray and threatening, or maybe it was just my mood.

Back at the company, I walked into the debriefing room. "Where is the rest of your team?" Colonel Zummo asked in a puzzled manner.

"I'm it; four/four is present or accounted for, sir. The rest of my men are shot to shit," I told him.

Someone had acquired a large barber chair for the colonel, and the way he sat in it, one would have thought it was a throne. He was seated in it in the middle of the room, the only light shining over his head. The other officers and men present stood behind him or at his side, like courtiers. He directed me to take a seat; all that was handy was an empty ammo crate. I felt like I was at an inquisition.

Just then Lieutenant Peter walked in, his head hanging down. "We got their gear, sir," he told the colonel. Then he glanced over and saw me sitting at the edge of the shadows. I would have sworn his face turned white. "You're dead. We found your hat. It was so full of holes and covered with so much blood, no one could have lived through that!"

That must have been Danny's hat.

"I wasn't wearing a hat," was my only response. I felt dead.

It didn't seem like I was really present at the debriefing. I made my report and was asked to repeat several parts. Colonel Zummo chastised me in what he might have felt was a fatherly tone for abandoning our equipment, but it didn't come across that way. And he was deeply disturbed by the report that I had booby-trapped a dead VC. Had I? he wanted to know. Yes, I had, I acknowledged. "Do you realize that is a war crime? That you could be court-martialed for that?" The reply, I didn't know, would have had an awful empty ring to it. It was a dirty fucking war. What difference did it make? I didn't answer.

Lieutenant Peter reported that they had seen one dead VC, our first victim I guess, as well as another one hanging in some bushes at the southeast corner of the oasis. The reaction force had only been on the ground long enough to collect our equipment, not to look for other bodies. "Your equipment is all shot to pieces," the lieutenant said, "and all we found were empty magazines. Your team put up one hell of a fight." I just looked at him; all I could manage was a sick grin. I had been aware of the amount of ammo I'd carried. I'd had thirty-six mags and twenty-five frags; I'd gotten back in with six of each. And I'd used some of Danny's ammo to boot, since his weapon was beyond use. I was tired and alone, and all I could feel was guilt.

The debriefing finally ended with me receiving a very strong warning from Zummo not to repeat any more of the things I'd done. For some odd reason, we were only given credit for one dead VC, despite Lieutenant Peter's telling them he'd seen two. Considering all of the hoopla about body count, maybe they really didn't care?

I returned to my barracks and, once alone, allowed myself to succumb to a good shaking fit. The other team that shared our barracks was in the field, so I had the place to myself. I really was alone. Every time I heard shots being fired out on the perimeter that night, I hit the floor. What sleep I got was very fitful. My head continued to ring from all of the explosions for days, or perhaps to this day.

The next morning, when I took my shower, I noticed red welts all over my body, as if I had chicken pox. The shrapnel had hit me, but for some reason, almost all of it had bounced off. When I began to roll my clothes up for the laundry, I felt a lump in one of the pockets. It was my book. There on one end was a small spot of dried blood, picked up when I'd shoved the book into my pocket as we left the field. That was all the blood I seemed to have shed from that fight.

Later that day, the lieutenant advised me that he was taking me off the duty roster for a while, particularly for field duty. At least that would give me a little time to visit with my team at the hospital.

After a few days, it was determined that Mark and Bill would be going home because of their wounds. No one could figure out how Bill had manage to walk to the chopper, his legs had been so badly cut up. But at least he would be able to walk again.

Mark had received a lot of damage to the back of his neck and head as well as numerous shrapnel wounds to the rest of his body. Keith had been lucky after all. The doctors told him that the bullet which hit his leg, had it followed a direct path, would have emasculated him. But it had been slowed down by a little P-38 can opener he'd been carrying in his pocket. His urinary tract was screwed up, and this would necessitate a long recovery period in Japan, but he would recover also.

The doctors told me Danny had taken at least twenty-seven pieces of shrapnel in his head. That many pieces had been removed before they quit counting, and there were many more in the rest of his body. Quite a few would remain where they were.

He would spend his recuperative time in country, but he would be down for a while also. The ARVN, Nghia told me, would be sent back to his unit and eventually medically retired. Too bad. He was still alive. As for my men, each in our own way had certainly been lucky, but the "it could have been worse" still had a hollow ring.

After about a week of downtime, I went to Lieutenant Peter. "Sir, I appreciate what you're trying to do for me, but I've got to go back out. If I don't, I'll never be able to do it again. The war ain't over yet." It never occurred to me to ask for a job in the rear. I was a LRP; our place was in the field.

He didn't like it and tried to dissuade me, but he finally gave in. Now I had five more new faces to deal with, and one of them was another fucking ARVN!

When that patrol ended, I returned to base camp with a definite feeling that the lieutenant must have arranged for me to be sent into the most totally uninhabited area of the whole country. It wasn't unusual for us to go out and not see anyone or hear anything of significance, but there were usually some sounds; shots being fired in the distance, explosions, something to report. We spent those days sitting in another oasis and had absolutely nothing to report.

I had been one scared little boy on the flight out, more so than usual. The flights to the field always terrified me, primarily because I was afraid of flying as well as the entering into the unknown, a cold LZ. But once on the ground, I felt like Antaeus, the Greek giant who drew his strength from the earth, his mother. One helluva paratrooper I was! But that nonpatrol was all it took. My nerve returned again, and I was back in the war.

Shortly after that last patrol, Lieutenant Peter approached me and handed me a couple of sheets of paper. It was a handwritten commendation from the men of my team, recommending that I be awarded the Bronze Star with V device for valor for my actions on October 14. They had all signed it. I felt completely overwhelmed. "It would seem to me that they have been somewhat effusive in their praise," the lieutenant said. I didn't know. I couldn't, and still don't, remember doing half of the things they had written. They had done this on their own without even telling me. Boy, was I going to have some words with those guys!

In fact, I very humbly thanked them for their praise, and we had a good round of laughs, some of the previous tension seeming to fade away. "We even got the ARVN to sign it," Mark said.

"Yeah, like we gave him any choice, the son of a bitch," Bill said ominously. There was a darkness to his grin. I wondered who'd held the gun to the ARVN's head?

"You know what the real pisser is?" I said. "To add insult to injury, most of that stuff that hit us was American. I saw a lot of the frags before they exploded, and everyone I saw was an M-26. And that M-79 kept popping rounds at us, too."

It really did rub me the wrong way, but under the circumstances it could have been worse. Had Charlie had more Chicom grenades or his homemade varieties, with cast-iron bodies like our old MK2 "pineapple" grenades from World War II, we would have been much worse off. Those were defensive grenades; they put out a smaller amount of shrapnel, but the pieces were much bigger and made much nastier wounds. They were designed, as I understood it, to be thrown from protected positions so the troops would make a bigger mess and not be endangered by their own shit. Offensive grenades were meant to be thrown while a man was attacking, putting out smaller pieces so if a man ran into his own stuff he wasn't likely to be injured as badly. Of course, theory and practice were on different planets. It was just a small observation that meant something to me at the time.

The fact of the men writing me up also made me realize that I had been remiss in my duties in not commending them for what they had done. LRPs for the most part were not Glory Hounds, seeking medals or commendations, at least not the men I knew personally. But my men had all hung in there and continued to fight despite some very serious injuries. I recommended Mark, Bill, and Keith for Bronze Stars, also, and wrote Danny up for a Silver Star. His act of throwing out a hot grenade and continuing to fight despite continually passing out impressed the hell out of me. I didn't know if I'd have had the balls to grab that grenade. There were, of course, some differing opinions when we later discussed the matter individually. I wouldn't argue against another's opinion, this time, but I went with my own feelings. And later, I also thought the men, or at least a couple of them, had tried to have my medal upgraded to a Silver Star.

None of this mattered. None of us got our medals. Someone along the chain of command lost all of the commendations, and there was no record of their ever having been submitted. And once again, for my part, it no longer matters. This was the second example to me of the recognition by my subordinates being more important than any award that might have been bestowed upon me by the army.

CHAPTER 28

Another patrol soon followed, and this one was a complete bust. It was supposed to be a river ambush on the west side of the Oriental. We weren't real certain we were going out, however. Teams 3/4 and 4/1 had been fired upon earlier that day by helicopters, this despite the fact of both teams having waved their signal panels at the ships as they'd made their firing passes. At first we wondered if Charlie had finally gotten some air support from the north. Then it was confirmed that the choppers were Hueys. There was a story running about of a Huey that had radioed in to their headquarters a while back that due to the heavy rains he was flying into, he was going to set down and return to base after the storm ended. That ship and its crew were never seen again, as the story went. Had Charlie found that bird and learned to fly it? Were we now going to have to contend with an air threat also? Turned out it was just some jerk from another chopper company, out hunting in an area he was not authorized to be in. None of our guys were hit, but I still hoped they reamed that pilot's ass good for him. It was dangerous enough without our own people shooting at us.

Our chopper swung in low over a rice paddy while I stood braced in the doorway, ready to jump. At the signal from the pilot, I jumped. The results were probably quite amusing to the other men, and embarrassing for me. There was only about ten or twelve inches of water in the paddy, but there was no bottom to the mud. I sank to my armpits immediately, my rucksack making a bad situation worse. The chopper pilot saw my dilemma and moved closer to the dike to off-load the rest of the team.

Probably the only thing that kept me from sinking completely out of sight was that the mud was so thick. I sloshed and swam, inch by inch, until I was able to grab the rifle of one of the other men, and they pulled me to the dike.

Everything was, of course, covered with mud. My pistol holster was full of it. Then I considered the rest of our situation. The dike we occupied seemed to be the only dry ground in sight. I looked toward the river and could see nothing but more swamp and trees for at least a hundred meters. One of the new men volunteered to see just how deep the water was and if we could get to the river. If he'd only been about six inches taller . . . We fished him out and made our sitrep to headquarters, trying to be diplomatic in saying, this place sucks!

It took headquarters an awful long time to figure out what to do. Several other teams were in the same fix. The rest of the day passed into dusk, and the tide began coming in. "Four/four to Headquarters. We have water rising rapidly. Request immediate extraction." It didn't hurt to remind them we were out there.

A decision as finally made to pull us out, but by then it was too dark. The water had risen to about three or four feet, and that was over the mud. It seemed a good probability that someone would drown if we tried to get out in the dark.

We'd retreated up the dike and finally found an old VC bunker that had been built into the dike. The top of it was a little smaller than a Ping-Pong table and was a good three to four inches above the water. It would be a tight fit, but it beat the alternatives as far as I was concerned.

"Four/four to Headquarters. Water is too deep for extraction. Will remain here till morning when the tide goes out." Unless we floated away first.

I'd been in some tight perimeters before, but six grown men with enough equipment for twelve, trying to get comfortable in an area barely large enough for three small boys? For once, I was really hoping Charlie did build strong bunkers.

With arms and legs entwined while we tried to rest on our equipment and at the same time keep our butts out of the water, we settled in for another long dreary night. Just about the only exciting thing to do was to watch the water level to see if it did rise any farther. There was also a matter of whether or not we were going to have to contest the "high ground" with a herd of river rats. I thought I was going to have to frag one persistent little bastard!

Extraction was accomplished fairly easily the next morning, despite the clinging mud not wanting to let us go. I was starting to worry about whether or not the chopper would have the power to pull us free as the last mud turtle scrambled aboard. At least we didn't have to worry about dropping off our gear before we went into the showers; everything needed a good wash down anyway.

I fully expected to be told to get the team ready to go back out the following day. That was of course the norm. However, this time we received different orders.

Several teams, at least one from each platoon, were told to pack up for a return to Bien Hoa. We would be briefed upon our arrival.

This set off a natural chain of speculation, accompanied by instant rumors. Ever since the company had formed, we had discussed, hoped for, and planned on that "special mission" that would put us in the history books. Being an all-Airborne outfit had formed the core of all such dreams. We had repeatedly discussed the possibilities of a jump into Cambodia, Laos, or North Vietnam, to take the war to the enemy in his sanctuaries. This would have been worth any price exacted by battle.

Upon arrival at Camp Lindsey-Lattin again, we found that none of these things were to be. But the mission we were given had plus factors of its own. Intelligence reports indicated Charlie was holding a number of American and ARVN prisoners of war in an area roughly twenty miles northeast of Bien Hoa, around the Song Be. All teams were to prepare to go in for an extended patrol, staying out well beyond the normal four to five days that our patrols normally ran. "How much longer?" we asked.

"Perhaps seven to ten days." I knew it was a good cause, and that the concept had worked in other wars, but . . . ?

Errol Flynn had made it look fairly easy in *Objective Burma*, but real soldiers like Merrill's Marauders and Orde Wingate's Chindits in World War II had used mules to carry their equipment. There had also been the occasional airdrop of supplies. I had seen the movie *Merrill's Marauders* with Jeff Chandler, and even given that Hollywood had prevailed against facts, it had still looked like much less than fun. The real men had been on real long range patrols in fairly large bodies. We were just kinda fuckin' around by comparison. Of course, going out in such small numbers as we did was not something many people really wanted any part of. I did not feel intimidated by the experiences of the last generation; I just respected them for what they'd been through and hoped, in time, they would respect us for our war.

Our mission would be to try to locate the camps where the prisoners were being held and, if possible, effect a rescue. At the very least, we were to pinpoint them so larger units could do the job. The whole thing was to be done very surreptitiously to prevent Charlie from knowing we were in the area and then having him spirit the men away, or worse, summarily executing them. No ambushing, and avoid contact at all cost.

Most of our equipment was standard, but there were a couple of specialty items. A number of British MK II-S Sten guns, World War II standard submachine guns with silencers, were acquired and issued to the team leaders. Test-firing of them revealed that the 9mm rounds they fired were almost totally silent. In turn, I let Crowe carry my 16 with its suppressor. We had a number of 5.56mm rounds bootlegged, using low velocity powder and soft lead bullets that did make the suppressor quite effective. With the standard ball ammo the sound would not be appreciably lessened, but we were told the sound would be distorted so anyone being fired upon to our front would not be able to locate our position. Anyone standing behind us would not have this problem. The lead bullets worked fine, except for one drawback; you had to hand-cycle each round. Their power was too weak to work the action of the rifles. The Sten would fire full auto with its standard ball ammo. We were being prepared to assassinate anyone who stumbled over us and not let the whole countryside know we had come a callin'.

They also provided us with High Standard .22 pistols for taking small game to supplement our rations, or for popping sentries if we could get that close. Head shots only. These were supposed to have silencers, but someone had screwed up; they had target-style bull-barrels, nothing more. I took mine along anyway. Who knew what use we might find for it?

There was also a special device for cutting chains in case prisoners were found. These had tungsten-carbide blades and were supposed to be able to cut any chain known. They were awfully damned heavy, considering the fact they were supposed to be good for cutting no more than one chain each. What if we found multiple prisoners with lots of chains attached? No answer.

Preparations were soon completed and insertions began, with the first three teams going in on October 28. Everyone was really geared up for this mission. Getting some of our guys back and hurting Charlie in the bargain seemed like a really great way to spend the war.

Once on the ground, we immediately set out toward the north, as indicated by map references. The ground vegetation was a very thick carpet of creeper vine with very broad leaves, something similar to a plant I'd seen all over Fort Benning. The going was slower than usual. We hardly seemed to gain any ground at all, when I looked up and noticed a hill in our line of march where the growth seemed to have given way to sunlight. This was only a hundred yards or so away, so we veered in that direction.

Suddenly Crowe and Jim Berry, my point man, disappeared in front of me, simply dropping through the growth. I stopped immediately, fearing we'd stumbled onto a huge punji pit. Very slowly, I knelt down and crawled forward. Just as I was about to peek into the ''pit,'' I heard Crowe and Berry quietly cursing, not in pain but disgust.

The creepers had grown out over a gully about fifteen feet deep, and both of the men had fallen through the growth and were lying in the mud and shallow water at the bottom. They were trying to right themselves and just rolling around on top of each other. I found it amusing, after having so recently thought I had lost them to a booby trap. Now I had to cover my mouth to keep from laughing out loud.

We started to pull them out, and then decided to join them.

We had to continue in that direction anyway. The rest of the team slid down the bank, making the descent a little more gracefully than Don and Jim. Both of them were unharmed, but their pride had taken some abuse.

In continuing up the opposite bank, we encountered a real problem. The brush and vines were so entwined that we were forced to remove our gear and crawl through, then have the other men push our gear after us. It took us well over an hour to move no more than twenty or twenty-five feet.

By the time we had cleared that mess, it was beginning to get dark. Since we had no real timetable to meet and the men were worn out (me, too!), I could see no point in moving any farther and then just crashing around in the dark. I decided to set up for the night where we were. We were on a gentle slope with good cover on all sides, but the brush was thick enough on the outer edges that it should prevent anyone from slipping up on us. A huge tree, ravaged by defoliants, dominated the area.

Everyone was beginning to relax a little before going into our normal nightly routine of listening and waiting. We began to hear voices to the southeast, and they seemed to be coming from the gully we'd just cleared. The different voices indicated a number of Vietnamese, laughing and talking as if they had the whole world to themselves. While I couldn't see them, I could follow their progress in the gully and knew exactly when they had found our tracks. The voices suddenly stopped. It was my guess that there was at least a squad down there.

The brush that had seemed like such a blessing moments before in its protective capacity now became a curse. We were supposed to avoid contact at all cost, but at whose cost? The enemy knew we were there. A first-year Boy Scout would have been able to tell from our tracks that we hadn't been able to get very far after climbing out of the gully. We couldn't slip away quietly in the fading light without giving away our exact location. My Chickasaw blood wasn't that thick. All we could do was hope they would think we were long gone. I doubted that completely.

We could hear splashing from the creek and the faint sounds of cloth against brush as they fanned out. By listening, I determined the gully had apparently gone just a short distance farther west and then had hooked back north and then to the northeast. This meant it ran in front of as well as parallel to our position.

I couldn't see any of this, but again, by the sounds, I could follow their movement. Everyone held their breath, listening and waiting.

The explosion nearby caught everyone by surprise. One of the enemy had tossed a grenade up from the gully, just searching. For them to waste the ordnance meant they were pretty certain we were still there. Otherwise it meant Charlie's supply system was improving a great deal. That first one hadn't inflicted any injuries, but as exposed as we were, I knew this would not be the case indefinitely.

I thought about the matter for quite a while. Snyder had left the company, and I wasn't sure how the new Three Fox would react. It didn't matter. When I got on the radio with headquarters, I discovered I was speaking directly to Zummo. Remembering October 13, I was not encouraged. "Four/four, this is Six. What is your situation?" he asked. "Just had a grenade thrown toward our position. Charlie is hunting for us. They found our trail, and we are trapped in our present position."

"Four/four, this is Six. You are under very specific orders to avoid contact at all cost. You will break contact immediately and continue your mission." Then another grenade exploded, much closer. A few moments later there was another one. We couldn't get away, and I didn't like letting this thing go on any longer without us doing something about it. I was no longer paying attention to anything Zummo had to say. He wasn't sitting there beside me, in danger, so orders or not, I had to act in the best interest of my team.

"Well, fuck this shit!" I muttered under my breath. "Okay, guys, you now how the gully runs. Let's throw out a few of our own frags and see if we can get lucky. No shooting and no talking. Try for air bursts as much as possible once your frags clear the brush." Here again, it was a matter of pulling the pins, releasing the spoon, and counting to two or three before throwing the grenades.

I was only carrying six extra mags for the Sten, all that had been available for issue, but I did have twenty-five frags. If push came to shove, I also had four pounds of TNT and the fuses to go with them. I could make an awful lot of noise all by myself.

The grenade battle began and probably lasted an hour, with the exchange of grenades being sporadic from both sides. We had a better idea of where they were but couldn't be certain whether or not we were inflicting any casualties. I thought I heard groans from time to time but wasn't sure. In the meantime I let my RTO talk to Zummo. I had nothing else to say to the man. Our luck seemed to be holding so far. But there was no end to this situation that I could see. We were advised that they were not going to pull us out. I guess Zummo thought it would make him look bad.

Then the situation changed.

The men were laid out on the hill in a row, one after another, running up the slope. Berry was first in line at the bottom, I was next, and then there was Ellis, a fairly new man that I had only been out with a few times. He was another "old man" of perhaps twenty-four or twenty-five. He had some gray hair and a dark moustache, so it was hard to tell. He also had a beautiful wife, from a photo I'd seen. I couldn't remember if she was Thai or Filipino. He was quiet, friendly, but reserved. I had avoided getting to know him. Just following my instincts.

I had my back to Berry and was facing Ellis. There was another explosion a short distance down the slope in front of Berry. Suddenly Ellis tensed, almost bowing backwards. His mouth flew open in a silent gasp of pain and surprise. "I'm hit, Sarge!" he whispered. I'd have screamed.

"Where?" I asked.

"In the back." Somehow the shrapnel had skipped over Berry and me, circled Ellis, and hit him in the area of his liver or kidneys. I wasn't that certain of human anatomy, but I knew it was a bad wound. No one else had been hit. Perhaps it had bounced off of one of the trees or bushes.

"Six, this is four/four. Got a man badly wounded. We'll try to break contact and get clear if you can get him out by McGuire Rig." I wasn't really ready to go back in. If they would only pull him out and resupply us with grenades, I was quite willing to continue with the mission.

The grenade battle continued until the choppers arrived. We threw trip flares into the gully to give the gunships a bearing and point of aim and then began pulling back a short distance, trying to locate a clearing. Not finding any clear spot anywhere close, we began to make our own. The brush, vines, and creepers were well over our heads, so we began throwing our bodies at them, beating them down and back, until we'd formed a small circle about ten or fifteen feet across. But it didn't seem to make a difference. While there were very few trees in the area, there were still enough close together, and all of them were tall enough to prevent the McGuire rig from being lowered without endangering the chopper. That would not have done the team any good either.

I finally gave up, and we continued our withdrawal until we found an LZ large enough to take Ellis out. The pilot indicated that the rest of the team should board also, so we did.

Upon returning to base the routine ass-chewing began. Ellis had already been dropped off at the dispensary. "Sergeant Ford, you were explicitly ordered to avoid contact." The man was like a fucking broken record.

"Sir, give me another man to replace Ellis and we'll go back out. It was a bad start, but we're still ready to do the job." You can't always have it your way in combat, but we were willing to try. No one wanted to quit this mission.

Zummo, for reasons he didn't bother to explain, decided against that. Our part of the mission was scratched. He did indicate that a court-martial was in the near future for me, but for reasons again unknown at the time, the matter was just dropped. Once again, I had come within a gnat's ass of winding up in LBJ and, once again, for reasons that I hadn't felt I'd had any control over.

The team was to return to Cu Chi in a few days, and the rest of the teams would continue with the mission.

None of them found any POWs, despite the teams having covered an awful lot of ground. In one case, a team was out for six days, and another one was out for seven. One team was attacked by Charlie when they stumbled into a base camp. A team member was wounded in the leg and eventually extracted while the rest of the team continued their mission. The last teams were pulled out on November 3. The closest they came to find the POWs was when one team found a bunker with eyebolts embedded in concrete, with chains and manacles scattered around to indicate there may have been prisoners kept there, but nothing else could be determined. The mission was a good cause and a great effort by the other teams, but their efforts would never make the back pages of a newspaper, let alone the history books. I was never able to determine if any prisoners had in fact been in the area or not. I knew of no Americans being rescued to that point or of having escaped, though. Lt. (subsequently major) Nick Rowe did make his spectacular getaway the following December. I always wondered who it was, in fact, that we were supposed to rescue. I'd have given my left nut to be able to do the job.

CHAPTER 29

Team 4/4 stayed around Bien Hoa for a couple of days until another supply chopper was headed toward Cu Chi. We were not a high priority item on the company menu for movement. While waiting, I managed to scarf up another bush hat. My "special" hat had been sucked off of my head by a chopper a while back and had been chopped to rags. Since then, I'd gone back to wearing the hat I had worn the night I'd gotten the shrapnel in my head. The new one I dyed black, using boot dye, just for the sake of being different.

Back at Cu Chi, I hitched a ride to the hospital to see Bill and the others. Mark had already been shipped out and would soon be on his way home. Lurch would be headed for Japan shortly, as well. I was afraid, once they left, I would never see them again.

I had heard on the radio while going to the hospital that Team 1/5, Fuson's team, was in contact and that one man had been seriously wounded. They had run into a bunch of VC, heavily armed, and one of the weapons had been a captured M-60.

As I was dropped off at the hospital, I spotted Bill limping along on crutches and yelled at him to follow me to the emergency room. I wanted to see what I could do to help. What, I had no idea.

The kid they carried in, I had known only by sight, a pale

redheaded guy with freckles, who'd been with the company for a while. Bill told me his name was Enczi.

We stood and watched helplessly; the doctors didn't need our help, and it looked like Enczi was beyond help. He'd been hit several times in the chest. They split him open and inserted some device that looked more like an instrument of torture. I was later told it was a rib expander. Whatever his chances were, the medical staff was doing everything they could for him.

Before long, all efforts to save him were suspended. He had never had a chance. Raymond Enczi became F Company's sixth combat fatality. First Platoon was certainly having some hard luck. Except for the first two, all of our deaths had been from that platoon. That was the night of October 31, 1968.

There was another change about to take place. Team 4/4 went back out on November 3, only to be pulled back in the following day. In the interim, Joseph J. Zummo, Lt. Col., Commanding, had been relieved of command. His replacement was Maj. George Heckman. For what it was worth, Captain Laizik, our new XO, told me in strictest confidence that the near massacre of my team on October 14 had been the final straw. Zummo was reported to have been drunk when he'd come out on the 13th, and that's why we hadn't been pulled out. That had surprised no one who knew the man, but the fact that someone had gone over his head did surprise everyone, and it had worked. Major Heckman was a new unknown, but no one believed he could be any worse.

Back home, as Camp Lindsey-Lattin seemed to have become for me, patrols began again in the familiar terrain of War Zone D. My first patrol upon our return, we had a *Hoi Chanh* assigned to go along with us. I was thrilled! His name was Tang and he was supposed to have been a Viet Cong major. He was of average height and build for a Vietnamese, perhaps five foot two, and maybe 110 pounds soaking wet. I judged him to be in his middle to late thirties. His English was very limited.

The patrol itself was quite uneventful from my point of view. There were the usual shots fired in the distance, trails observed with an occasional indication of recent VC activity or habitation. We did have one VC pass our impromptu ambush position one night, but if I hadn't been facing that direction, I never would have known it. He passed by us, running swiftly and silently, and was gone like a phantom.

About midafternoon the next day, we heard a number of VC coming down the trail. Our ambush was prepared this time, and we set ourselves to hit them. It looked like this one was going to be a good one; they didn't seem to suspect our presence at all.

The unseen enemy, instead of walking into our kill zone, suddenly turned off the trail and moved into an apparent clearing about fifty feet to the east of us. They stopped, and from the sounds made, it would be a good guess that they were setting up for the night. "What a trip!" I thought. "Wait till I tell Mom about the time I camped out with a bunch of VC!"

Tang listened nervously to their conversations for a while, and I attempted to have him relay anything he'd heard back to base by radio and then have base tell me if the enemy were saying anything that would be of value to us. Yes, they were spending the night, I was advised.

We did have a dilemma. The VC were too far away and there was too much brush between them and our position to try to engage them or to sneak up on them. They were also too close to call for artillery or gunships. The latter might have worked if not for the thick canopy overhead. When a team is in imminent danger, one is justified in calling such support as close as necessary. For a routine slaughter, it wasn't worth the risk.

Oh well, all we had to do was to relax, listen, and wait. There really wasn't anything much more unusual in this situation than what we normally had to live with. Those guys were really talking up a storm. Once again, I tried to have Tang relay anything they were saying back to base, but again that was a mistake. He was just too nervous to keep his voice below a whisper. I finally had to take the radio away from him and physically cover his mouth to shut him up before he gave us away to the folks next door. I didn't want to be unneighborly.

The rest of the day passed quickly. Our alert status was certainly enhanced, but it was really no big deal. I thought Tang was going to die of heart failure before it was all over, not that it would have been any loss. The team took it in stride, even the new men. After dark, I was just glad Hackley wasn't with us any more. He'd have given the whole show away with his snoring.

For reasons unknown to us, the VC left the next day quite early and moved back down the trail in the direction they had come from, once again denying us the opportunity to ambush them. Damned inconsiderate! I directed an artillery mission in the direction they had gone, but of course, the results would never be known to us.

CHAPTER 30

Not long after the return to Bien Hoa, Bill Walsh shipped out for home. I would miss his cool presence in the field. Danny Arvo would come back before long, but he no longer seemed to be with it. October 14 continued to haunt him, and the only relief he seemed to find was in staying high as much as possible. Quite often, when he would switch to alcohol, he would begin to cry. "I did okay that day, didn't I, Sarge? I didn't let you guys down, did I?"

I would sit and hold him. "Yeah, Danny. You did fine. I was proud of you." I didn't know if my assurances helped him, but it was the best I could do for him.

Keith came back after a while, also, but his first few missions, he'd found his leg wasn't up to the grind of patrol. He probably should have also been sent home, but someone felt he was fully field ready. It was just another example of a cold, uncaring system that was more concerned with having the bodies present than of the welfare of the individual. In effect, I really had lost my whole team.

About the 13th of November, a company runner came to get me. We had a warning order. Lieutenant Peter would be leading this one, with me acting as *segundo*. This was to be a heavy team for another special mission.

"Approximately six weeks ago," Lieutenant Peter told us at our pre-mission briefing, "an air force Piper Cub radio-relay plane was lost on a routine flight about eighteen miles northeast of here. There were no distress signals sent out nor any other calls indicating problems. Yesterday, a Cobra gunship on another routine overflight spotted what appears to be the wreckage of that plane. The area is heavily patrolled and very definitely VC territory. There were no signs of any survivors."

I wasn't sure this was exactly our kind of mission and said so to the lieutenant. "Why doesn't the air force send their own recovery people?"

"I agree with you, Sergeant," the lieutenant said, "but since one of the officers on board was with the 11th Armored Cav, and they have one of their companies quartered just down the street, perhaps someone thought it would be good public relations. Besides, everyone else is tied up on other operations at this moment.

"There are a couple of interesting factors to this mission," he continued. "The two missing crewmen are both majors, one air force and one army. Both of them are qualified pilots, and no one is certain which man was flying the plane. And interestingly enough, they both have the same last name—Cunningham. If, as I suspect, we find them still with the plane, it will be necessary to maintain the integrity of each corpse. For that purpose, we will be taking body bags with us. Once the remains are recovered, they will be airlifted out of the site."

A picture suddenly popped into my head; if Charlie hadn't found the guys, all we would probably find would be two grinning, yellowed skeletons. I had always read that the jungle will strip the skin from your bones in just a matter of days. This was six weeks later.

The lieutenant took me with him on the overflight the next day. We spotted the wreckage easily enough, and I wondered how it had gone undetected for so long. It was lying on its port side, the starboard wing pointing up into the sky. There were a lot of tall trees close by, so rappelling in was out of the question, or so I thought. The nearest LZ was a good two thousand meters away. That never sounded like much, if you said it real fast and didn't know the significance of its distance on the ground to a grunt. Most of the upper vegetation in the area was gone, whether from defoliants, bombs, or artillery, I couldn't tell. That meant the stuff on the ground was going to be loads of fun to hump through.

We didn't spend too much time over the site in case Charlie was watching and got suspicious. The last thing any of us wanted was to run into a reception committee. We flew back to base and began our preparations. The lieutenant took care of coordinating with the air force and artillery this time, as well as drawing the SOI (signal operating instructions) and codebooks. I saw to it that everyone packed their gear and took the proper equipment.

As usual with a heavy team, we would be taking two M-60s. The rest of the equipment was standard fare. Each man had eight canteens of water, anywhere from twenty to thirty magazines for their rifles, one claymore each, five smoke grenades, five trip flares, one to two aerial flares, one hundred rounds of M-60 ammo, etc. The assistant machine gunner carried at least four hundred rounds.

There were specialty items like binoculars and LAW rockets, at least two for the team for bunker busting, and that damned Starlight Scope. They were supposed to be great for picking up movement after dark, but they required some sort of ambient light, such as stars or the moon. Even a campfire or lit cigarette would have helped. In triple-canopy jungle, they weren't worth a good goddamn. I wondered if I just didn't have mine adjusted properly, or what. The trouble was, we were required to carry them anyway, no matter what the terrain was like. This was an additional five pounds I'd have preferred to leave behind. We were already carrying a weight almost equal to our own body weight. But the orders were pretty specific about what we had to carry with us. I always wished those who made up the rules had to carry the loads we did. I usually carried the scope myself rather than stick someone else with the extra weight. We had also been ordered that, since this device was Top Secret, if the team was in danger of being overrun, our first concern would be to destroy the scope so it wouldn't fall into enemy hands. Without pushing the issue, I determined that was not on the top of my priority list, should such a situation arise.

I still had that Sten gun from the previous special mission, so decided to take it along, as I hadn't had the opportunity to use it in its proper mode yet.

As usual, I'd been out with most of these men at least once, but there were a few fairly new faces. Everyone had to start somewhere. George Christiansen, whom we lovingly called "Psycho," would be one of the machine gunners. For this patrol, I decided that I would walk point, with Psycho walking slack behind me. I figured I'd just let the lieutenant run the show. He wasn't bad about butting in, but I was getting burned out on leading and didn't mind relinquishing the top slot from time to time. Besides, point was the spot most likely to catch any shit, and I wasn't ready to quit playing yet.

Psycho was a good man and one helluva LRP, even if he was always bitching about having to carry the 60. But, at over six feet and weighing about 185, he was a natural for humping the big gun. We called him Psycho because he was always trying to devise new methods for killing Charlie, and that's what it was all about. He'd even managed to have a fancy semiauto shotgun sent to him that he'd put to use a time or two. Worked great in sweeping a sampan.

Psycho was bitching from the start about someone stealing some of his ammo. Since there were several other teams getting ready to go out at the same time, it wasn't unheard of for someone else to swipe another guy's gear to save himself another trip to the ammo bunker or supply room. "Just get more ammo," I told him, "and stop being such an asshole." He did, but it didn't improve his disposition.

We inserted just after 1500 hours on November 15. I didn't like this. As far as we had to go, I'd have preferred going in early, getting there quickly, and getting the hell out. We had no illusions about Charlie not having found the plane. I fully expected to find the area crawling with enemy soldiers and/or loaded with booby traps. However, ours not to reason why, etc.

A LOH (light observation helicopter) would fly overhead, keeping us on our heading. Its presence meant that we could bust brush. There wasn't any point in trying to maintain noise discipline with a chopper hovering over us. We moved off to the south. As I expected, the going was rough. The ground was saturated with water, and it was a toss-up whether the mosquitos or the brush was thicker. I quickly decided the best use for the Sten gun was to push the bush and vines down as I tried to break trail. With the weapon's magazine running at a right angle to the barrel, it worked great as an improvised bush crusher. I made a point of also watching the ejection port so it wouldn't be full of debris if I needed it as a weapon. Long experience still prevailed; if Charlie heard the sound of breaking brush, he might think it was an animal or another VC. But if he heard us talking in English, that would be it. Still, Psycho kept up a constant stream of muttered curses as we moved. Couldn't say I really blamed him; my smaller body barely made a dent as I passed through all of that shit. He was forced to break his own trail. With the machine gun nestled in his arms, I knew he was going through hell.

Everyone went into a mind-set, pushing on, following the LOH, making minor course corrections to remain on heading. We tried to ignore the heat, humidity, and the bugs. The water was always ankles- to knee-deep; the sweat was stinging as it hit each new abrasion made by the wait-a-minute vines as well as our equipment rubbing us raw. We should have been used to that by now, but then you never did get used to it. We got a ten-minute break every hour, but the breaks kept getting shorter as we tried to cover a little more ground before darkness set in. Other than whispered instructions or subdued curses as someone would slip or stumble, there was no talking to relieve the monotony or to pass the time.

We finally stopped about 1900 hours and set up our RON on a small hill that might allow us a slight chance to keep our butts out of the water for a change. The LOH returned to base, and we were on our own. Response time, if we got into trouble, would be at least thirty minutes. This was no big deal; we were used to being alone. We hadn't seen or heard a thing from Charlie all day. I certainly didn't mind this under the circumstances, but I'd have felt better if we had seen some sign or heard something. No one liked surprises.

"Sergeant Ford, over here," the lieutenant whispered. I crawled over, retaining my weapon and ammo. "Aloft advises we've covered almost one thousand meters, and we're still on course. We have almost that far to go. If we get an early start, we should be at the crash site by midafternoon." He waited for my response.

Shit, I thought, is that all? Aloud I said, "Well, sir, at least

we know those guys aren't in any real rush, if they are there.''
What more could I say?

"No, that's fairly certain. Aloft also hasn't seen any signs of
the enemy. Everything is going according to schedule.''

I returned to my rucksack and prepared my meal. Everyone
ate in silence, each man lost, as usual, in his own thoughts.
Then everyone settled back for the night. Three men would be
on guard at any given time. Not long after darkness had fully
descended, we began hearing sounds in the jungle nearby; no
one needed to ask. Charlie was looking for us; a lot of them,
but they never came near our little hill.

"We could call artillery in on 'em,'' I whispered to the lieutenant.

"No. We have a mission, and I don't want to compromise it
just to kill a few VC,'' he replied. I couldn't say I always agreed
with all of his decisions. I'd never missed an opportunity yet to
try to hurt Charlie.

Morning found us still alive; I guess it always amazed me to
find it so. We had our gear packed by 0700 hours and moved
out as soon as the LOH returned. Then followed the same mind-
bending routine of humping on, breaking through one barrier
after another.

Most of the last thousand meters was covered fairly quickly.
Then came the tricky part; none of us believed Charlie hadn't
found the plane, so we fully expected to run into booby traps.
An hour or so of searching as we covered the last couple of
hundred meters proved us wrong, but to no one's disappointment. There were no indications that anyone had been near the
wreck, but we discovered quite quickly that no one had left it
either.

The lieutenant, Jim Beake, and I approached, after setting up
our defensive perimeter, somewhat extended due to the area to
be watched and the relatively small size of our team. Psycho
would handle the defense, and I had full confidence in his abilities.

We, the recovery team, took several moments to accustom
ourselves to the stench as we drew closer to the plane. I would
never have believed the smell could be so bad after so many
weeks. I looked at Jim, a tall blond kid from Illinois. He was
turning green, but I wasn't sure I was doing any better at holding
down my breakfast. I thought of several witty things to say but

figured it was best to hold my peace. I could be right in the middle of showing how tough I was when everything came up. No thanks.

We walked carefully around the plane and examined everything. The pilot had obviously been killed instantly during the crash; the left wing had caved into the cockpit and caught him at the bridge of his nose, then drove straight back through his skull. It would seem as if there had been no pain, just instant oblivion. I doubted if he would be identifiable by dental records, as there seemed to be so little of his face left for us to gather. It also surprised me just how much meat and tissue was left; he was a mess.

The passenger just as obviously hadn't been killed upon impact. The pilot's seat, positioned forward, had slipped back upon impact and had pinned both of his feet, doubling them over. The tibia and fibula in both of his legs were broken in two places. There was a first-aid kit open beside him. His .45 auto was missing from its holster; perhaps he'd thrown it away, not wanting to appear too aggressive if Charlie found him. Or maybe he hadn't wanted to be tempted by the idea of suicide. My guess was that it had taken him a couple of days longer to die, unless he'd been lucky, and shock had set in and taken him sooner. I hoped so at any rate. The smaller bones of both men's hands were missing, probably carried away by animals. "A lonely fucking way to die," I commented to no one in particular.

We then set about gathering the parts separately and scooped them into the body bags we'd brought along. Jim and I had the primary task of recovery while the lieutenant supervised. Not that there was that much room in the cockpit, but for once I wished I'd had the good sense to delegate the job. Both of us wore heavy rappelling gloves while we worked, and there was no doubt in my mind that I was going to throw the damned things away when this job was done. It didn't seem to make any difference; the rotting tissue just soaked through. Besides, the smell got into my nose and would take days to clear away.

In the course of gathering everything else up, I discovered that the passenger had been carrying a CAR-15, the submachine gun version of the M-16. It had been badly bent in the crash and was no longer serviceable. The pilot had been carrying a K-frame Smith and Wesson .38 revolver, unloaded for some reason. It was rusted beyond use. There was also a strobe light and a URC-10 emergency radio, but these had been with the pilot, inaccessible to the passenger. Perhaps if he could have reached them . . .

After getting everything sorted out and put into the bags, we called for the helicopters to come pick up the bags. The ship lowered the ropes in, and we tied them off. I'd have thought the surrounding trees were too tall to make it, but they seemed to have plenty of clearance. Why hadn't we been allowed to rappel in, then? Who knew or would say?

I watched as the bags lifted out and thought that it was a helluva way to go home.

Seeing that it could be done, I asked the lieutenant if we might be able to get the choppers to come back after they'd dropped off their loads and take us to the nearest LZ by McGuire rig. Again for reasons unknown, when he checked with headquarters, this request was denied. We'd have to walk out.

The final part of the act was to deny Charlie any use of anything left in the plane. We placed one thermite grenade on the engine block in hopes that there was enough fuel left to get a fire going. Hell, running out of gas was probably what had made them crash, I thought. Then another thermite was tossed into the cockpit. Once we were certain the fire was going well, we began our withdrawal. As we made our way through the brush and headed north toward our LZ, I could hear the distinct sounds of the small-arms ammo aboard the ship cooking off.

The return trip was somewhat anticlimactic. We had another long, cold night in the bush, and Psycho was still bitching about the heavy load he was carrying. He didn't miss a chance to remind me, either, that I wasn't doing a very good job of breaking trail for him, but he was almost diplomatic about it. His complaining was finally lost in his gentle breathing as he fell into a well-deserved rest. There were no indications that Charlie was looking for us that night.

The next morning, we were up and moving before the crack of dawn, all but running now. The rear security had spotted movement and believed Charlie was following us. Before long, we heard a shot; the VC often used single shots to signal each other. As we neared the LZ, Psycho and I both fired up a few bushes in case anyone was hiding in them. The choppers came in fast, and we had the luxury of the cool wind blowing across our sweat-soaked bodies for the flight back to the base.

Our mood upon returning to the camp should have been seen as understandably jubilant; we'd completed our mission and made it back safe without any casualties. We wanted to get the debriefing over with as soon as possible and then break down our gear and relax. I was one of the first people to enter the debriefing shack and noticed a couple of air force types, as well as army personnel, who were not from the company. No doubt friends of the now-departed. In my exhilaration, I took them for a very somber bunch. I quickly figured out that they'd already seen the bodies; now they wanted to know the whys and wherefores. I couldn't think of much that we had to tell them that would make them feel better. Their friends had died, separately and, for all practical purposes, alone.

Then down the sandbagged stairs of the bunker came Lieutenant Peter, bouncing like he was back from a college football game. "Team four/four, reporting back from the body snatch," he yelled. Then he saw the other officers. Talk about the air getting suddenly icy!

I had my gear broken down and sorted out quickly and headed for the NCO club for a tall scotch and water. I had hardly gotten through the first glass when I heard screaming coming from the area of 4th Platoon barracks. That yell sounded familiar, I thought. I returned to the barracks area and found out what the problem was. There stood Psycho, draped in dozens of belts of machine-gun ammo. All I could see was his head, hands, and feet. "Motherfucker!" he kept shouting. "That's what made my load so heavy, Sarge. Guess I got too good at packing my ammo. No one took that extra three hundred rounds I couldn't find. I was carrying it!" George usually carried anywhere from four to five hundred rounds of ammo himself, while the rest of us would carry an additional one hundred rounds. He'd just continued packing his modified claymore bag full of ammo and had then packed in a few more rounds for good measure. He'd been carrying over a thousand rounds of ammo all by himself, over seventy-five pounds of ammo alone, not to mention his water, grenades, and everything else we normally carried, just shy of the kitchen sink.

I had a good laugh at George's expense and wandered back to the club to finish the rest of the day in relative comfort.

CHAPTER 31

The day after that last mission, Rick Diers approached me and asked if he could borrow "my" Sten gun for his next patrol. Team 1/7 was going out with a new team leader, and Diers was going along for the ride. He was short and really didn't have to go, but from what he told me, it was his idea. We took the submachine gun out to the test-fire pit and ran a couple of magazines through it. Everything seemed in proper working order. Not that I really doubted it, but I did love to hear the soft spitting sounds made by the rounds breaking through the silencer. Diers took the weapon and went off to get more ammo.

Two days later Diers was dead. His team had run into an estimated platoon of NVA and had become engaged in what some had described as a "fun firefight," at first. Diers had been hosing down the jungle and having a ball with the Sten when debris fell into the cavernous ejection port and jammed the thing. He was lying on the ground, trying to clear the weapon, when he'd been hit in the crotch. The two guys who'd told me the story couldn't see how he'd been hit; he'd been lying behind them, and they'd been sitting up, firing away, shoulder to shoulder. There was no way that round could have gotten past them to hit Diers, but it had. The bullet had severed the femoral artery, and Diers had bled out before the team could be extracted. He had been their only casualty. That made seven for the company.

The team had also reported that their opponents were in full uniform and wearing pith helmets. By this fact and the tactics they'd used, it was felt the enemy had been regular troops instead of local militia. It looked like some real heavy-duty company had moved into our neighborhood. Things were going to get worse.

Diers's death also caused some speculation among those who'd professed to know him a little better, not that many claimed to know him well. He'd always seemed to march to the tune of a different drummer. Some still suspected he'd sloughed off his duties when Team 1/5 had been hit, the day Henrickson and the other two had been killed. I had to wonder if he'd had a premonition and had volunteered to go out on a patrol he didn't have to in order to make amends. Whatever the case, he was now with his teammates forever.

There was one final scene to be revealed. I was visiting with Dvorak when Diers's footlocker was opened so his personal effects could be inventoried to be sent back to his family. One of the first things I saw was a MKII Gerber knife. Not many of the other guys had those, and Frazier's had disappeared some time back. I picked up the knife and looked at the serial number. Since Mike and I had ordered ours at the same time, the serial numbers of both were within just a few digits. Yes, this was Mike's knife. Mike still had his scabbard, and this one didn't have one.

"Ya think he stole it?" someone asked. I didn't know and decided not to address the issue. The old saw of never speaking ill of the dead never set well with me. If someone was an asshole while they were alive, I couldn't see how death made them any more noble. Diers was dead, and I hadn't known him that well. I would get Frazier's knife back to him. What was the point in pursuing the issue?

Luck was not to change for 1st Platoon. Just over a week later, a heavy team composed of men from 1/3 and 1/6 made contact with another large body of either VC or NVA. Seven men had been wounded, one seriously. All that they could account for had been two dead VC. This was not a fair trade-off. Two of the men hit had been friends of mine, Dvorak and Bernard Ford, my "cousin." Everyone commented frequently on the striking family resemblance, other than the fact that Bernard was a lot darker than I was. The other men wounded were fairly new men; Ralph Boldt and Jim Kovach had been with us a little longer but Bruce Cotton, Ben Buchanan and Ken Holmes had only been with the company for a few weeks. One hell of a way to be introduced to the realities of combat.

And it wasn't over yet. Before he'd been evacuated, Dvorak had tried to make a point of warning headquarters *not* to send anyone back into that area, telling them that the LZ watchers seemed quite alert and had lots of company. Someone didn't listen. On December 3, Team 17/12 (i.e., 1/7 and 1/2) ran into a real bad situation. The enemy were reported to be an extremely aggressive bunch of NVA or VC, no one was sure which. A new shake-and-bake E-6, Larry Cunningham from Mississippi, was killed almost immediately. It turned out he'd been hit by a very small piece of shrapnel that had penetrated the base of his skull. Two other men were reported missing when the chopper they were running for was hit by an RPG round that destroyed the slick. A pilot and door gunner had been wounded but had escaped from the burning ship.

The fight had raged on, with six more of our men being wounded when the enemy company had tried to overrun the team. If it had never been the case since John Wayne, the cavalry definitely came to the rescue that day in the form of D Troop, 3/17 Cav, our reaction force. The team also had an awful lot of support from our gunships, the pilots flying much lower than was prudent, but that was the kind of thing they were good at. The enemy was driven back, and our guys pulled out. Our two missing men were found in the wreckage of the downed chopper, burned beyond recognition. Another man, Freeman Evans, died the next day.

Later, after the team's equipment was returned to the company area, I went to the supply shack. The equipment that had belonged to Rosenkrans and Urban, the two men killed when the chopper had exploded, lay off to one side. I looked the stuff over and noticed three charred fingers, seemingly welded to the barrel of what was left of one of the M-16s. I tried to imagine the pain and suffering, and then stopped myself. That kind of shit could make you crazy. I hoped the men had died quickly. What more could you ask for a buddy that had no chance?

The war had ceased to be fun. On one hand it had turned into a very serious and ugly slugging match, while others of us couldn't find any contact, no matter how hard we looked for it.

One of the teams had captured some documents in mid-

November that actually gave everyone a brief boost. According
to the Viet Cong "intelligence" sources, since 1965 one million
five hundred thousand Americans had been killed in battle, along
with eight hundred thousand ARVNs. We had also lost over four
thousand aircraft and another three thousand vehicles had been
destroyed. That seemed to indicate that I'd been killed at least
five times.

The rumor mill had it for some time that the company was
going to be broken up soon. What would become of us, no one
seemed to know.

I, for one, didn't care. After a few too many close calls, I felt
my nerve beginning to slip, but I fought it. What I didn't realize
was that I was starting to lose it, going just a little beyond the
bend. I countered this by volunteering for and seeking more
dangerous action. All to no avail. It seemed like the more willing I was to take chances, the less action I saw. I began to feel
like I could dribble a basketball through a minefield and not get
any more serious an injury than jammed fingers.

Jim Beake told me I'd gotten into one bad habit; every time
he would turn around in the chow line or when he would step
out of the shower, I was pointing a pistol at him and snapping
the hammer on an empty chamber. My excuse was, "Ya gotta
be alert all the time." I think Jim made it up. What I did know
was that I kept volunteering for one-man, stay-behind ambushes, explaining to Staff Sergeant Maggart that I could handle
the situation. He never told me no, he just kept putting me off.
I'd get to do it next time, okay? I just bided my time and made
my preparations for what might come.

Lieutenant Peter approached me one day with a change of
plans. We'd gotten in a new man, S. Sgt. James Barnett. He was
a big, blond Nordic-type. We were told he had served a previous
eighteen-month tour with the 101st Tiger Forces, a very badassed bunch of people with the Screaming Eagles recon unit. At
six feet four and about 235 pounds, I figured Barnett had been
a team all by himself.

"Sergeant Ford, Staff Sergeant Barnett will be taking over
team 4/4 for the time being. I think it's time you took a little
break, shared some of the responsibility. You've done a good
job, but you'll be going home soon. Staff Sergeant Barnett might
be a little rusty, though, so you'll stay on as his assistant to help

him relearn the ropes, okay?'' The lieutenant had tried to let me down easy, but I still felt like I'd been slapped.

It could have been worse. For a lifer, Barnett was easy to get along with. He was apparently one of the victims of an army decision not long before to bring back a lot of senior and/or experienced personnel who had already done their time, due to a shortage in experienced people in Vietnam.

Several seemingly uneventful patrols followed, and about all that happened was that we walked a lot. There were a couple of insignificant night actions, with us shooting off a lot of ammo, but there were no casualties and no enemy bodies to count, so it hardly seemed worth the effort. Barnett apparently felt the word *recon* belonged back in the LRP dictionary. I lost more weight that December than in all of the previous months combined. On one of these patrols, I had taken a dextroamphetamine one night and unintentionally got high. I spent all night calling in a sitrep on a flying saucer, actually just a star traversing the heavens.

One incident with Barnett probably brought me as close to death as any time I could remember. (As I said, Barnett was a big man, and his strength was incredible. We had an old M-1 carbine lying around that was beyond repair. We wanted to make certain. Little ol' me took it out and stuck it through the O ring on a trailer hitch and tried to bend the barrel. Despite my best efforts, all I did was strain my back. Barnett walked up and took the barrel and gave it a gentle pull and bent the thing almost double. I was impressed!) During one brief break between patrols, a bunch of us were horsing around one hot afternoon. Some men began tossing dirt clods, taken from split sandbags, at each other, and soon a general melee was in progress.

I found one clod that was almost as big as my head and probably weighed eight to ten pounds. I picked it up and lobbed it into the air about fifteen or twenty feet. Barnett walked under it just as it started back down. It exploded on his back.

Barnett arched his back in pain, his fists shaking in the air, and his yell was something out of a horror movie. I was certainly concerned that he might be hurt, and then in absolute terror when he swung around and glared at me like a crazed bull.

I was dead! Holy shit, I was gonna die, and there wasn't a thing I could do about it. My rifle was locked up in the supply room.

Slowly he began to stalk me. I cowed down, ready to accept the inevitable. I felt one catcher's-mitt-sized hand grab my neck, and the other paw grabbed my thigh. In an instant I was suspended a good seven feet in the air in Barnett's grip. Where, I wondered, would I land?

After an eternity, literally suspended between heaven and earth, he slowly lowered me back to the ground, almost gently. Holding my shoulders, none too gently now he shook me, maybe just a six on the Richter scale. "Don't ever do that again," he hissed through clenched teeth, then he stalked off. If I'd had any moisture in me, I probably would have pissed my pants.

A couple of days after this incident, we were sitting in the barracks enjoying our music and recounting stories of derring-do. I had been listening to "Light My Fire" through someone's headset when another man walked in, holding a can of Coors beer. My God! The elixir of life, at least in Oklahoma. I grabbed the can from his hand and downed it. Very uncivilized conduct, but one should not tempt the heathens.

Afterwards, I was sitting on my bunk talking to Barnett and several other people. I looked up to see Tang running down the aisle between the bunks. He had a maniacal look on his face, as if he'd completely lost control of himself. He ran on until he came to a footlocker that stood in his way, jumped onto the surface, and then leapt at me. I just sat there, having no idea what his problem was but unmoved by the threat. I was just too mellow. Barnett was a little more alert; he stood up and grabbed Tang by the throat with one hand while he was still in midair and began to shake him like a rag doll. "What's your problem, boy?" In an instant, Mot had arrived to rescue Tang from the barbarians, as if his presence would really have any effect. I still hadn't forgiven that son of a bitch for lying to me about the ARVN we'd had to take along in October. None of us could determine what had set Tang off, but Mot intimated that he was very upset with me, that I had taken too many chances and endangered this man too often. Was that all!? Shit, that was old hat. I wasn't the team leader any more. That burr must have been rubbing on him for an awful long time and had suddenly surfaced. Tang had lost it. In fact, there seemed to be developing a near rebellion within the ranks of the *Cheiu Hois*. I could have cared less. Some of the officers and senior NCOs quelled the

riot, marshaled the natives away, and we returned to our partying.

Camp Lindsey-Lattin really was like home to me. Even if the
field had ceased to be fun, there were several plus points to our
isolated area that still made being in Vietnam bearable. There
were separate clubs for the officers, NCOs, and enlisted men.
The NCOs had the best, in my humble opinion. There was
plenty to drink most of the time, a jukebox full of the latest hits,
and several slot machines. I couldn't leave the damned things
alone and always lost. We also had several pretty Vietnamese
barmaids. While I didn't have much luck running a line on them,
they were still interesting to watch in their *ao dai*s as they gently
floated around the room. Plenty of fantasies were had.

One day Bob Green and I were talking, all the while staring
at one luscious lovely, tall and slim, and very pretty in any part
of the world. Bob had commented about how easy it would be
to take her back home and how easily she'd fit into the proper
society. I watched her for a while, having my own fantasies,
then commented. "Yeah, but what if you were at a party some
night, and she was the hostess. She's standing with a group of
your friends and suddenly gets tired of standing, so she drops
into their traditional squat. What would your friends think then?"

Bob almost dropped to the floor, he was laughing so hard.
The girl under discussion may or may not have heard what I
said. Not that I intended to embarrass her, it had just been a
thought. She was, in fact, a doll. I'd also never seen an Oriental
blush before. It took Bob a few minutes to compose himself,
but the idea stayed with him for a while and he continued to
crack up for the rest of the evening, every time the mental picture returned.

The best club manager we had was Sgt. Lonnie Miles. Everyone liked Lonnie. One time, he'd arranged for a stripper to
entertain us. Everyone was really looking forward to the show.
My feelings were that as long as there were women who didn't
mind exposing their bodies, I didn't mind looking.

During the afternoon prior to the event, though, I got into
trouble, again. There was a surprise shakedown of wall and
footlockers. A lot of empty morphine Syrettes had begun to
show up around the company area. Someone obviously had a
serious drug problem. This seemed ridiculous to me; all I knew

about were the alcoholics and potheads. We had no drug problem. It later turned out that one of our mail clerks was hooked on the stuff. That was the only case of serious drug abuse I ever knew of. All of the rest of the consumption of alcoholic beverages or marijuana was just each man's way of winding down after a patrol or as a means of dealing with the stress.

When Staff Sergeant Jones came to my wall locker, I was really hoping he wouldn't see the bag of loaded magazines stashed in the corner, a clear violation of company policy. It wasn't an intentional screwup on my part, just an oversight. I wasn't usually in the habit of disobeying orders, at least not in a way that I was likely to get caught.

It could have been worse. At that time, I was fairly well into Jones's good graces, unlike other times when he'd wanted to shoot me. All that I got was a severe ass-chewing, and then I and a few other miscreants were assigned to clean out the latrines. This was the infamous shit-burning detail. We had to pull out the half fifty-five-gallon drums full of feces, pour in diesel fuel, and burn the mess, then bury it in deep holes. Our guys usually didn't have to do this chore; the company paid the local civilians to do it. Unless of course, they wanted to make a point to someone that orders were meant to be obeyed. The work was hard enough and nasty enough that most of the men worked very hard at avoiding such an honor. Some detail for a hard-charging buck sergeant, but it beat an Article 15!

The job took several hours, and by then we knew the show had started. No time to waste on showers or changing clothes; she'd be gone by then. We trooped on over to the club to join our brothers in the frolic.

There were probably fifty or sixty men surrounding the stage, actually little more than a bandstand about six or eight inches high, the platform being little more than twelve feet by eight feet across. It was hard to see the girl; most of the guys were taller than I was, or they were standing on chairs. Not to be left out of the fun, we began to worm our way through the crowd and soon made it to the front. And sooner still, our odoriferous presence gave us all the elbowroom we needed. Don't know if it really made any difference to the girl or not. Having all of those screaming LRPs standing around while she disrobed certainly took some of the starch out of her smile. Still, it was a great show. Lonnie's popularity went up another couple of notches.

CHAPTER 32

Lieutenant Peter had been after me for a while to take another R & R. I thought about it a lot and finally settled on one to Vung Tau, in country. The way things seemed to work, often when you didn't want it that way, had I taken an R & R out of country I'd have been out of the field for at least ten days. I had reached the point where if I went more than seven days or more out of the field, I got really restless and jumpy.

During this period, I also got to attend my only Bob Hope USO show. It was wonderful. Ann-Margret stole the show as far as I was concerned. I'd gone with Jim Berry and my "cousin" Bernard. Between the three of us, we managed to keep our one pair of binoculars quite steamed up. We saw it in Long Binh, along with about five thousand other GIs, so there was no way we were likely to get a front-row seat. Bob did introduce a Medal of Honor recipient from the Korean War. As I recall, the man had not only gotten the Medal, but was awarded a special gold pin in the shape of an entrenching tool, since this was the weapon he'd used to dispatch about eighteen enemy soldiers. I was duly impressed.

Not long after, I made a trip to the Long Binh PX with several other guys, just for a chance to move around. We once again were assailed by every passing MP, "Where's your helmet, soldier?" Our response remained the simple, "LRPs don't wear helmets!" You'd have thought after all that time they'd have gotten the message.

Along the way, we stopped off at a small roadside stand for

a couple of bottles of "33" beer, known far and wide as "Old Tiger Piss." Couldn't say I would argue the point. We were soon joined by a number of ARVN soldiers. They made me nervous. I never had much respect for their fighting capabilities, if the enemy was armed. They were armed, we weren't, other than my little two-shot .38 derringer. I didn't see that as giving me much of an edge against their carbines and 16s, so I became the epitome of the "beautiful American." We toasted each other repeatedly over our great victories and promised to remain friends for life. We even exchanged addresses. Since I couldn't conceal my name tag on my uniform, I made up the rest. I sure felt sorry for some guy named Bob Ford in Champagne, Mississippi, wherever the hell that was, once he started receiving all of the correspondence and requests to come visit.

Christmas of 1968 was spent on patrol, again with nothing of significance to report. One of our E-7s, Sergeant First Class Malichi, had died of a heart attack on Christmas day, the only casualty for the company that day. A couple of teams had made contact and had gotten several KIAs and prisoners, but we'd lucked out again. Two teams that did make contact came back with a distinct impression that Charlie could have had them but was more interested in chasing them out of the area rather than engaging them. All in all, it seemed like we were seeking but not finding.

The word was finally official. The company was going to be broken up, effective some time in January, but the date hadn't been set. Higher authority had decided to convert all thirteen Long Range Patrol companies into Ranger companies. This left a lot of us with more questions than answers about our fate. (My feeling on the matter was that the very things that had made us effective in the field had condemned us. LRPs were mavericks, very independent minded and resourceful and not the least interested in the opinions of any who had not shared the same dangers we had faced. We were probably, man for man, one of the most willing bunch of malcontents who wanted to pursue the war to ever come down the pike. But, quite admittedly, we didn't give a damn about higher authority or the Mickey Mouse that went with garrison. That could well have been our downfall. I was just pleased to learn that the Rangers who followed us were just as bad. Good in the field and lousy garrison troops.)

Very few of us had been Ranger qualified. We just saw ourselves as super grunts who had learned our trade by OJT (on the job training). We wondered if we would be excluded, if these companies would be all Ranger-qualified personnel and if the rest of us would be sent back to the line? There were some assurances that we would be a part of these units, but we just didn't know what to believe.

I was concerned also, but it was really a moot point for me. I was going home. I had thought frequently of extending again and had a number of buddies try to talk me into it. I can't say I never wavered, but I stuck to my guns. Originally, I was supposed to go home at the end of January, but someone had noticed that I had taken an extended extension leave. They figured I owed them another nineteen days. By the military way of counting, my DEROS was moved back, from January 26 to February 27. Logical to me, I think?

New Year's Eve 1968, we were tear gassed by some guys from the 11th ACR, quartered down the road. It may have been in retaliation for some prank pulled off by some of our guys. Naturally our gas masks were locked up in the ready bunker, strapped to our rucksacks. I discovered that a poncho liner makes a fair substitute when all else fails.

The new year of 1969 began with the strains of Paul Mauriat's "Love is Blue" being played over the Armed Forces Radio station, accompanied by a thousand rifles and machine guns firing into the air all over the base, as well as dozens of large and small explosions. It seemed like I'd been through that before. At least this time, we didn't have any casualties.

A few days later, my team went back out again. Sometimes I was allowed to lead, other times Barnett was in charge. Once more, there was nothing to report. The day after we had gone out, a kid named Aubain died from wounds received on December 3. He was just a few weeks shy of his twenty-first birthday. That made five for that patrol and twelve for the company, besides the three we'd lost not as a result of combat action. The general impression was that most of the old-timers had at least two Purple Hearts each, but maybe that was just a slight exaggeration.

An Indiana National Guard unit, Company D/151st Infantry, LRP, had joined us in late December. By all accounts, they were a very well-trained outfit. To us they looked like a bunch of green kids. That isn't being unkind; an eighteen-year-old who's been shot at a few times does look older than the most highly trained but inexperienced thirty-year-old man.

Frazier and DeFer spent a little more time helping to train them than I did, but we were all involved to greater or lesser degrees. In effect, we ran them through something of a "jungle school," showing them some of the things we'd learned and assisting them in getting acclimated to the country. For my part, it was primarily taking them on long marches until they'd gained their stamina. They would also be getting some of our people when we split up, as well as the fact that some of our personnel joined them on their first few patrols.

Other parts of the company were divided up into nonentities called the 78th and 79th Infantry Detachments. This made no sense as far as we were concerned, then or now, and it never was explained to my full satisfaction. Most documents showed we had ceased to exist as of mid-December, but we were still F/51 and would remain such until we became Companies O and P of the newly reorganized 75th Infantry (Ranger).

On January 15, the team got another warning order. I got another one of my gut feelings and told the lieutenant that I wasn't going out. I had no reason or excuse, I just didn't want to go. Probably, no certainly, had a cherry done that, or the officer had been anyone but Lieutenant Peter, I would have been in serious trouble. I got away with it.

The day after the team was inserted, they were ambushed. Four of our guys were wounded, two seriously, including Staff Sergeant Barnett. He had jumped between two of the men when a grenade had been thrown at them and had absorbed most of the blast with his body. A bullet or large piece of shrapnel had also gone through his jaw, taking out several teeth.

Two of the guys, Jim Fenner and Phillip Solomon, both fairly new to the company, were hit lightly, comparatively speaking, but incapacitated for the period of the action. The other man was hurt more seriously. Jim Beake and George Christiansen, the men Barnett had taken the blast for, were almost completely worn out from having to carry all of the wounded and their equipment to the waiting chopper. I could just imagine how much fun carrying Barnett was. Bear that Barnett was, his recovery wasn't expected to take long. He was recommended for the Medal of Honor. I think this is one of those cases where, had he died, he'd have gotten it. Still being alive, he got, as I was told, the second highest award, the Distinguished Service Cross.

Since two men hadn't been hit and no one had been killed, maybe my premonition, if that's what it was, had been off just a little. I would never know, but I suffered no guilt for having missed that patrol. I'd been pushing my luck too long.

On January 22, Team 4/4 went back out but was extracted the following day. Team 1/6 came out five minutes later. We were now, according to the brass, on stand-down. For how long, no one knew.

Everyone was expecting Charlie to do a replay of the previous Tet Offensive, so while we may have been on stand-down, that didn't mean we weren't on alert. I was placed in charge of one of our company's reaction teams, to be prepared to rush to any point on the perimeter that might need assistance. It struck me as being a very hollow honor.

That didn't mean we had no time off. On January 30, I went to one of the NCO clubs off base with several buddies, again for a change of scenery more than anything else. Most of the buddies I went with were not sergeants, but once again, if anyone had noticed that half of the men had the same name tags on their shirts as the other half, they let it slide.

Another new man, I'll call him Bullet Head, had invited himself along, much to everyone's disgust. He'd come into the company just a short time before with many tales of derring-do and heroism when he'd been with other units. At first he'd been interesting, and then things were noticed. His stories were never the same from day to day, and to hear him tell it, he'd been in on and a major participant in every great battle since Dien Bien Phu. The topper was when he told the story about how his brother had died in his arms, with thirty variations at least; how he'd once thrown a bayonet at a running VC and hit him dead center in the back at thirty yards; the loss of the tip of one finger from napalm burns at "Carpenter's Valley," a debacle that occurred when a company commander named Carpenter had mistakenly called in the strike on his own position instead of the enemy, etc. You get the drift? The guy was a real jerk.

To top it off, it seemed like every time a patrol came up, he got sick. The word "coward" and the term "full of shit" were whispered, but not too loudly. This guy was larger than Barnett by a couple of inches and about fifteen pounds or so heavier. A very formidable hunk of real estate.

This particular night he joined in and instantly pissed off everyone in sight. For one thing he never had any money. His records had been "lost," and he couldn't get paid. As tough and brave as we saw ourselves, when he "requested" a loan, which was never repaid, few turned him down.

He also decided he didn't like the presence of a "bunch of fucking legs" in the bar. Bad move, idiot, it was their fucking club! Since the 101st had moved out, we were the only Airborne unit left on base. While we were proud of our status, we also had enough pride not to push the issue. We seldom got into fights, over that factor at least.

As soon as the inevitable fight broke out, Bullet Head disappeared out the side door, another of his famous tricks. We managed to extricate ourselves without too much loss of face or flesh and returned to the company area.

I immediately reported Bullet Head for violation of orders, being a specialist fourth class in an NCO club (conveniently overlooking the fact that one of my guests had been a private first class), as well as a few other infractions, probably including Lincoln's assassination. Lieutenant Peter placed the asshole under barracks arrest, and I was ordered to guard him. Shit, fucked up again, Ford! I thought.

Bullet Head had to make the inevitable threats about what he was going to do to me. Being no dummy, and with my rifle locked up, I pulled out my Gerber and lay it where he could see it. With a lot more confidence than I felt but with many drinks under my belt, I told him, "Do what ya gotta do, but lay hands on me, motherfucker, and you're gonna die!" It damned sure didn't hurt to try to run a bluff.

The night drifted on, and we finally turned in. I could have cared less if he ran off, I needed my sleep. Sometime during the night I had to answer nature's call. As I got up, I remembered the knife and picked it up, laying it on the top bunk. As I fumbled around for my flashlight, I must have knocked the knife off. It hit my foot and certainly hurt like hell, but I thought it was the blunt end that had hit, until I started to walk off. For a moment I thought I'd stepped in some mud; in the barracks? I shone my light on my foot; it was a good one. Blood was gushing everywhere. Being somewhat anesthetized from a goodly supply of Cutty Sark, I shrugged it off, wrapped a field dressing around my foot, completed my business, and went back to bed.

The next morning I couldn't walk. Not being willing to ask Bullet Head for assistance, I crawled to the orderly room to get a ride to the dispensary. It only took a few stitches, as well as a ten-day, no-field-duty profile.

The accident was embarrassing enough. I always seemed to do more damage to myself than Charlie had ever managed, but there had to be one last play out for some asshole to run. The new Three Fox had decided I had inflicted the wound deliberately.

"This time, Sergeant Ford, you will pay. This time you are going to be court-martialed. I've heard about some of your stunts. You knew you were to receive a warning order today, and you deliberately inflicted injury on yourself to avoid field duty." Fortunately Lieutenant Peter had, as they say, anticipated the command. He was present at this last tirade.

"Lieutenant, Sergeant Ford had not, I repeat, not been advised of any such thing. I was going to tell him today. As far as he knew, we were still on stand-down. Besides, he's close enough to his DEROS that he probably presumed he was excused from further field duty." Well, it was half-right; the injury was an accident, and as far as I knew, we were on stand-down. But I'd already decided, come what may, I wasn't going out again.

Case closed. However, it turned out that it made no difference what the lieutenant thought of what I'd done. That patrol, as well as all others that had been scheduled to go out, had been canceled. Company F, Long Range Patrol, 51st Infantry (Airborne), ceased to exist as of February 1, 1969.

The next two weeks seemed like a vacation. No morning formations, we could sleep as late as we wanted and spend the rest of the day enjoying ourselves. For me, this involved getting as much of a suntan as possible before going home. I liked the idea of going back in the dead of winter and being the only one with a tan.

I also spent a good bit of the day sipping on my scotch and water. The thing that really rubbed me raw was the fact that I had to have my subordinates buy my bottle for me; I was too young to enter the base package store. I was still a couple of weeks short of my twenty-first birthday. That might allow me to buy a bottle as well as to vote, not that I considered that any great privilege. Politics and politicians were not things held in great esteem. They were just a small step above whale shit on the ocean floor. I could buy a drink in the club, but not a bottle. Military logic?

At one of our parties one night, old Bullet Head had tried to weasel his way in again. Psycho and a couple of others had run him off. He was not welcome, and everyone was tired of his bullshit. He left in a huff but returned very soon brandishing a 16. He stated that he was going to teach someone a lesson. He charged forward, stepping across the two-foot plus drainage ditch that ran down the east side of the barracks row, and was acting like he was going to create some havoc.

Idiot! You don't have to get close to a man with a rifle. He let himself get too close, and Barnett attacked. He stepped forward and grabbed the rifle away from Bullet Head and knocked his dick in the dirt. Bullet Head was then hauled off to await charges. He deserted shortly after that.

I was told later that he'd arrived at a Special Forces compound that was being run by a sergeant major who was the father of one of our lieutenants. Bullet Head had finally lost it. He had appeared wearing his dress khaki uniform with row after row of ribbons to attest to his valor. But instead of having the appropriate ribbons with oak-leaf clusters to designate subsequent awards, he'd just added more ribbons. Someone wearing three or four separate Silver Star ribbons has some explaining to do. I never heard what became of the dummy.

A week or so after the company officially ceased to exist, D/151 lost their first man killed in action. I didn't know all of the circumstances but what I did hear was that his team had made it back to their extraction LZ and then had left the dead man in the jungle when the had been pulled out. Over the protests of some of their officers, Major Heckman made them go back in the next day and get him.

Many of our people, myself included, thought this was a really stupid act and could not be explained away. Some of our men pointed out the fact that in all of the previous months of action, we had never left a man behind. I agreed, but after a time, I'd had to look at things more realistically. Yes, we had a good record in that area, as well as many others. But it was also recognized that we had some really great support from our slick pilots and crewmen, the gunship personnel, as well as the different reaction forces that came in to pull us out when we found the water too rough. The air force and artillery people had done an admirable job. We could be proud of ourselves, but there could never be any forgetting the support we'd had. Had a team ever been forced to E & E, it would have been almost certain someone could have been killed or wounded and may well have had to have been left behind. I was just glad it never came to that.

But those men with D/151 were still green. They had a lot to learn. And it would seem they learned their lessons very well. That company finished out the rest of its tour with only one more man killed in action, with two more killed in accidents. That speaks well of them. We just had a little too much arrogance to be understanding at the time.

CHAPTER 33

All too soon it was over. Different groups of men began leaving to join their new outfits. Some went to Long Binh for final processing to the 82d Airborne. A few were transferred over to D/151. My group would be going to Quang Tri, up near the DMZ, to join the 5th Infantry Division (Mechanized) as the nucleus of Company P, 75th Infantry (Ranger). Rumor control had it that Quang Tri was experiencing daily mortar and rocket attacks, and a ground assault by the enemy was expected at any time. A lot of our short-timers had gotten orders early to go home. Not me. I was being sent into the fire once again. I never did learn who was responsible for that little screwing. Long Binh was the closest disembarkation point; I had two weeks to go. I felt like someone wanted me dead.

It was hard to say good-bye to guys who, in many cases, had become like brothers. We'd shared so much laughter and pain together. No one wanted to say the words. "See ya," was about the most anyone could say as they'd pat each other on the back and run off to their waiting trucks. Many of the guys still had a lot of time left in country, and the war wasn't over yet.

Frazier, one of my closest friends, had extended his tour again and was going to O/75. I wondered if I would ever see him again.

There was also a great deal of anger and resentment over our breakup. No final parade, no presentation of awards, or ceremonial taking down of the flag. No "job well done." We felt like we had done a good job. We'd been told so often enough. We gave more than we received, both from the army and the enemy. No one seemed to care. I felt like we were being sent off into exile in shame. It was a dirty end to a damned good outfit.

We had added something to the history of the 51st Infantry, for whatever it might be worth. Battle streamers now included the Valorous Unit Award, embroidered SAIGON–LONG BINH, and the Vietnam Cross of Gallantry with Palm, embroidered with VIETNAM 1968. Campaign participation now included the Counteroffensive, Phase III; Tet Counteroffensive; Counteroffensive, Phase IV; Counteroffensive, Phase V; and Counteroffensive, Phase VI. It would be up to historians to determine if they meant anything. To me it sounded more like we had done little more than respond to Charlie's aggression, when in fact, we had usually taken the war to him, and generally on our terms.

It finally came, our turn to head off to Quang Tri. I could not avoid the fact of still being in charge of my part of our group, but I managed it without much trouble. We loaded onto the trucks to take us to Bien Hoa International for the last time. As we off-loaded, the stitching in the Vietnamese holster I had bought for my Browning split, dropping my pistol to the dirt. For some reason, that seemed to be an ominous sign. Dropping one's weapon in the dirt was always a good reason to knock out at least ten push-ups. Despite my reservations, I couldn't say extending still hadn't left my mind. I think that was the final signal. Fuck it!

I had one last laugh at a REMF as we prepared to depart. I noticed a big, fat major sitting in the terminal, wearing the collar brass of a paymaster. The son of a bitch was wearing a steel pot, flak jacket, and had a gas mask on his hip as well as a .45 auto in its holster on his hip. And he was all but sweating blood as he sat eyeing the throng of soldiers passing around him, clutching his briefcase to his chest. The fat motherfucker probably thought he had the key to the winning of the war in his possession.

Those last two weeks in Quang Tri were a real bust. Fortunately for me, the ground attack that had been expected never materialized, and in fact, the rockets and mortars quit raining down on the base. I hardly heard a shot fired the whole time I was there. Well, there were the occasional coughs from artillery passing overhead, going out to Charlie land. One distinct passing I heard reminded me of a freight train. Someone told us those were salvos being fired from the USS *New Jersey*.

The weather was lousy, with rain or drizzle constantly wetting everything down, including our spirits. It was also much colder than we were used to. Reminded me of the weather around Monterey, California. The only "combat" I saw were our nightly forays against the legs. Our designated company area had barracks with half-wooden walls, the rest of the wall being screening. The rest was just roofs and floors and little else. We determined what we needed to make the place more civilized and then went out and stole it from other units. Almost every raid was successful.

There was one major blunder, however. Someone had made the mistake of parking a truck loaded with mess-hall supplies too close to our compound. We could always use extra chow. One case we carried back to our lair contained four number-ten cans of unsweetened cherries. Since we couldn't eat them in that form, we tried to figure out how to ferment them for hooch, bootleg liquor. I wouldn't be around long enough to enjoy the results. The problem was, once again, that there was either no liquor available or the legs were hiding it. I also heard that the base commander was a real stickler and didn't care for alcoholic beverages. Who knew?

I turned twenty-one a couple of days after our arrival. Knowing the true character of my buddies, I didn't tell anyone. It didn't help; someone found out and told everyone. Getting doused with a couple of cans of unsweetened cherries, then being thrown into the almost-freezing showers at night, and having my birthday "licks" administered with a wet broom by a dozen men was not my idea of fun. But, hey! What are friends for? I caught a mild case of pneumonia but wasn't about to report it. They might put me in the hospital, and I'd miss my plane.

While completing my processing out, our new commanding officer, Lt. Jeffery Milson, made one final offer. He'd promote me to staff sergeant on the spot if I would extend my tour again. This had often been promised, but then usually just as quickly withdrawn due to my known attitude problem. I could and would do what was required of me in the field, but there was just too much Mickey Mouse to contend with for me to be able to keep my mouth shut.

I couldn't say I had no last-minute thoughts about staying. I had been through a lot and seen a lot. I had changed and would never be the same again. Whether that was good or bad, only time would tell. Dozens of faces flashed through my mind, guys I knew I would remember long after I'd forgotten their names. We'd been family. But I had made it without having any of my men killed. Charlie had had forty-four chances at me, as I'd had that many patrols. I didn't want to tempt the fates any more.

"No sir. Thanks, but I'm going home."

EPILOGUE

Of course, it didn't end there. I thought I was through with Vietnam, but perhaps it wasn't through with me. I found garrison life at Fort Benning, Georgia, just as much a pain in the ass as I'd expected. I quickly volunteered to return to Vietnam, but the orders never came in, not even after I had waited almost fourteen months, until my discharge date arrived.

Still, being in the army after Vietnam did have certain advantages over the experiences of a lot of vets who'd returned and were immediately discharged. For one thing, I never had to endure the harassment a lot of vets received from ignorant civilians. But once again, I found that certain members of the military can be just as bad. Many officers and NCOs who had never been over there were really hard to get along with. And not being allowed to wear the F Company shoulder scroll meant I had to wear the II Field Force patch with the Airborne tab. No one could figure out what that represented, and after having to explain it one time too many, I had the 173d patch sewn on all of my uniforms. This really burned me, but there seemed no recourse.

Another advantage was occasionally being able to see other men who had been with the company. Bill Schmidt, one of our company clerks, was my roommate for a while after we got an unauthorized apartment, just off base, in Columbus, Georgia. On December 5, 1969, several members of the company, mostly men who had gone on to P/75, had a reunion party at my apartment. Those attending, in many cases, had just gotten back home. Some of those who attended included Tom Snow, Rick

King, Guy Andes, John Ring, and Jerry Brock. It was a great party.

I was finally discharged from the army in June 1970, but after only eight months, I reenlisted. While I didn't specifically volunteer for Vietnam, I had put myself in a position where it was likely to come up. I'd gotten married in October of 1970, but I wasn't really ready for the domestic life. I did volunteer for Ranger School, to prove something to myself, graduating with what I always figured was the lowest score to get through. It was just very hard for me to adapt to their way of doing things. One of my classmates was Ted Godwin, another man from F Company. He seemed to get through without any difficulties, but Ted always was a better soldier than I was. All I knew was combat.

Orders finally did come in; I was either going back to Vietnam or to Germany. I wanted no part of Germany, but to appease my wife, I protested the orders for Vietnam. I had, I tried to explain to those in charge, already served my time in Vietnam. Why was I being sent back when so many people I knew who had the same MOS and rank never went? "That tour," I was told, "didn't count because you got out of the army." The bullshit never seemed to end.

Vietnam in 1972 sucked worse than before. We weren't allowed to fight, but they kept sending men to the field. I bounced around in different units, my attitude being much worse that time. I even spent a month as a company clerk, typing out orders for Bronze Stars and ArComs (Army Commendation medals) for men going home. The Bronze Stars were reserved for officers and E-6s, while the rest of the men got the ArComs. I was told that, since I was typing up the orders, I could give myself a Bronze Star. Shit! I somewhat politely told the officer in charge that all I wanted from that outfit was out. I got it. The next day I was returned to the field. After a disagreement with a .45 auto, I was medevaced to Okinawa, and when I returned to Vietnam, my unit, the 196th Light Infantry, had been disbanded. Ten days later, on July 27, 1972, I left Vietnam for the last time, exactly five years to the day I had first arrived in country.

The last man from F Company I was to see for many years was Jack Schmidt, at one time the platoon sergeant for 3d Platoon. He was the first sergeant of Company B, 75th Rangers, when I joined them after my departure from Vietnam. We did not of course have much to say to each other, but I did once again begin wearing my II Field Force combat patch. That's about as close to brownnosing as I ever came. However, I didn't remain with Company B for very long. There were entirely too many E-5s and 6s in that company who never went to Vietnam, and they didn't like my attitude because I wasn't gung ho enough to suit them. I very reluctantly terminated my Airborne status, but I'd had enough shit to last a lifetime, I thought. After fourteen months of the army, I got out once again.

A four-year hitch with the coast guard followed, just for something different to do, but this did not help me put the past behind me either. I finished that hitch and found myself at loose ends once again. I finally, unintentionally at first, found myself an officer with the El Reno, Oklahoma, police department, in the town where my first wife had lived. Police work was and is in many ways like being in combat; 95 percent of the time waiting for the other 5 percent to blow up in your face.

A lot was missing, though. After so many years of not having any contact with anyone from F Company, I almost began to feel as if the whole thing had never happened, as if it had all been just a dream. It made me feel like the only survivor. I finally made contact with Bill Schmidt again; I still had his wedding announcement from his first marriage and contacted his, as it turned out, ex-in-laws. That was a beginning, but I needed to find some of the other men, particularly my men from Team 4/4. I wanted desperately to know if in the intervening years they had come to blame me for what had happened on October 14, 1968. I had been in charge. Had our near disaster been my fault?

And quite honestly, I began to fret an awful lot about not getting that damned medal. After months of writing letters to every service organization, I received a letter from Mark Eastman, the last man I expected to hear from. Less than two weeks later, I got a letter from Bill Walsh (there were thirteen Bill Walshs listed with the Veterans of Foreign Wars; they all got letters and many of them responded, wishing me luck with my quest), and the same day, a phone call from Danny Arvo, his opening line being, ''Four/four, Negative contact.'' Keith Morris continued to elude me until late 1990. I was extremely gratified to find that none of them blamed me, and in fact were all very supportive.

I eventually came to one conclusion; not getting that medal did have a profound effect on my life. Had I gotten it, it would have been tangible evidence of "deeds of derring-do." I might well have been content to sit back and rest on my laurels, so to speak. Having no such proof of what I did, I was compelled to continue my quest for fame and acclaim. Now, after many years of tilting at windmills, I no longer feel the need to prove anything to anyone, including myself. Perhaps, at last, the war is over.

Things have grown since finding my team. Nine of us from F/51, Walt Butts, Speedy Gonzales, Mark Eastman, Tom Grzybowski, Charlie Mundo, Bill Walsh, Don Fant, Dennis Lovick, and I met at Colorado Springs, Colorado, in July 1990, at the 75th Ranger Regiment Association's reunion. The first sergeant and I made up after over twenty-two years of my carrying a grudge over one little incident that can remain personal between us; we all had a great time, and decided to form our own association in conjunction with the 75th. Yours truly was drafted as the director. I have been greatly assisted in this effort by Speedy, and working more quietly behind the scenes is Jack Meli, both of Austin, Texas. They are also doing monumental work in preparing for our first reunion next month. We also found our first honorary member, Mr. James W. Graves of Colorado Springs, a veteran of the 5th Ranger Battalion at Omaha Beach, during the Normandy Invasion in World War II. He has given us a great deal of support in our venture. Rangers stick together.

This association has become a labor of love. Speedy and I are determined to locate all of our people, even some we didn't like. There have been disappointments; a number have passed on since the war, or we learned they died later in other units. But the search goes on.

I received much assistance and encouragement in writing this book because all felt the story must be told. Granted that most of it is my story, but I was just a small part of the whole. I was probably one of the youngest team leaders, the youngest, no doubt, being Mike Frazier. I feel very honored to have so much support. I hope these men, my brothers, like the story.

I might also mention, Company F, 51st Infantry, is alive and well again. It was reformed in 1984 in Stuttgart, Germany, with the 7th Corps, now as a Long Range Surveillance company and is now designated, Co. F, LRS, 51st Infantry (Airborne), with the 511 Military Intelligence Battalion, 207th MI Brigade. As of this writing, they have just returned to Germany, having seen action during Operation DESERT STORM. I spoke recently to their company commander, Capt. Don Clarke, and learned that they suffered no casualties in what he described as their "one hundred hours of battle," but he also relayed that the company is being disbanded again. Another example of the army's attitude, if it works, fix it? We, the men of "old" F/51, salute our younger brothers and wish them well. There will be other wars; too bad Uncle Sam has to wait until they are running before he allows the creation of specific units to do the job.

APPENDIX A

       The following activity board was compiled using, in part, information contained in the F Company yearbook. This work has again been mentioned frequently in my book because it was so important to all who were able to obtain copies of it back then, as well as in providing me with further information and a feel for the times once again. It was something tangible to hold on to when all else seemed forgotten or lost.

       The original activity board covered the period of 22 November 1967 to 24 June 1968, coincidentally when I was prepared, more or less, to take over leadership of Team 4/4. Having no idea of the methodology used to compile the original, I took the after-action reports, typed at that time and held all these years, then provided to me by Clyde Tanner of Lockport, New York, for my own or association business. It was then a matter of sitting down and pulling everything together. In many cases, it may not be scientifically correct, but if in error, it's only by a small degree. I just felt it important to let the world know what we did, and that we were there. A few other categories have been added that I felt were important, and some numbers have been changed from the original that was sent out in the association newsletter, due to additional information.

ACTIVITY BOARD
22 November 1967 to 23 January 1969

NUMBER OF DAYS OPERATIONAL	438
NUMBER OF LIGHT TEAMS INSERTED	638
NUMBER OF HEAVY TEAMS INSERTED	133

NUMBER OF TIMES ENEMY SIGHTED	808
NUMBER OF TIMES CONTACT MADE WITH ENEMY	403
NUMBER OF ENEMY KILLED, PHYSICAL BODY COUNT	293
NUMBER OF ENEMY KILLED, PROBABLE, VISUAL REPORT	189
NUMBER OF ENEMY WOUNDED, VISUAL REPORT (NOT COUNTED AS PROBABLE)	54
NUMBER OF ENEMY WEAPONS CAPTURED	45
NUMBER OF ENEMY TAKEN AS PRISONERS OF WAR	45
NUMBER OF ARTILLERY MISSIONS FIRED IN OUR SUPPORT	292
KILLED IN ACTION/DIED AS A RESULT OF COMBAT ACTION	12
DIED NOT AS A RESULT OF COMBAT ACTION	3
WOUNDED IN ACTION	139
MISSING IN ACTION	NONE
OTHER FRIENDLY KILLED IN ACTION	4
OTHER FRIENDLY WOUNDED IN ACTION	7

APPENDIX B

Company F, Long Range Patrol, 51st Infantry (Airborne)

The following is a roster of the men who have been documented as having served with the company at one time or another during its brief time in history. The roster was compiled from various records, now considered public documents, or from orders I still have. The list was then cross-referenced with the Vietnam Casualty Directory as prepared by the Vietnam Veterans Memorial Fund. I knew the names of some of our casualties but not all of them; this book provided all of the names plus a few who died after leaving the company, either during the time of its existence or after it was disbanded, or in a couple of cases, they may have transferred out.

As luck would have it, shortly after I had completed this task, I received the list of names of our dead from several other sources. At least my tally was correct concerning those we lost while with the company. Those who died later were more tricky.

There were a couple of errors. David A. Fowler is listed as having been killed in 1970. David called a couple of months ago and assured me it wasn't so. That was another man with the same name. Similarly, several of our people were absolutely convinced that Mike Frazier was no longer with us. Mike did the same thing, calling and telling me he was still alive and kicking. In Mike's case, I had never believed it anyway. Not until I'd seen him laid out with a stake through his heart. I don't mind being wrong in a good cause.

Only two or three names have been deleted from my original

roster; in these cases they were men I have been informed left us before we began field operations. We all knew of men we wished we had never been associated with, but as my dear wife Jan said, they were all a part of the company, the good, the bad, and the ugly. Let history judge them, but let all men know them. These were our men.

Ranks and platoons shown are those I have records of. These may be in error, but I must go with what I have. Ranks also indicate those they held during that time. Many remained in the service, and I am pleased to report that quite a few of our people achieved the rank of full colonel, in the case of officers, or command sergeant major among the enlisted personnel. No general officers are on record yet. The records are not entirely complete, nor have all of the men been accounted for. The process continues. Other information, pertaining to those since dead but not confirmed, is yet to be fully established. All attempts at protection of privacy have been taken into account, but the records still stand. I do have documentation pertaining to the loss of several people under less than honorable circumstances as well as dates when most of the people either arrived or departed. However, I'll let this record stand as it is.

COMPANY F, LONG RANGE PATROL, 51ST INFANTRY
(AIRBORNE)
APO SAN FRANCISCO 96266
REPUBLIC OF VIETNAM
25 Sep 67–1 Feb 69
COMPANY ROSTER

1. Vincent Accardy   PFC   2d Plat.
2. Michael A. Akins   PFC   4th Plat.
3. Herbert D. Alcorn   Sgt.   2d Plat.
4. George D. Alexander   Sp4.   2d Plat.
5. James F. Alexander   Sp4.   4th Plat.
6. Seferino R. Alvarado   Sp4.   2d Plat.
7. William J. Alvarez   Sp4.   HQ.
8. Ronnie E. Alvord   PFC   3d Plat. 1-11-47 to 3-5-68, died in accident, Hutchinson, Kans.
9. Eugene J. Anderson   S.Sgt.   3d Plat.
10. Myron L. Anderson   Sp4.   1st Plat.
11. Benjamin F. Andes   PFC   3d Plat. "Guy"

12. Maurice E. Arnold   Sgt.   2d Plat.
13. Daniel W. Arvo   PFC   4th Plat. "Danny the Kid"
14. Roy A. Aubain   PFC   3rd Plat. 1-23-48 to 1-4-69, died result of wounds received 12-3-68, St. Thomas, V.I.
15. John A. Auer   Sp4.
16. Richard P. Auten   Sp4.   2d Plat.
17. Bruce Avant   Sgt.   2d Plat.
18. Bob E. Baker   Sp4.   HQ.
19. Timothy M. Baldwin   PFC   3d Plat.
20. Catalino Barajas   SFC   2d Plat.
21. James E. Barbic   PFC   HQ.
22. Warren D. Barfield   PFC   1st Plat. "Dave"
23. Bobby K. Baker   PFC
24. Rodney K. Baker   Sp4.
25. Marshall G. Barnes   Sgt.   HQ.
26. James R. Barnett   S.Sgt.   4th Plat.
27. Thomas Barthelow   Sp5.   HQ.
28. Robert F. Bass   Sgt.   1st Plat.
29. James A. Beake   Sp4.   4th Plat.
30. Jerry D. Beck   S.Sgt.   3d Plat. 8-13-48 to 4-6-69, KIA with O/75 Rangers, Dallas, Tex.
31. Michael B. Becker   Sp4.   HQ.
32. Brian J. Benedict   PFC   2d Plat. Reported deceased 8-29-72.
33. Dicky M. Bennett   Sgt.
34. Jimmie Bergeron   S.Sgt.   4th Plat.
35. Ross S. Barkhahn   PFC   2d Plat.
36. Jerold D. Berrow   Sgt.   HQ.
37. Jim R. Berry   Sp4.   4th Plat.
38. Frank Bighames, Jr.   S.Sgt.
39. Kenneth R. Blair   PFC   1st Plat. 12-19-48 to 8-12-68, KIA, Marbleton, Ga.
40. Freddie Blankenship   Sp5.   HQ.
41. Ralph Bleskan   SFC
42. John J. Blososky   Sgt.   HQ.
43. Terry A. Boat   PFC   2d Plat.
44. Ralph L. Boldt   Sp4.   1st Plat.
45. James G. Bolger   PFC   2d Plat.
46. James E. Bolton   Sgt.   2d Plat.
47. Henry Bonvillian   Sp4.   2d Plat.
48. Ben R. Botiller   Sp4.   3d Plat.

49. Larry Bowling   Sgt.   Commo.
50. Sandy Boyd   Sp4.   2d Plat.
51. Gene D. Boyer   Sp4.   3d Plat.
52. Jimmy L. Boykins   Sp4.   3d Plat.
53. Estelle R. Bramlette   Sp4.   HQ. "Sonny"
54. Emerson Branch, Jr.   Sp4.   2d Plat.
55. Emerson Branum   Sp4.
56. Frederick D. Bratton   PFC   1st Plat.
57. Hugh J. Brewer   Sp4.   Commo.
58. Jerry M. Brock   Sgt.   2d Plat.
59. David R. Brooks   Sp4.
60. Gerald P. Brown   Sp6.   3d Plat.
61. Robert H. Brown, Jr.   Sgt.
62. Ronald K. Brown   S.Sgt.   S-2.
63. Willie D. Brown   Sp4.   1st Plat.
64. Willie T. Brown   PFC   3d Plat.
65. Robert H. Bryant   Sp4.   4th Plat.
66. Benjamin M. Buchanan   PFC   1st Plat.
67. Harold W. Buntin   Sp4.   1st Plat.
68. John Burke, Jr.   S.Sgt.   3d Plat.
69. John J. Burke   PFC   4th Plat.
70. Paul M. Burns   PFC
71. James H. Butcher   Sp4.   Commo.
72. Walter B. Butler   Sp4.   4th Plat.
73. Walter P. Butts   1st Sgt.   4th Plat.
74. Herman J. Bynum, Jr.   Sp4.   1st Plat.
75. Daniel C. Caccia   Sp4.   HQ.
76. Charles S. Calaman   PFC   4th Plat.
77. Stephen Calderon   Sgt.   Commo.
78. Robert E. Caldwell   Sp4.   4th Plat.
79. Dennis L. Cameron   Sp4.   1st Plat.
80. Richard L. Carlson   Sp4.   Commo.
81. Emory G. Carlton   PFC   4th Plat.
82. Clark Carnahan   Sp4.   4th Plat.
83. Donald D. Carnahan   Sp4.   1st Plat.
84. Norman Carraher   PFC   2d Plat.
85. Willie C. Carson   PFC
86. David E. Carter   S.Sgt.   2d Plat. 2-27-41 to 8-10-69, KIA with P/75 Rangers, Hamilton, Ohio.
87. Howard M. Cartwright   Sp4.   Commo. "Mike"
88. Gilberto Chaires   PFC   2d Plat.

89. John D. Chichester   PFC   1st Plat.
90. George Christiansen   Sp4.   4th Plat.
91. Paul E. Cicala   Sp4.   HQ.
92. Anthony E. Cicerano   Sp4.   2d Plat.
93. Dwight F. Clements   Sp4.   3d Plat.
94. Donald D. Clemons   Sp4.   1st Plat.
95. Thomas J. Corvell   Pvt.
96. Bruce W. Cotton   PFC   1st Plat.
97. James R. Cowles   Sgt.   1st Plat.
98. Billy J. Cox   Plat. Sgt.   HQ.
99. Jeffery E. Cox   PFC   3d Plat.
100. S.C. Crabtree   1st Sgt.   HQ.
101. Robert J. Cresci   Capt.   1st Plat.
102. Don A Crowe   Sgt.   4th Plat. Deceased 4-10-75.
103. Larry L. Cunningham   S.Sgt.   1st Plat. 6-10-45 to 12-3-68, KIA, Louisville, Miss.
104. Dwight D. Davis   Sp4.
105. James H. Davis   Sp4.   4th Plat.
106. Stephen S. Davis   PFC   3d Plat.
107. Robert M. DeFer   Sgt.   2d Plat.
108. David L. Deshazo   Sgt.   2d Plat.
109. Robert Dickerson   Sp4.   4th Plat.
110. Richard W. Diers   Sgt.   1st Plat. 12-19-47 to 11-21-68, KIA, Pinellas Park, Fla.
111. Russell E. Dillon   PFC   Commo.
112. Walter L. Dixon   Sp4.   Commo.
113. Eric L. Dodson   Sgt.   4th Plat.
114. Fred Domcszewiez   Sp4.   1st Plat.
115. Geoffrey L. Douglas   PFC   4th Plat.
116. Charles L. Drew   Sp4.   4th Plat.
117. Patrick A. Duffield   Sp4.   1st Plat.
118. David Duncan   Sgt.   HQ.
119. Bruce E. Duval   Sp4.
120. Edward L. Dvorak   Sgt.   1st Plat.
121. Mark G. Eastman   Sp4.   4th Plat.
122. Duane P. Eaton   Sp4.   HQ.
123. Daniel S. Edwards   Sp4.   Commo.
124. Robert C. Edwards   S.Sgt.   1st Plat.
125. Dale O. Eggers   PFC   HQ.
126. Arthur L. Elkins   PFC   Commo.
127. William J. Elliott   Sp4.   HQ.

128. William D. Ellis   Sp4.   4th Plat.
129. William J. Ellis   Sp4.   2d Plat.
130. Horace R. Ellison   S.Sgt.   3d Plat.
131. Edwin L. Emanuel   Sp4.   2d Plat.
132. Kenneth M. Emmick   PFC   Commo.
133. Raymond M. Enczi   Sp4.   1st Plat. 7-26-48 to 10-31-68, KIA, Elyria, Ohio.
134. Leslie W. Ervin   Sp4.   2d Plat.
135. Clark W. Etterman   S.Sgt.   2d Plat.
136. Freeman Evans   Sgt.   1st Plat. 5-26-49 to 12-4-68. Died result of wounds received on 12-3-68, Gordon, Ga.
137. Raymond W. Ewing   Pvt.   3d Plat.
138. Donald D. Fant   Sgt.   HQ.
139. Ramon Favela   Sp4.   2d Plat.
140. Gary W. Fenton   S.Sgt.   4th Plat.
141. James C. Fenner   PFC   4th Plat.
142. Michael J. Feller   PFC   1st Plat.
143. Robert J. Fields   PFC
144. Desmond H. Fitzsimmons   PFC   2d Plat. Reported deceased 1977.
145. Madison Flowers   Sp4.   1st Plat.
146. Dennis R. Foley   Capt.   HQ.
147. Bernard M. Ford   Sgt.   1st Plat.
148. Gary D. Ford   Sgt.   4th Plat.
149. James C. Foreman   S.Sgt.   4th Plat.
150. Joseph M. Formelio   Sgt.   3d Plat.
151. Carl M. Forrest   Sp4.   1st Plat.
152. David A. Fowler   PFC   Commo.
153. Ralph C. Fox   Sp4.   4th Plat.
154. Michael D. Frazier   Sgt.   2d Plat. ''Brazzaville''
155. Wilmer E. Fridley   S.Sgt.   4th Plat.
156. Michael M. Fuson   Sgt.   1st Plat. Reported deceased.
157. Daniel J. Gadna   Sp4.
158. Patrick A. Gairns   PFC
159. James L. Gallegos   Sp4.
160. Willi A. Gallian   Sgt.
161. Paul D. Gann   PFC   HQ.
162. Michael W. Garner   Sp4.   HQ.
163. Ellis Gates, Jr.   Sp4.   2d Plat.
164. George W. Gentry   Sp4.   4th Plat. Reported deceased.
165. Gary S. George   Sp4.   3d Plat.

166. Domenic Giandomenico, or Giandanico Sp4. 2d Plat.
167. Robert C. Gilliam Sgt. 1st Plat.
168. Herschel L. Givens Sp4. Commo.
169. Thad Givens Sp4. 2nd Plat.
170. Clodie Gladney, Jr. S.Sgt. 3d Plat.
171. Teddy J. Godwin Sgt. 2d Plat.
172. Stanislas Gonkiewitz Sp4.
173. Robert R. Gonzaga Sgt.
174. Tiofilo Gonzales Sgt. 3d Plat. "Speedy"
175. Gary E. Goodner PFC Commo.
176. Douglas Goodnight Sp4. 4th Plat.
177. John H. Gordon Sp4. 1st Plat.
178. William B. Gray Sp4. 2d Plat.
179. Robert M. Green Sgt. 4th Plat.
180. Roger S. Green Sp4. 4th Plat.
181. Thomas W. Green, Jr. Sgt. 2d Plat.
182. Thomas Grzybowski Sp4. 3d Plat.
183. Jeffery Hackley Sp4. 4th Plat.
184. Nolan L. Haddock PFC 2d Plat.
185. Dennis Hagan Sp4. Commo.
186. Cleveland E. Hall PFC HQ.
187. Donald C. Hall S.Sgt. 2d Plat.
188. Noah O. Hall, Jr. Sp5. HQ.
189. Claude P. Hamilton Sgt. Commo.
190. James A. Hardy PFC
191. Frank. J. Harper Sgt. 3d Plat.
192. Tillman J. Harrel PFC
193. Shelby D. Harris Sgt. 4th Plat. "Don"
194. Samuel L. Harvey, Jr. Sp4.
195. Joseph F. Havrilla S.Sgt. 2d Plat.
196. Lloyd H. Heath Sp4. 2d Plat.
197. George M. Heckman Maj. HQ.
198. Mack J. Henderson Sp4. 2d Plat.
199. Lewis B. Hendricks Sp4.
200. Jan V. Henrickson Sp4. 1st Plat. 3-11-48 to 8-12-68, KIA, Hartley, Del.
201. Jaime T. Hernandez Sp4. 3d Plat.
202. Margarito Hernandez PFC 1st Plat. "Chico"
203. Edward T. Higgins PFC 4th Plat.
204. Kevin W. Higgins Sgt. 3d Plat.
205. Richard P. Hill S.Sgt. HQ.

206. Ronnie J. Hill   Sgt.   2d Plat.
207. David L. Hillard   Sp4.   Commo.
208. Anthony Hockenberry   Sp4.   HQ.
209. Kenneth R. Holmes   Sp4.   1st Plat.
210. Hershell Hoskins   Sp4.   2d Plat.
211. Bruce R. Houghton, Jr.   Sgt.   2d Plat.
212. William J. Houser   Sp4.   HQ.
213. Charles R. Hughes   Sgt.
214. Mark. A Humberger   PFC   3d Plat.
215. Michael A. Hyson   Sp4.   4th Plat.
216. David N. Inwood   1st Lt.
217. Dennis Jackson   Sp4.   Commo.
218. Fred Jackson, Jr.   Sp4.   HQ.
219. Charlie Jacobs   Sgt.
220. John E. Jacobson   Sp4.   4th Plat.
221. Melvin Jennings   Sp5.   HQ.
222. Glenn E. Johnson   PFC   1st Plat.
223. Jerry W. Johnson   PFC   3d Plat.
224. Paul E. Johnson   PFC
225. William Johnson, Jr.   Sp4.   4th Plat.
226. Ray J. Jones   S.Sgt.   4th Plat.
227. Andrew Jordan   Sp4.   3d Plat.
228. Ronald J. Kaiser   PFC   1st Plat.
229. Lawrence Kalamajka   Sp4.   HQ.
230. John P. Kane   Sp4.   3d Plat. "Jack." Deceased 8-6-91.
231. George A. Kanes   Sp4.   4th Plat.
232. John J. Kanicsar   Sgt.   3d Plat.
233. Robert P. Kapczynski   Sp4.   Commo.
234. Ronald A. Kaplan   Sp4.   4th Plat.
235. George M. Keller   PFC   4th Plat.
236. Michael J. Kelley, Jr.   PFC   4th Plat. 6-27-48 to 4-25-69,
     KIA with O/75 Rangers, Syracuse, N.Y.
237. Melvin Kent   PFC   4th Plat.
238. Richard J. King   Sgt.   1st Plat.
239. William M. King   Sp4.   2d Plat.
240. Ronald J. Klein   PFC
241. Ronald J. Kluemper   Sp4.   1st Plat.
242. Daren L. Koenig   Sp4.   Commo. 1-26-48 to 4-6-69,
     KIA with 0/75 Rangers, Hannibal, Mo.
243. John R. Kohler   PFC   2d Plat.
244. Van Kominitsky   Sgt.   4th Plat.

245. James W. Kovach   Sp4.   1st Plat.
246. James E. Kozak   Sp4.   Commo.
247. Harold E. Kubin   Cpl.
248. Joseph A. Kuehn   Sp4.   1st Plat.
249. David A. Kuenhert   Sp4.
250. Keith Lafee   PFC   4th Plat.
251. Warren L. Lahara   Sp4.
252. Peter R. Laizik   Capt.   HQ.
253. Timothy L. Lambert   Sgt.   3d Plat.
254. Richard L. Lapan   Sp4.   3d Plat.
255. Allen W. Larson   PFC   4th Plat.
256. John H. Lattin, Jr.   1st Lt.   2d Plat. 3-24-44 to 12-15-68, KIA, Columbus, Ohio.
257. William L. Lavender   S.Sgt.   1st Plat.
258. Charles R. Lawson   Sgt.
259. Stanley E. Ledford   PFC   4th Plat.
260. Dennis P. Lee   Sgt.
261. Earl H. Lequire   Sp4.   2d Plat.
262. Ronald C. Lewis   S.Sgt.   4th Plat.
263. John R. Libert   Sp4.   3d Plat. ''Tiny''
264. Joseph Lieben   Sp5.
265. William H. Liggett   PFC   1st Plat.
266. Daniel H. Lindsey   Sp4.   2d Plat. 9-18-47 to 12-5-67, KIA, Orlando, Fla.
267. Barry Linington   Sp4.   2d Plat.
268. Richard L. Littlefield   Sgt.   1st Plat.
269. Melvin E. Littles   PFC   4th Plat.
270. Anthony J. Longo   Sp4.   4th Plat.
271. Dennis W. Lovick   Sgt.   4th Plat.
272. Charles Luczynski   Sp4.   1st Plat.
273. Bobby J. Lukasheay   Sgt.   3d Plat.
274. Shelby N. Luman   Sp4.   HQ.
275. Lawton Mackey, Jr.   Sp4.   2d Plat.
276. Thomas H. Maggart   S.Sgt.   4th Plat.
277. Frank C. Majka   Sp4.   1st Plat.
278. Bobby Malichi   SFC 1-9-36 to 12-25-68, Died, Bennettsville, S.C.
279. Robert G. Mall   PFC
280. Donald V. Mann   Sp4.   HQ.
281. Robert C. Mann   PFC   4th Plat.
282. John W. Manuel   Sgt.   4th Plat.

283. Edwin A. Markut   Sgt.   1st Plat. "Al"
284. Reece L. Marple   Sgt. 12-29-45 to 5-11-68, KIA, circum-
     stances and unit unknown, Jellico, Tenn.
285. Olin Marsh   Sgt.   4th Plat.
286. Jeffery P. Martin   Sp4.   2d Plat.
287. Paul G. Martin, Jr.   Sgt.   4th Plat.
288. Richard J. Martin   PFC   4th Plat.
289. Thomas L. Mattox   Sp4.   2d Plat.
290. William C. Maus   Lt. Col.   HQ.
291. Robert M. Maxson   Sgt.
292. Benjamin J. Maxwell   PFC   4th Plat.
293. Greg C. McClish   PFC
294. Richard E. McCoy   Plat. Sgt.   4th Plat.
295. James R. McElwee   Sgt.   1st Plat.
296. John McFolley   Sp4.   4th Plat.
297. Gerald J. McGarry   Sgt.   HQ.
298. Gerald E. McGough   1st Lt.   HQ. "Snuffy McGuff"
299. Robert D. McIntosh   Capt.   HQ.
300. Michael J. Meadows   Sp4.   2d Plat.
301. John W. Meli   Sgt. "Jack"
302. Thomas P. Meyer   Capt.   HQ.
303. Steven J. Miles   Sp4.   2d Plat.
304. John R. Millender   Sp4.   2d Plat.
305. August I. Miller   PFC   Commo.
306. Douglas L. Miller   1st Lt.
307. James W. Miller   Sp4.   3d Plat.
308. Roger W. Miller   Sgt.   2d Plat.
309. Rodney K. Mills   PFC 12-19-48 to 5-5-70, KIA, circum-
     stances and unit unknown, Alma, Mich.
310. Jeffery W. Milson   1st Lt.
311. Jose Montez   Sp4.   3d Plat. Deceased October 1972.
312. Bruce Montplaisir   Sp4.   Commo.
313. Kenneth R. Moore   Sp4.   3d Plat.
314. Keith O. Morris   PFC   4th Plat. "Lurch"
315. Charles E. Morrow   Sgt.   Commo.
316. William B. Mortenson   SFC   HQ.
317. Richard L. Moyer   Sp4.   1st Plat.
318. Charles Mundo   Sp4.   1st Plat.
319. Charles M. Muscat   SFC   Commo.
320. Delbert Musgrove   S.Sgt.   HQ.
321. Charles W. Nelson   PFC   4th Plat.

322. Keith R. Nelson Pvt.
323. Nelson H. Newhouse Capt. Commo.
324. Larry W. Nicholls PFC 2d Plat.
325. David B. Nichols Sp4.
326. Brian O'Sullivan Sgt. 3d Plat. "Sully"
327. Seer Odom, Jr. Sgt. 4th Plat.
328. Joe O. Olivo, Jr. Sp4. 4th Plat.
329. Geronimo Oplinger Sgt. 3d Plat.
330. Samuel Pacurari Sp4.
331. Richard Pallares Pvt.
332. Robert F. Palluch PFC 4th Plat.
333. Gordon Panton 1st Lt. HQ.
334. Clarence Passey Sp4. 3d Plat.
335. David A. Peace Sp4. 4th Plat.
336. Malachi Pennington PFC 4th Plat.
337. Don C. Perry Sgt.
338. Donald A. Peter 1st Lt. 4th Plat.
339. Francis Peterson Plat. Sgt.
340. Wayne C. Pledger Sgt.
341. John L. Plunkett Sgt. 4th Plat.
342. Ronnie Pochowski Sp4. HQ.
343. Eugene Porter S.Sgt. HQ.
344. Richard Powell PFC
345. Robert Pressnall Sp4. 1st Plat.
346. James S. Prestwood 1st Lt. 2d Plat. Died December 1986.
347. Harry D. Pruitt Sp4. 2d Plat.
348. Albin F. Radzik Sp4. 3d Plat.
349. William J. Ragland PFC
350. Thomas P. Rallo PFC
351. Howard W. Randall Capt. HQ.
352. Bernard Rankevich Sgt.
353. David P. Raxter Sp4. 4th Plat.
354. Wayne G. Reese Sp4. Commo.
355. Michael P. Regula PFC 4th Plat.
356. Norman A. Reid Sgt. 2d Plat.
357. Richard F. Rennolet Sp4. 1st Plat. 5-12-49 to 4-14-68, Died, Aberdeen, S.Dak.
358. David S. Rezney Sp4. 4th Plat.
359. Lenson N. Riggs Sp4. 1st Plat.
360. Jerome K. Riley Sp4. 4th Plat.

361. Patrick L. Rine Sp4.
362. John L. Ring Sgt. 1st Plat.
363. Bernard Rinkevich Sgt. Commo.
364. Joseph R. Rivera PFC
365. Roger L. Roberts Sgt. 1st Plat.
366. Bobby E. Robinson PFC
367. Franklin Robinson S.Sgt. 1st Plat.
368. Jennings Robinson Sp4.
369. Robert A. Robinson Sp4.
370. Victor L. Robinson PFC 3d Plat.
371. Castro F. Rodriguez Sp4. 3d Plat.
372. Edward R. Rodriguez Sp4. 3d Plat.
373. Fredrico C. Rodriguez Sp4.
374. Joseph Rodriguez PFC
375. Julio Rodriguez Sgt. HQ.
376. Larry R. Rose Sp4. HQ.
377. Leslie D. Rosenkrans Sp4. 1st Plat. 7-19-48 to 12-3-68,
     KIA, Auburn, Mich.
378. Johnny B. Rowe Sp4. Commo.
379. John W. Sahm Plat. Sgt. 1st Plat.
380. Charles P. Sailes Sgt. 2d Plat.
381. Thomas N. Santa Sp4. 4th Plat.
382. Jack R. Schmidt Plat. Sgt. 3d Plat. Deceased.
383. William H. Schmidt Sgt. HQ.
384. Kenneth Schweitzer Sp4. 4th Plat.
385. Randall W. Scrum Sp4.
386. James W. Seay S.Sgt.
387. Steven J. Sheffert Sgt. Commo.
388. Walter W. Shreiner Sp4. 2d Plat. "Smokey" Reported
     deceased 6-22-79.
389. Phillip E. Siemion Sp4. 3d Plat.
390. Robert G. Sill PFC
391. Basilio Silvestri PFC HQ.
392. Robert Simmons S.Sgt.
393. Stanley W. Simmons S.Sgt. 2d Plat.
394. George D. Simpson PFC 1st Plat.
395. Patrick Singleton Sgt.
396. Franky Skipper Sp5. HQ.
397. Robert L. Slade PFC 1st Plat.
398. Eugene N. Slyzuik Sgt. 3d Plat. "Gene"
399. Max E. Small Sp4. Commo.

400. Bobby L. Smith   S.Sgt.
401. Clyde L. Smith   Sp4.   Commo.
402. Dean V. Smith   Sp4.   Commo.
403. Howard C. Smith, Jr.   Sp4.
404. Sherman Smith   Sp4.   Commo.
405. Thomas H. Snow   Sp4.   1st Plat.
406. Albert J. Snyder   1st Lt.   HQ.
407. Phillip N. Solomon   PFC   4th Plat.
408. John A Souza   PFC   3d Plat. "Al"
409. Michael S. Splawn   Sgt.   3d Plat.
410. Bailey L. Stauffer   PFC   4th Plat.
411. Robert D. Steele   Sp4.   Commo.
412. Daniel Steuernagle   Sgt.   2d Plat.
413. Franklin Stoneburner   Sgt.   Commo.
414. Gerald Stratton   1st Lt.   1st Plat.
415. John T. Stringer   S.Sgt.
416. Ralph Sutterfield   Sp4.   4th Plat.
417. Franklin Swann   Sp4.   2d Plat.
418. Norman C. Taitano   S.Sgt.   HQ.   "Tai"
419. Clyde F. Tanner   Sp4.   HQ.
420. Terrance Teasley   Sp4.   1st Plat.
421. Harold L. Thomas   Sp4.
422. Leroy Thomas   S.Sgt.
423. Tommy L. Thomas   Sgt.   4th Plat.
424. Gerald L. Thompson   Sp4.
425. Ronald W. Thompson   Sp5.   HQ.
426. Ronald W. Thorne   Sp4.   2d Plat.
427. Leland J. Tibbles   PFC
428. Joseph J. Tootle   Sp4.   4th Plat.
429. Manuel Torres   Sgt.
430. Herbert Tortice   PFC   1st Plat.
431. Sammy E. Treat   Sp4.   4th Plat.
432. William F. Trenum   Sp4.   4th Plat.
433. Steph Trinsjstick   PFC   3d Plat.
434. Calvin J. Treser   PFC   1st Plat.
435. Alvie A. Turner, Jr.   Sp4.   1st Plat.
436. Victor H. Turner   Sgt.   4th Plat.
437. Alfred Turnipseed   Sgt.   HQ.
438. Willie H. Twiggs   Sp4.   4th Plat.
439. David L. Urban   Pvt.   1st Plt. 4-27-43 to 12-3-68, KIA, Chardon, Ohio.

440. Terry W. Vance   PFC
441. Steven F. Vargo   Sgt.   1st Plat.
442. Richard D. Vincent   Sp5.   3d Plat.
443. Robert P. Viney   Sgt.
444. Dennis R. Vitias   Sp4.   HQ.
445. Tony L. Wade   Sp4.   1st Plat.
446. Gregory H. Waibel   Sp4.   3d Plat.
447. Fred H. Wake III   Sgt.   2d Plat.
448. James G. Walker   Sp4.
449. Robert Walker   Sgt.   HQ.
450. Gunther A. Wallner   Sp4.   3d Plat. "Wally"
451. Harold E. Walsh   Sp4.   Commo.
452. William M. Walsh, Jr.   PFC   4th Plat.
453. Landers Washington   S.Sgt.   4th Plat.
454. Michael Waskiewicz   Sp4.   3d Plat.
455. Gary J. Weitzel   1st Lt.   Commo.
456. Alan F. White   S.Sgt.   Commo.
457. Willie Whitfield, Jr.   PFC   1st Plat 12-18-47 to 8-12-68,
     KIA, Columbus, Miss.
458. Robert Wilkerson   Sgt.   1st Plat.
459. Colin K. Williams   Sgt.   3d Plat. "Kelly"
460. Louis Williams   PFC   1st Plat.
461. Perry B. Williams   PFC
462. Winston L. Williams   PFC   HQ.
463. John W. Willis   PFC   3d Plat.
464. James D. Wilson   Sgt.
465. Stephen B. Wilson   PFC   2d Plat.
466. John Witherspoon   Sp4.   1st Plat. "Spoon"
467. James A. Wolf   PFC   3d Plat.
468. Hershel R. Womack   Sp4.   3d Plat.
469. Charlie Wright   S.Sgt.
470. John H. Wright   Sp4.
471. Torrence J. Wright   PFC
472. Joseph J. Zummo   Lt. Col.   HQ. Deceased 11-10-91.

ABOUT THE AUTHOR

Gary Douglas Ford was born in Alvin, Texas, but grew up in both Texas and Oklahoma. He enlisted in the army in June 1966. After almost seven years in the army, with non-Vietnam duties primarily at Fort Benning, Georgia, and Fort Carson, Colorado, in training or support, he got out, only to reenlist in the Coast Guard. Duties with the Coast Guard included sixteen months on the cutter *Boutwell* as a gunner's mate and two years with base security, Kodiak, Alaska. Awards and decorations include the Purple Heart with First Oak Leaf Cluster, the army and Coast Guard Good Conduct Medals, and the Combat Infantry Badge. He is both Airborne and Ranger qualified. He has received an Associate Degree in Police Science from Oklahoma State University Technical Institute as well as an Associate Degree in history from El Reno Junior College, El Reno, Oklahoma. He has been employed with the El Reno police department since 1979 and is currently a patrol lieutenant and shift supervisor. He and his wife, Janice, were married in May 1990 and have seven children. This is his first published work, but he hopes it will not be the last.